STUDIES IN IMPERIALISM

general editor John M. MacKenzie

Established in the belief that imperialism as a cultural
phenomenon had as significant an effect on the dominant
as on the subordinate societies, Studies in Imperialism
seeks to develop the new socio-cultural approach which
has emerged through cross-disciplinary work on popular
culture, media studies, art history, the study of education
and religion, sports history and children's literature.
The cultural emphasis embraces studies of migration and
race, while the older political and constitutional,
economic and military concerns are never far away.
It incorporates comparative work on European and
American empire-building, with the chronological focus
primarily, though not exclusively, on the nineteenth and
twentieth centuries, when these cultural exchanges were
most powerfully at work.

Emigration from Scotland between the wars: opportunity or exile?

MANCHESTER
UNIVERSITY PRESS

STUDIES IN IMPERIALISM

Emigration from Scotland between the wars: opportunity or exile?

Marjory Harper

MANCHESTER
UNIVERSITY PRESS

Manchester and New York

distributed exclusively in the USA by
ST. MARTIN'S PRESS

The right of Marjory Harper to be identified as the author of this work has been asserted by her in accordance with the Copyright, Designs and Patents Act 1988.

Published by **MANCHESTER UNIVERSITY PRESS**
OXFORD ROAD, MANCHESTER M13 9NR, UK
and ROOM 400, 175 FIFTH AVENUE, NEW YORK, NY 10010, USA
http://www.man.ac.uk/mup

Distributed exclusively in the USA by
ST. MARTIN'S PRESS, INC.
175 FIFTH AVENUE, NEW YORK, NY 10010, USA

Distributed exclusively in Canada by
UBC PRESS, UNIVERSITY OF BRITISH COLUMBIA,
6344 MEMORIAL ROAD, VANCOUVER, BC, CANADA V6T 1Z2

British Library Cataloguing-in-Publication Data
A catalogue record for this book is available from the British Library

Library of Congress Cataloging-in-Publication Data applied for

ISBN 0 7190 4927 X hardback

First published 1998

05 04 03 02 01 00 99 98   10 9 8 7 6 5 4 3 2 1

Typeset in Kuenst 480
by Special Edition Pre-Press Services
Printed in Great Britain
by Bookcraft (Bath) Ltd, Midsomer Norton

CONTENTS

LIST OF FIGURES

LIST OF MAPS

LIST OF PLATES
appearing after page 112

GENERAL EDITOR'S INTRODUCTION

Emigration has long been central to Scottish historical identities. Yet it is only in comparatively recent times that historians have sought to illuminate a phenomenon that has often been associated with powerful emotions, myths and polemics. Through intensive and highly sophisticated research on the social and economic, political and cultural aspects of migration, the field has now become central to a new Scottish historiography which seeks to place the history of Scotland within its wider contexts. Marjory Harper's work, starting with an important and detailed study of emigration from northeast Scotland, has been influential in developing these studies.

In this book she examines emigration in the years between the two world wars of the twentieth century. Until recently, this seemed to be the neglected era in migration studies, but increasingly scholars are turning their attention to the period. Marjory Harper seeks to place the Empire Settlement Act of 1922 in its proper context. If this act appeared to herald a period of more intensive state involvement in emigration, much discussed but never implemented in the century before the First World War, in fact its implementation was at best only half-hearted and fraught with much controversy. The tradition of voluntarism, promoted by the large number of agencies involved in migration, continued in much the same mould as in Victorian and Edwardian times.

The great strengths of the book lie in the remarkable range of sources the author has used, the light shed upon a variety of voluntary agencies, the hesitant nature of much state involvement, the character of emigration propaganda, and the tensions and strains that all this activity placed not only on relations with the dominions but also on local and national politics. They also reside in the extent to which she has been able to survey the experiences of fishing, crofting and agricultural communities of the highlands and islands, the northeast and the borders as well as the industrial populations of the central belt. The arguments for and against migration lay at the heart of the political process in the 1920s, and they were reflected in the reactions of the press, the churches, philanthropists, social commentators and politicians in the period. But, above all, migration was about people – individuals caught up in economic forces beyond their control who were persuaded to seek a form of exile in order to carve out a hopefully better future. Individual experience is at the core of this study, for we hear many emigrants' voices talking of the character and consequences of emigration, of successes and failures, and of hopes and disappointments.

Diasporas invariably have powerful effects on their core populations. Scottish nationalists have long hoped that former migrants – particularly those settled in the United States and Canada – would play their part in the struggle to bring state and nation back into alignment. Cultural nationalists have also sought inspiration from overseas communities. Clan and other Scottish associations continue to have an extraordinary number of branches in North America, Australasia and elsewhere, and the role of such exchanges and interactions in the maintenance and development of Scottish identities remains of considerable concern. All those interested in the effects of these connections on Scottish politics, social analysis and literature will find much of interest here.

John M. MacKenzie

PREFACE

War memorials throughout Scotland testify not only to the enormous human cost of the conflict of 1914–18 but also to the large number of Scottish emigrants who returned from Canada, Australia and New Zealand to serve in imperial regiments. The First World War is often portrayed – and rightly so – as a watershed in economic, social and cultural terms, as well as in political terms, and at first glance it may appear that it also formed a watershed in the history of emigration. Certainly the Empire Settlement Act of 1922 marked an unprecedented commitment by the British government to promoting and funding emigration from a country perplexed by unemployment and political unrest to an empire that was threatening to fall apart, while, in a Scottish context, the 1920s saw a unique and startling inter-censal population decline, the result of both internal and external migration, particularly from urban areas.

But emigration is not only a consistently controversial issue which is guaranteed to produce widely differing interpretations between and among academics, governments and participants. It is also an issue notoriously prone to clichés, half-truths and one-dimensional perspectives, and closer examination of its inter-war manifestations suggests that some of the apparent innovations of the 1920s were characterized as much by continuity as by change and that, as in previous generations, official policy was only one aspect of a complex and multifaceted phenomenon. The considerable legacy of Victorian and Edwardian emigration reflected in the war memorials provided a foundation and a model for much of the later movement, in which traditional influences were reinforced rather than totally remoulded by government intervention.

The study presented in this book evaluates the surprisingly neglected phenomenon of Scottish emigration in the 1920s. Focusing on the relationship between the new colonization schemes spawned by the Empire Settlement Act and the long-standing influences of family and community networks, private enterprise, philanthropic sponsorship and professional agent activity, it seeks to establish whether Scots were persuaded to settle in North America and the Antipodes by the same priorities that had persuaded their Victorian predecessors or whether the experience of war, depression and government intervention had produced a new breed of emigrant. The sources on which the evaluation is based include, from the Whitehall perspective, the voluminous official publications emanating from the Overseas Settlement Department of the Colonial (later Dominions) Office, which chart the course of the numerous schemes promoted under the 1922 legislation, while Public Record Office statistics of emigrant shipping, compiled by the Board of Trade, include useful data on the origins and occupations of passengers, as well as age, gender and family profiles and ports of embarkation and debarkation. Scottish official sources include the invaluable files of the Department of Agriculture and Fisheries, which shed detailed light on the often tortuous history of highland emigration, and these records are supplemented by a rich seam of highland material in the records of the Canadian Department of Immigration and Colonization. The crucial contribution of professional agents to Scottish emigration is also documented in meticulous detail in Canadian Immigration Department files, as is the role of philanthropists who, on both sides of the Atlantic, harnessed the funding facilities of the Empire Settlement Act to their programmes of rescue, rehabilitation and relocation. The records of Scottish institutions involved in such programmes provide a vital complement to the transatlantic sources. The obvious Canadian bias of the study is dictated largely by the wealth of material in Canadian archives, in contrast to the unfortunate paucity of relevant information that could be identified in repositories in Australia and New Zealand. Although Canada remained the favourite destination of Scottish emigrants throughout the inter-war period, significant numbers went to the Antipodes and, to a lesser extent, South Africa, but lack of access to archival evidence in those countries has resulted in their experiences remaining, for the purposes of this study, a largely closed book. Deficiencies in antipodean material have been addressed to some extent by having recourse to the Scottish provincial newspaper press and farming periodicals, not least the correspondence columns, while the journals of some of the juvenile emigration societies also contained letters from recruits in Australia. Newspapers unfailingly provide a wealth of promotional, cautionary and descriptive information that was readily available to would-be emigrants, while anecdotal evidence, primarily about Canadian and American experiences, has been gleaned from interviews with emigrants who were still alive in the 1980s and 1990s and from material in local government archives, such as the school-leaving registers, which record 156 emigrants out of approximately 3,718 leavers from Kittybrewster School, Aberdeen, between 1916 and 1932, and 128 emigrants out of approximately 4,177 leavers from Sunnybank Public School in the same city between 1912 and 1930.[1]

This book could not have been researched, written and published without encouragement and assistance from an army of individuals and institutions. I am particularly indebted to Jane Brown for drawing to my attention obscure documents hidden in the bowels of the Scottish Record Office's West Register House. Elsewhere in Edinburgh, Christine Johnston of the Scottish Catholic Archives gave me invaluable assistance in my quest for information about the enigmatic Father Andrew MacDonell, and I was warmly welcomed by the staff of the Free Church of Scotland College, the Scottish YMCA and the Church of Scotland Social Work Department when I visited their premises to research Christian colonization schemes. I owe a huge debt of gratitude to Ged Martin, Director of the Centre of Canadian Studies at Edinburgh University, for introducing me to the world of Canadian Studies on both sides of the Atlantic, for giving me the opportunity to air my ideas at conferences and for encouraging me to persevere in my work. Ewen Cameron and Alexander Murdoch of the Department of Scottish History, Margaret Mackay of the School of Scottish Studies, Harry Watson of the Dictionary of the Older Scottish Tongue, and Andrew Walls of the Centre for the Study of Christianity in the Non-Western World, all of the University of Edinburgh, have all offered wise advice and stimulating discussion.

In Scotland's other capital city, the staff of Glasgow University's Business Records Centre gave me access to newly-acquired Trustee Savings Bank records, while, a little further south, I was delighted to renew my links with Quarrier's Village, especially with Bill Dunbar, and to delve again into the treasure-trove archive of the Orphan Homes. In the north, Robert Steward ensured that I made best use of my time at the Highland Council Archive, and I also spent an enjoyable week among the newspaper files and school records held in the Western Isles Public Library in Stornoway. Nearer home, the late Gilbert Buchan and Annie Noble of Inverallochy kindly allowed me to tape their personal recollections of emigration from northeast fishing communities, and I received helpful correspondence from Babs Jenner, Greta MacKenzie and Geoffrey Palmer. On the other side of the Atlantic, I have been enlightened and stimulated by conversations with Marilyn Barber, Bruce Elliott, Michael Vance, and Ferenc and Margaret Connell Szasz. National Archives of Canada staff in Ottawa were unfailingly helpful and efficient, as were the staff of the City of Vancouver Archives and the University of British Columbia, the Glenbow Archives, Maureen Williams of St Francis Xavier University, and Twila Buttimer of the Provincial Archives of New Brunswick. I am also grateful to Diana Pardue of the Ellis Island Oral History Project, who first alerted me to the existence of interviews with Scottish immigrants, and to Janet Levine, who then arranged for me to purchase relevant tapes.

The biggest debts have been incurred closest to home. In acknowledging the assistance provided by Aberdeen University Library, particular mention must be made of the staff of the Department of Archives and Special Collections, who have frequently steered me in the direction of valuable source material that might otherwise have eluded me. The Geography Department helpfully supplied the maps, and Anne MacLeod provided Gaelic translation. Colleagues and students have made valuable suggestions, encouraging me to articulate my research and justify my conclusions.

I am particularly grateful to Donald Withrington for facilitating the publication of a revised version of my study of Christian colonization schemes in the *Records of the Scottish Church History Society*, and to Peter Payne for publishing a fuller version of Andrew MacDonell's experiences in *Northern Scotland* in 1994. Allan Macinnes has awarded me generous amounts of research time as well as providing a wider context for my work through his 'Scotland and the Americas' research project, and has given me valuable contacts and advice.

At an institutional level, I have benefited from two periods of research leave awarded by the University of Aberdeen, one in 1994 to undertake initial research and writing and another in 1998 to complete the manuscript, while a generous Faculty Research Award from the Canadian High Commission allowed me to make a final research visit to Canada in 1998.

Finally, my thanks go to my husband, Andrew Shere, not only for frequent technical assistance but for patiently living with this book in its various stages of preparation throughout the last four years.

Notes

1 Aberdeenshire Archives (AA), GR6S/A47/3/1-3, GR6S/A71/3/1-4. The children went to a range of destinations, primarily in North America, but also including South America, India and Africa as well as the Antipodes.

LIST OF ABBREVIATIONS

AA	Aberdeenshire Archives
BOAS	Board of Agriculture for Scotland
CNR	Canadian National Railway
CPR	Canadian Pacific Railway
DIC	Department of Immigration and Colonization
DO	Dominions Office
ESA	Empire Settlement Act
GH	*Glasgow Herald*
Hansard	Hansard's Parliamentary Debates, fifth series
HN	*Highland News*
LSB	Land Settlement Branch (of the Canadian Soldier Settlement Board)
NAC	National Archives of Canada
NFU	National Farmers' Union
NRAS	National Register of Archives (Scotland)
OSC	Oversea Settlement Committee
OSD	Oversea Settlement Department
P&J	*Press & Journal*
PANB	Provincial Archives of New Brunswick
PANS	Public Archives of Nova Scotia
PP	Parliamentary Paper
PRO	Public Record Office
SCA	Scottish Catholic Archives
SF	*Scottish Farmer*
SFS	*Scottish Farm Servant*
SFSU	Scottish Farm Servants' Union
SG	*Stornoway Gazette*
SHR	*Scottish Historical Review*
SNFU	Scottish National Farmers' Union
SOSBW	Society for the Overseas Settlement of British Women
SRO	Scottish Record Office
SRTN (SM)	*Scottish Red Triangle News (Scottish Manhood)*
SSB	Soldier Settlement Board
TSB	Trustee Savings Bank
WHFP	*West Highland Free Press*

CHAPTER ONE

A tradition of emigration

Establishing the tradition

In the course of the nineteenth century emigration was woven indelibly into the fabric of Scottish life and lore. Between 1825 and the outbreak of the First World War at least 1,841,534 emigrants left Scotland for non-European destinations, constituting an exodus which had profound psychological, as well as demographic, implications.[1] In particular, there developed a historiography of enforced diaspora, fuelled by polemicists, poets and novelists, which portrayed the movement from Scotland primarily as an outflow of unhappy highlanders who, having been driven into exile by policies of clearance and eviction, sought to reconstitute their disrupted lifestyles across the Atlantic or in the Antipodes. Serious recognition of the multi-dimensional and geographically widespread nature of the Scottish exodus was impeded by the dominant image of the impoverished highland emigrant, just as hagiographical studies of the achievements of individual Scots abroad retarded scholarly investigation of the overall economic, social, cultural and political impact of the Scottish presence. Although a more investigative approach was adopted in Margaret Adam's four articles on eighteenth-century highland poverty and emigration published in the *Scottish Historical Review* between 1919 and 1922,[2] a broader basis for the study of Scottish emigration in all its diversity was laid only in 1966 with the publication of Gordon Donaldson's book, *The Scots Overseas*. Two years earlier its author, in his inaugural lecture as Professor of Scottish History at Edinburgh University, had advocated a new approach to the subject which would involve the study of such hitherto neglected issues as Scotland's overseas connections,[3] a plea that has been answered in the last three decades by numerous published investigations of the social and economic roots and repercussions of Scottish emigration, and by an enduring interest in the subject at undergraduate and research levels. This Scottish research is part of a much wider international tapestry of interest in migration studies, which, since the 1960s, has focused more on quantitative analysis of the socio-economic background and motives of the migrants than on debates about their settlement and assimilation overseas. Spearheaded by scholars such as Charlotte Erickson and Dudley Baines, the comparative approach has encompassed a growing recognition of the complexity of migration movements, the impact of migration on the donor countries, and the importance of return migration, while acknowledging the continuing challenge posed by piecemeal research.[4]

Emigration became a significant European phenomenon in the century before the First World War. Over fifty million Europeans went overseas – primarily from Britain and Ireland in the first half of the century, from parts of Scandinavia and several German states around 1850, and from Italy and other areas in southern and eastern Europe by the early 1900s – the United States being the main destination in all cases.[5] Although Scots accounted for only 12 per cent of extra-European departures from the British Isles in this period, the loss of almost two million people from a country whose total population in 1911 was only 4,760,904 represented a considerable drain of human resources and had clear demographic effects. From the European perspective, Baines estimates that only Norway and Ireland – with very low population growth rates – lost a greater proportion of their natural increase of population through emigration.[6] Gross emigration as a percentage of Scotland's natural increase of population rose from 27.6 per cent in 1855–60 to 54.1 per cent in 1881–90 and 84.3 per cent in 1901–10, and exceeded the natural increase in 1907, 1910 and 1911–13. The corresponding English and Welsh figures were 22.2 per cent in the 1850s, 42.5 per cent in the 1880s, and 46.3 per cent from 1901–10, and Scottish net emigration also consistently exceeded the English and Welsh movement as a percentage of natural increase.[7] Indeed, an intensified Scottish exodus at the turn of the century meant that between 1901 and 1914 emigration was taking place at almost twice the English rate, with 11.2 departures per 1,000 population, compared with 6 per 1,000 in England and Wales.[8]

Like their English, Welsh and Irish counterparts, Scots were attracted in the greatest numbers to the United States, but whereas the USA received most emigrants from Britain and Ireland in every single year from 1835 to 1909, the Scots' preference for Canada was maintained until 1847, and demonstrated on six subsequent occasions,[9] before Canada re-emerged as the favourite destination of all but Irish emigrants from 1910–14. Australia, New Zealand and British South Africa, in that order, absorbed most of the residue of emigrants from both Scotland and the British Isles at large. Whereas emigrants in the first half of the nineteenth century were often likely to settle permanently overseas, improvements in transport from the 1850s, in conjunction with changing occupational opportunities, made temporary emigration an increasingly realistic alternative. From

[2]

1894, when statistics of inward movement become available, we can attempt to quantify return migration, albeit imprecisely, since by no means all those entering the British Isles were returning expatriates. As far as Scotland is concerned, an outward movement of 824,325 in the years 1895–1914 was countered by an influx of 320,646, or 39 per cent of overall movement, compared with 45 per cent for the British Isles as a whole.[10] A breakdown of inward movement by selected locations indicates that a greater proportion of Scots returned from the United States (45 per cent) than from either Australasia (32 per cent) or British North America (21 per cent), a ranking that is paralleled, at a consistently higher level, by the influx into the entire British Isles.[11]

The steady movement of emigrants was underpinned by an ongoing public and political debate, originating with the departure of a disquieting number of industrious highlanders across the Atlantic in the second half of the eighteenth century. Opposition at that time had focused on the damaging repercussions for national prosperity and security resulting from such a depletion of economic and military manpower, but, by 1815, mercantilism was giving way to Malthusianism as a burgeoning population across the British Isles, reinforced by demobilized soldiers, threatened to create massive unemployment, disrupt poor relief and provoke social conflict. Emigration therefore came to be perceived in seventeenth-century terms, not as a threat, but as a safety valve which – provided adequate state funding was forthcoming – would rid the country of a redundant and potentially dangerous surplus population. The new Malthusian theories spawned a few small-scale, state-sponsored colonization schemes in Canada and Cape Colony, but excessive cost, limited success, economic recovery and the government's non-interventionist philosophy combined to bring about the termination of these experiments by the mid-1820s. The principle of exporting a surplus, pauper population was also opposed by the emerging Wakefield school, which favoured careful selection of recruits fitted to undertake the 'systematic colonisation' of Britain's valuable, but misused, overseas empire. Wakefield's principles were to influence Colonial Office policy for more than a generation as the Antipodes and, to a lesser extent, the Cape and Natal (though not British North America) were settled under the auspices of the Colonial Land and Emigration Commission. The Commissioners, who regulated the sale of crown lands and the application of the profits to subsidize the passages of eligible colonists, assisted more than 370,000 emigrants during three decades, until the settler colonies began to put their growing powers of self-government to use by assuming responsibility for their own immigration policies.

Public demand for overt and extensive state funding for emigration, which had been silenced by the Commission's success and the buoyant economy of mid-Victorian Britain, re-emerged in the 1880s in response to prolonged recession, coupled with the refusal of the self-governing colonies to adopt any policy which would allow Britain to export her unemployed surplus population. The lobbyists, headed by the National Association for Promoting State-Directed Emigration and Colonisation, argued that state funding would solve at a stroke the twin problems of overpopulation in Britain and labour shortage in the colonies, and also promote the unity of the empire. The government made a token response by appointing a select committee in 1889 to enquire into the feasibility of publicly assisted emigration. It also conceded to a recommendation of the Napier Commission by advancing £10,000 towards the settlement of 465 Outer Hebrideans on the Canadian prairies in 1888 and 1889, but the venture was beset by financial and administrative difficulties and simply confirmed the government in its *laissez-faire* stance. Throughout the century public support for state-aided emigration had always been most vociferous at times of economic crisis and, as the economy began to recover, the conclusion of the select committee in 1891 that there were 'no grounds' for systematic state-aided emigration effectively silenced the state emigrationists, consigning emigrants who were unable to finance their removal to the care of a variety of charitable societies.[12] Despite this setback, however, the combination of organized lobbying with a new concern for imperial unity and opportunity ensured that the emigration debate remained as vibrant at the end of the nineteenth century as it had been at its beginning and sowed the seeds of subsequent legislation.

Yet if we seek to chart the ebb and flow of Scottish – and British – emigration in the nineteenth century in tandem with the vicissitudes of official policy we might be disappointed, for much of the political debate did not contribute significantly towards the actual movement and contributed even less towards the development of a tradition of Scottish diaspora. The British government's consistent priority was to avoid positive intervention while broadly sanctioning imperial colonization and discouraging movement to the USA. Legislation – whether to impede or encourage an exodus – was infrequent and largely ineffective, particularly in respect of the always-controversial state-funded colonization, and although 339,000 emigrants from Britain and Ireland were assisted by government schemes between 1846 and 1869, the assistance was indirect and they represented only 7 per cent of all emigrants at that time.[13] So although emigration took place within a broad framework of official policy – which was clearly responsible for the strategic Canadian settlements in the 1810s, bounty emigration in the 1830s, and the Hebridean colonies at Killarney and Saltcoats in the 1880s – government involvement was intermittent and half-hearted, and the movement was rooted more firmly in a multiplicity of individual and regional factors that shaped its volume and direction. Thus, in Scotland it was the highland landlord lobby which campaigned for both the anti-emigration Passenger Act of 1803 and the facilitating legislation of 1851[14] and unofficial bodies such as weavers' societies and the Otago Association which capitalized on the government's limited support for emigration in order to devise assisted schemes tailored to the needs and interests of Scottish participants. Crucial personal encouragement and assistance offered by pioneer emigrants to relatives and friends at home led to the development of clear patterns of chain migration, while professional emigration agents, many of them sponsored by the destination countries, directed the steps of otherwise uninformed emigrants by means of increasingly sophisticated recruitment campaigns. A notable upsurge in emigration to Canada at the end of the nineteenth century, for instance, was partly the result of the federal government's vastly increased financial commitment to overseas agency activity.[15] And the fact that Scottish emigrants, like their counterparts elsewhere in Britain and Europe, left in large numbers when the domestic economy was buoyant, indicates the consistently magnetic pull of overseas inducements publicized by professional agents and private correspondents, often in contrast to the crisis-induced temporary experiments of governments and welfare organizations.

Who were the Scottish emigrants of the nineteenth century whose departure has been so powerfully mythologized as a diaspora and who seem to have made an impact disproportionate to their numbers on a variety of destinations? To describe emigration as little more than a flight of the impoverished is at odds with much contemporary evidence[16] for, contrary to popular perception, they were not all highland refugees but a diverse collection of individuals from all regions, social backgrounds and occupations, many of whom were described by concerned commentators as the flower of the population. Yet, although their motives for emigrating were as varied as their origins, these emigrants nevertheless successfully constructed a single, enduring image of Scottish identity overseas, achieving this corporate identity through formal and informal mechanisms which they developed both as ethnic anchors and as practical tools for their economic or social advancement. While the highlanders' culture and experiences combined to create in them a particularly emotive and dominant image of diaspora, which they couched in terms of enforced exile rather than positive choice, lowlanders tended to be pragmatic rather than romantic and were much more inclined to acknowledge motives of self-interest and personal ambition. But while they created different theories of diaspora and had different perceptions of its purpose, in practice there was often little difference in the way that they demonstrated and capitalized on their national identity overseas. Highland emigrants might be set apart by their Gaelic language and might have regarded the cultivation of celtic contacts primarily as a means of preserving a traditional culture which had been lost to them in Scotland, but that did not prevent them from using those contacts in pursuit of their economic and social betterment. Conversely, lowlanders – who might have been more inclined to highlight the practical economic applications of the emblems of diaspora – often came to value the cultural function of those emblems, particularly if the experience of emigrating had provoked in them, perhaps unexpectedly, a feeling of rootlessness. And the emblems themselves were often identical, for both highlanders and lowlanders made equal use of the formal mechanisms of church, school and Scottish association, and the informal mechanisms of correspondence, family, community and agency networks to demonstrate their ethnic identity and stimulate secondary emigration.

Tradition revised or reaffirmed? The impact of war and depression

The dislocating experience of world-wide conflict had significant repercussions for both the theory and practice of emigration. The outbreak of hostilities in August 1914 inevitably disrupted international movement, and from 1915 to 1918 only 150,462 people left the British Isles for non-European countries, 20,602 of them from Scotland. Nationwide, the inward movement exceeded the exodus by 20,883 in those years, and Scotland received 4,176 more individuals than it lost through external migration. The much greater disturbance of European migration patterns continued after 1918, when – as a result of intensified economic and political nationalism, totalitarianism, and the introduction of immigration quotas by the United States – the exodus from eastern Europe in particular never returned to pre-war levels.[17]

In Scotland, however, wartime decline was quickly reversed after the return to peace ushered in a renewed outflow that was to have notable demographic effects on the country. Although absolute figures never quite reached the 1911 peak of 88,852, the volume of Scottish emigration during the 1920s – aggravated by a steady southward drift and the ongoing demographic repercussions of heavy male mortality in the war, and combined with a relatively low inward movement – meant that the exodus exceeded the entire natural increase of Scotland's population in the inter-censal period 1921–30. In that decade, despite a natural increase of 352,386 individuals, or 7.2 per cent, the actual population of Scotland as a whole declined by 0.8 per cent, from 4,882,497 to 4,842,980, with every region except the western lowlands registering an absolute decline.[18] The drop was most marked in the highland counties (13.8 per cent), followed by the far north (11.3 per cent) and the northeast (1.4 per cent), and was lowest in the eastern lowlands (0.1 per cent). This remains the only period since records began in which Scotland's actual population has declined absolutely between censuses. Wales experienced a similar phenomenon, with an inter-censal population decline of 63,460 overall, reflected in ten of its thirteen counties. In England, however, the population rose by 6 per cent, from 35,230,225 to 37,354,917, and whereas Scotland suffered a net loss from emigration of 80 in every 1,000 people, England lost 5 in every 1,000, with only 7 counties experiencing a drop in population.[19] Even in Ireland there was a growth of 0.5 per cent, or 19,200 individuals, in the inter-censal period 1926–37.[20]

The Scottish movement, like that from the British Isles as a whole, was concentrated very markedly in the 1920s (Figure 1). The 494,733 Scots who journeyed beyond Europe between 1920 and 1930 accounted for 91 per cent of all such departures in the inter-war period, with a peak of 88,584 in 1923 as those bound for the USA rushed to beat the imposition of quotas. The scenario of high emigration and relatively low inward movement[21] was then reversed dramatically in the 1930s, for in the eight years 1931–38, while a total of 33,595 emigrants left Scotland, there was a simultaneous influx of 76,869 – well over double the number of emigrants. The biggest disparity was in 1932, when only 3,444 Scots emigrated, but 16,623 individuals entered the country from non-European locations, many of them disillusioned returnees from the 1920s exodus. That trend was paralleled to a slightly greater extent in Ireland, with a return rate of 129 per cent in the 1930s, and to a lesser extent in England, with an exodus of 202,548 and an influx of 342,111, these countries also experiencing their biggest disparities in 1932.

The Scots' choice of destinations corresponded to and reinforced immediate pre-war trends (Figure 2), although with a change of emphasis in the inward movement. Not all went overseas, for the English census reveals a growing presence of Scots south of the border. Between 1921 and 1931 there was an increase of nearly 10 per cent in the number of Scots-born people in England and Wales, which rose from 335,517 to 366,486, with a particular concentration in London and the southeast. Although the accessible counties of northern England continued to account for fairly large numbers, the increasing focus on the south during the 1920s reflects the greater impact of industrial depression on the north.[22] Between 1919 and 1938 197,325 emigrants went to Canada, 178,378 to the United States, 97,386 to Australasia and 20,964 to British South Africa. The same period saw an influx of 62,725 from Canada (32 per cent of the exodus), 49,714 from the United States (28 per cent), 22,477 from Australasia (23 per cent), and, notably, 13,623 from British South Africa (65 per cent). England and Wales showed a similar preference for Canada (229,909 passengers), followed by Australasia (177,461), the United States (107,946) and South Africa (91,385), but the Irish continued to patronize the USA

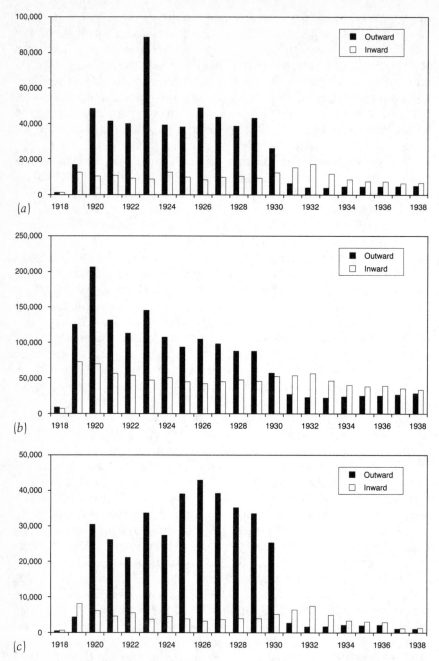

Figure 1 Movement of emigrants (including return movement) between constituent parts of British Isles and extra-European countries, 1918–38. (*Cont. on next page*)

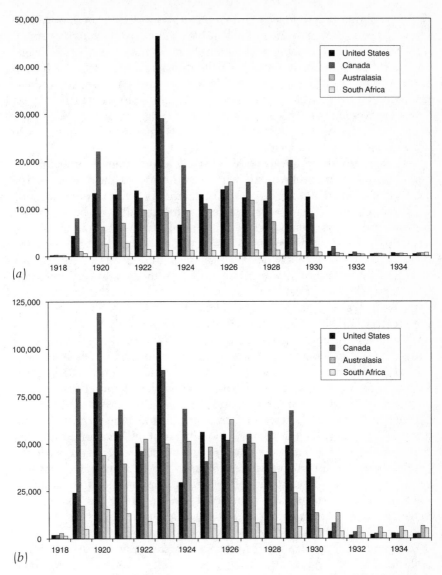

Figure 2 Destinations – emigrant movement from (a) Scotland and (b) the British Isles to the United States, Canada, Australasia and South Africa, 1918–35. (Data from Carrier and Jeffery (1953), pp. 96, 100)

(*Figure 1 cont.*) (a) Scotland; (b) England and Wales; (c) Ireland. (Data from N. H. Carrier and J. R. Jeffery, *External Migration. A Study of the Available Statistics* (London, HMSO, 1953), p. 93)

[9]

(251,706) rather than Canada (73,704), Australasia (29,968) or South Africa (4,690). The high proportion of English/Welsh and Irish inward movement from South Africa (86 per cent and 69 per cent of the exodus, respectively) paralleled the Scottish statistics, but the inward movement of Irish from the USA (17 per cent) was noticeably lower than that from Australasia (29 per cent) or Canada (26 per cent). As might be expected, the biggest inward movement took place to England and Wales, accounting for 49 per cent of the outflow to the United States and 44 per cent of movement to both Canada and Australasia.

Return migration in the 1930s was largely a consequence of worldwide depression and unemployment, just as the outward movement of the 1920s had been an attempt to escape the earlier onset of those conditions in Britain combined with a determination to capitalize on better opportunities still promised overseas. The economic dislocation in Britain after 1918 was not dissimilar to the depression that had followed the Napoleonic wars a century earlier, as was the resort to emigration, although the government's attitude to that remedy was very different. The depression was felt with varying intensity across the British Isles, with South Wales, Tyneside, Clydeside and Belfast probably experiencing the greatest hardship. Yet, although the expulsive catalysts of depression and lengthening dole queues affected the whole of Britain, they were particularly acute in Scotland, where the worst affected area was also the area of greatest population density. Even before the war, cracks had started to appear in Scotland's narrowly based, export-dependent economy and, after the artificial wartime boom and misplaced optimism of 1918–19, Scottish industries relapsed into deep-seated and long-term structural decline, plagued by foreign competition, unfavourable exchange rates, the growth of economic nationalism overseas and obsolescence of products. Having benefited disproportionately from the buoyant market in capital goods before the war, Scotland suffered both disproportionately and protractedly when that market contracted, and in 1935 the nationalist journalist G. M. Thomson wrote bitterly of a country in which, he said, 'the hands of the clock have begun to move backwards'.[23]

The greatest shrinkage was experienced in the heavy industries. Shipbuilding firms struggled for contracts as naval limitation treaties curbed admiralty orders, while the merchant marine contracted in the face of falling exports. Shipyard amalgamations and integration with an increasingly marginalized Scottish steel industry could not deflect the impact of falling orders and obsolete techniques. Employment in shipbuilding in Scotland dropped from 100,000 in 1920 to 50,000 in 1925 and to 10,000 in 1929–32, with unemployment rates rising from 2.42 per cent in 1920 to a startling 75.8 per cent in 1932.[24] At the same time the iron and steel industries fell victim to English, Welsh and overseas competition; in 1927 over half the iron furnaces in Scotland were dismantled in an ineffective rationalization policy, and between 1925 and 1936 the steel industry shed 5,000 workers in a similar futile attempt to rationalize and compete. The coal industry was also in long-term decline, battered by foreign competition, bad management and the challenge of alternative sources of energy. The industry contracted by a third, and in 1932 34 per cent of all Scottish miners were unemployed.[25] Away from the west-central belt with its interdependent heavy industries, Dundee's jute trade could not compete with cheap Indian labour in a slack market, and Aberdeen's granite industry wilted in the face of low demand and cheap foreign competition as well as high American import tariffs. Fishing and farming were also in the doldrums. The herring-fishing industry suffered a 30 per cent drop in tonnage between 1913 and 1929 with the loss of vital markets in the USSR and, later, in Germany, and the countryside was further depopulated as the price of cereals plummeted in the face of cheap foreign imports and, as in the 1880s, arable land was increasingly converted to pasture.

Scotland's economic problems were exacerbated by a failure to replace dependence on the established but ailing staple industries with investment in new secondary manufacturing industries such as aircraft, cars and consumer goods. Perhaps Scottish entrepreneurs were culpable for their lack of vision and initiative; perhaps Scotland was too remote to attract investment in the new era of national and multinational corporations and electric power, when proximity to financial centres and markets was more important than proximity to raw materials; perhaps would-be investors perceived the Scottish workforce as reactionary. Whatever the reasons, the failure to diversify successfully – even after central Scotland was awarded Special Area status in 1934 – aggravated the problems caused by industrial shrinkage and produced massive unemployment. According to Thomson, Scotland between the wars had an unemployment rate 50 per cent higher than that south of the border, an employment growth rate 50 per cent below England's and a steadily declining proportion of both national income and industrial production.[26] In January 1933 30 per cent of Scotland's insured population – around 400,000 people – was unemployed, and average wages for those who were in work were consistently lower than in England.[27] Only one government training centre was located in Scotland, at Springburn, and although it trained 400–500 men a year, this by no means met the demand, and 75 per cent of Scottish applicants were sent to English centres. In any case, the retraining centres were of limited use since admission was governed by opportunities for subsequent placement and, as the depression deepened, several centres closed down. The other abortive remedial policy of the late 1920s, the transfer of surplus workers from depressed to prosperous areas, failed because of all-round resentment and a contracting labour market across the country. Attempts to extend industrial transference to the dominions were, according to the Industrial Transference Board, 'disappointingly slow' because of the 'numerous and restrictive' formalities of migration procedure under the Empire Settlement Act (see page 16) and the expensive passage rates borne by unassisted emigrants, both of which discouraged young men from taking up that more promising option.[28]

Despite such images of a demoralized labour force, Scottish emigration, as in the nineteenth century, continued to be castigated by its opponents as an enforced diaspora of the young and industrious, albeit from a largely different source. While highlanders remained important, both as emigrants and as emblems of unwilling exile, it was recognized in the 1920s that greater numbers of industrial workers were leaving from the depressed central belt. A new political dimension was also added to the debate, as Scottish Nationalists attributed the high outflow to a lack of self-government, and the Labour Party demonized emigration as a government-inspired device for avoiding the extension of state welfare provision. Yet, surprisingly, neither the intensity of the inter-war exodus, the outcry of its opponents nor the recommendations of its advocates has produced, among contemporaries or historians, anything like the sustained interest that was generated by the outflow of highlanders in the eighteenth and nineteenth centuries. Perhaps urban-industrial emigration, lacking the romantic appeal of the highland clearances and failing to fit neatly into the established definition of diaspora, did not inspire detailed study; at any rate, its significance – although acknowledged – has not been deeply investigated in any social, economic, political or even demographic history of inter-war Scotland.

The criticisms of nationalists and socialists were not only a protest against the consequences of economic depression but were also a reaction against an assertive imperialism that is reflected in the historiography of British emigration in the inter-war era as well as in the actual movement of population. In *Migration within the Empire*, published in 1924 as the twelfth and final volume of a multi-volume study of the British empire, the authors deplored the 'negation of policy' represented by the *laissez-faire* attitude of the Victorians, whose fitful, uncoordinated approach to migration had, they claimed, impeded comprehensive and effective imperial colonization. In that year of the Wembley Empire Exhibition they advocated long-term government-directed, government-funded programmes to fill the dominions with British settlers rather than the 'unrewarded toil' of private promoters whose worthy ventures had been hamstrung by insufficient means and authority. Yet they also commended the controversial colonization schemes of child emigrationists and highland landowners such as Lady Emily Gordon Cathcart, whose former tenants, allegedly successfully settled in Saskatchewan, retained a 'gratifying memory' of their benefactor while at the same time culpably neglecting to repay their debts to her.[29] Four years later J. W. Gregory, Professor of Geology at the University of Glasgow, reinforced the case for assisted emigration in a whiggish survey of migration theory and practice in which the donor countries of western Europe were portrayed as conferring the benefits of civilization and economic development on largely passive receiver societies in America and the Antipodes. Yet the role of migration in relieving overpopulation and unemployment, improving living conditions and preventing the development of an unfavourable ratio of white to coloured races was, he predicted, under threat as a result of restrictive immigration policies in the United States and, to a lesser extent, Australia.[30]

By 1929 W. A. Carrothers was sounding a more pessimistic note from a British standpoint. In a book that relied mainly on official sources to examine more than a century of emigration, he confirmed the positive importance of assisted empire migration but bemoaned the failure of the ESA to achieve its potential in an era of increasing economic dislocation, falling birth rates and social welfare schemes that counteracted the lure of a new life overseas.[31] Three years later, in a more positive study that was sponsored by the Royal Empire Society, Australian scholar A. G. Scholes reinforced and expanded Carrothers' particular commendation of government-supported juvenile migration schemes, which he claimed had met with 'wide approval' and 'uniform success' in redistributing the population of the empire.[32] And, not surprisingly, G. F. Plant's study of emigration through the Colonial and Dominion Office window, although not published until 1951, provided a retrospective endorsement of the theory that inspired the inter-war experiments, while acknowledging their practical limitations in an age of 'economic disharmony'.[33] Having been secretary of the Oversea Settlement Committee from 1919 to 1936 and of its successor, the Oversea Settlement Board, from 1936 to 1937, Plant wrote from personal experience and a desire to analyse the past history of empire migration in order to formulate future policies for strengthening the Commonwealth, economically and defensively, through a continuing – but carefully regulated – redistribution of labour.

Empire settlement strategies

The interventionism which characterized the government's emigration policy in the 1920s and 1930s was not simply the product of war or depression but the implementation of concepts that had been debated since the early 1800s. The dawn of the new century had seen a strong revival of the positive imperialist ideology which advocated government-sponsored colonization as a vital tool in securing the increasingly fragile economic, political and racial cohesion of the British empire.

Philanthropists, imperialists and eugenicists joined forces to clamour for a more interventionist policy, not only to counteract cyclical unemployment and periodic unrest in Britain but also to strengthen the imperial relationship in the face of external economic competition and internal social and political tensions. As these concerns began to penetrate the bastions of Westminster and Whitehall some minor concessions were made to the emigrationists' case, but both the Colonial Office and Parliament continued to resist demands for a U-turn on *laissez-faire* emigration policies.[34] That stance was not decisively eroded until after the war, although another assault on non-intervention was made before 1914 by the standing emigration committee of the Royal Colonial Institute. This pressure group ensured that the Dominions Royal Commission, appointed in 1912 with a remit to examine all aspects of imperial development, trade and commerce, gave serious consideration to issues of migration, and its subsequent submissions helped to persuade the Commission that migration was a vital but neglected part of imperial strategy.

> Natural resources and their development are a fruitful theme for discussion. It is clear, however, that this development cannot be achieved without adequate man-power. Hence it comes that of all the problems which lie before Imperial statesmanship none is more important and none more fascinating than that of migration. Its successful organisation lies at the root of the problem of Empire development and largely upon it depends the progress of the immense territories of the Dominions and the increase of power of the Empire as a whole. It is a problem which attracts no less the philanthropist than the statesman, for while to the latter the creation of strong and vigorous communities in distant lands appeals with the greatest force, to the former the possibility of endowing large numbers of the younger generation in the Mother Country with opportunities for happiness and prosperity greater than those which they possess in the land of their birth, opens vistas for successful endeavour such as may be found in no other department of social amelioration.
>
> It is a problem which requires, in our judgment, far more sustained attention than it has hitherto received. Of all the subjects which we have investigated we have found none in which scientific study and scientific treatment are more necessary to replace the spasmodic fluctuations of opinion which have governed the discussion of emigration problems in the past.[35]

By the time the Dominions Royal Commission issued its 1,919-page final report in 1917 the demands of war had precipitated a new age both of multifaceted government intervention and of even greater concern about the future of the empire. It therefore became somewhat easier for the emigrationists to press their case for the establishment of a central emigration authority and for state funding of empire settlement, initially for ex-service personnel and subsequently for civilians. A tour of the dominions by Rider Haggard in 1916 had elicited general support for the settlement of veterans on dominion lands, while at home the Ministry of Labour predicted that such a scheme would be both popular and necessary.[36] But the emigrationists still had many battles to fight. The government, somewhat reluctantly, appointed an Empire Settlement Committee in 1917 under the chairmanship of Lord Tennyson to investigate how to put the Dominion Royal Commission's recommendations into effect. Although it recommended that war veterans be offered both land settlement schemes and free passages, nothing was done, on the grounds that domestic reconstruction should take precedence over empire development in the post-war world. The fruit of Tennyson's report was the stillborn Emigration Bill of 1918, which aimed to unify the administration of overseas settlement through the creation of a central emigration authority, which would also have extensive powers over agents, passage brokers and voluntary societies.[37] By greatly increasing state control without giving a clear indication of future policy, the bill pleased neither the supporters nor the opponents of emigration, and its abandonment in October 1918 seemed to herald a return to *laissez-faire* policies.

Such a prospect was reversed by renewed public interest in emigration when hostilities ended and domestic resettlement proved difficult to implement. A government Emigration Committee was appointed at the Armistice, envisaged as a makeshift transitional body which would oversee the renewed exodus. In April 1919 that committee – by then renamed the Oversea Settlement Committee (OSC) – was given a remit to devise and co-ordinate free passages and assisted emigration schemes for ex-service personnel and their dependents during a limited period, initially a year, beginning on 1 January 1920. In fact the scheme, introduced largely to appease veterans restive at unemployment and poor housing, lasted until March 1923 and assisted a total of 86,027 emigrants from 269,696 applicants. Free third-class passages were awarded to those who could prove war service and were approved by the government of their chosen dominion after initial selection by local officials of the Ministries of Labour and Pensions. Supplementary assistance with outfitting and incidental costs was given by the National Relief Fund to certain approved but impecunious individuals and also to voluntary organizations engaged in training and shipping recruits. Forty-two per cent of the emigrants went to Australia, 32 per cent to Canada, 16 per cent to New Zealand and 7 per cent to South Africa under a programme which accounted for 12 per cent of all British emigrants to the empire between 1919 and 1922.[38]

The appointment of Lord Milner as Secretary of State for the Colonies and Leo Amery as Under-Secretary was crucial in converting the government to a more wholehearted and longer-term policy of empire settlement and development. Both were committed to the idea of imperial unity and to state-aided colonization as a means of promoting it. Amery in particular was responsible for convincing the Cabinet and the Treasury that sponsored empire settlement was an effective and relatively cheap way of dealing with the growing spectre of mass unemployment and anticipated class conflict in Britain. At the same time, proposed rural settlement programmes in unexploited areas of the dominions were meant to reassure commercial and government interests there that the new policy was not simply a cosmetic version of 'shovelling out the paupers' but a viable tool for applying British funding to the economic development of those countries. Much was made of semantics – particularly the distinction between 'emigration', with its negative connotations of expatriation, and the more positive relocation implied by 'overseas settlement' or 'colonization'.

The imperialists' ideas were enshrined in the Empire Settlement Act of 1922 (ESA), which made provision for the British government to spend up to three million pounds a year for fifteen years on loans and grants for assisted passages, land settlement schemes, training courses and other approved ventures in partnership with dominion governments or with public and private bodies in Britain or the dominions. This initiative was a marked departure from the government's traditional reluctance to regulate or assist emigration and also contradicted the emphasis of the fiscal policy of the 1920s on stringent economy. It managed to escape the Geddes Axe on public expenditure because it went some way to assuage manifold public and government anxieties about the economic, political and military security of Britain and her empire in an uncertain post-war world. At the same time most of the dominions welcomed the prospect of British funding for land development, while shipping companies and emigration societies were relieved at the absence of inhibiting regulatory clauses.

Restrictive American immigration policies in the 1920s also helped to focus public interest on opportunities within the empire. Since at least the 1880s the United States had been moving away from a policy of unrestricted immigration and its traditional image as a receptacle for the downtrodden of Europe. It became particularly worried about the allegedly seditious potential of a new influx from southern and eastern Europe, which was perceived as threatening jobs and Protestant domination, and whose influence Congress tried to counter by contract labour laws, stricter exclusion of undesirables, higher head taxes and the adoption in 1917 of a literacy test for immigrants. The retention of native ties among German and Irish settlers during the First World War, compounded by fears of Bolshevism, complicated America's foreign policy and further inflamed feeling against 'hyphenated Americans', leading not only to isolationism but also to emergency legislation to restrict immigration. The provisional act which established a quota system in 1921 was a response to fears of a massive European influx swamping an already depressed labour market, and it limited the number of immigrants of each nationality during the forthcoming year to 3 per cent of the number of persons of that nationality in the USA at the time of the 1910 census. After being renewed for two years in 1922, this legislation was superseded by the National Origins Act, which reflected a more fundamental racism and rejection of the melting-pot theory. Quotas of 2 per cent were worked out on the basis of the 1890 census, with an upper limit of 150,000 on immigration in any one year, and the system was weighted heavily in favour of north and west Europe. From 1924 to 1927 the UK's quota was 84,007, but the main purpose of the National Origins Act was to replace the percentage principle by 1927 with a system that calculated quotas in proportion to different nations' contributions to the existing American population. This would have doubled the British quota at the expense of the nordic countries, giving the UK a quota larger than the total of all other countries in northwest Europe, but, before its effect could be fully felt, the depression brought all European immigration to a virtual standstill.[39] The main impact of American quotas on empire migration was probably to divert to the dominions, particularly Canada, would-be emigrants who had missed the American deadlines or were confused about the quota regulations.

Between May 1922 and March 1936 a total of 405,230 people – 36 per cent of all empire migrants in that period – left the British Isles under the auspices of the ESA (Figure 3), at an overall cost to the government of £6,099,046.[40] They left through a variety of passage and settlement schemes both promoted and co-ordinated by the OSC, a body which, administered by civil servants from the Colonial (later Dominions) Office, brought together for the first time representatives of the diverse government departments, societies and organizations with an interest in emigration. The emigrants were remarkably evenly divided among men, women and children and, in a continuation of pre-war practice, particular encouragement was given to both juveniles and single females. In 1919 the major women's emigration societies were reconstituted as the Society for the Overseas Settlement of British Women, which the following year received a Treasury grant and recognition as the women's branch of the OSC. Under the ESA reduced fares were offered to household workers going to the dominions, with further reductions in 1925 and 1927. Although New Zealand made the most attractive offer, it accounted for fewer women than Australia, which initially offered domestics a free grant of one-third, and a loan of two-thirds, of the third-class fare, subsequently reducing the passage from £33 to £11. Canada, which accounted for 80 per cent of domestics who emigrated under the ESA, agreed in 1922 to advance the £16 third-class fare, and in 1925 reduced the passage to as little as £3 for some destinations.[41]

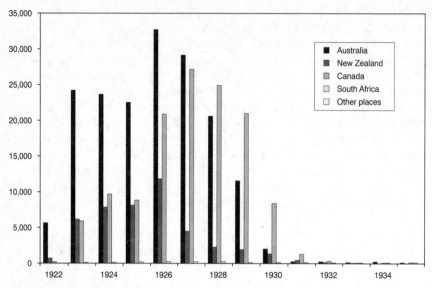

Figure 3 British emigration under the Empire Settlement Act, 1922–35. (PP 1936-37, Cmd 5200, *Report of the Oversea Settlement Committee for the period 1 April 1935 to 31 March 1936*, Table 2, p. 8)

Overall patterns of empire settlement mirrored the female preferences. Forty-six per cent of emigrants under the ESA went to Canada and 43 per cent to Australia, but only 11 per cent to New Zealand and less than 1 per cent to South Africa. Despite British confidence in the complementarity of interests between the core and periphery of the empire, the dominions' priorities in immigration policy did not always conform to British presuppositions – especially by the depressed 1930s as the limits of settlement were reached, labour needs were increasingly met internally and sex ratios became more balanced. South Africa's ambivalent attitude to British settlers, which predated the war, continued to be dictated by domestic politics thereafter as Afrikaner nationalism militated against overt British imperialism, while the persistent quest for white racial dominance shut out migrants without skills or capital – the very categories targeted by the ESA. At the same time, however, increasing fears of black domination led to a selective, largely tacit, recruitment of affluent British settlers, mainly under the auspices of the 1820 Memorial Settlers' Association, which sponsored a total of 10,000 settlers between 1920 and 1946, most of them would-be farmers with a minimum of £1,500–£2,000 capital. The élitism of South Africa's immigration policy and its insistence on the settlers' possession of substantial assets, which set it apart from the other dominions, stemmed from the country's economic limitations as well as political fears and meant that the ideology of empire settlement took only a very partial root there.[42]

Physical and economic limitations and the complaints of the labour movement about housing and job shortages also combined to inhibit large-scale assisted emigration to New Zealand, although the government welcomed the revival and extension of assisted passages. From 1918 to 1922 the New Zealand government itself subsidized the transfer of 14,967 selected immigrants, mainly female domestic servants, who were given entirely free passages. That allowance was continued under the British-funded ex-service personnel scheme, which saw the introduction of 12,671 immigrants, and the jointly funded ESA, which brought in a further 44,734 settlers.[43] In an attempt to demonstrate even-handedness towards farmers, industrialists and manufacturers, the New Zealand government modified the pre-war nomination system in 1920 to allow open nomination by any New Zealand resident of any person in Britain, irrespective of relationship or occupation, provided that the nominators guaranteed employment and accommodation. The continuing influence of the rural lobby, however, was seen in the extra immigration schemes that operated in addition to nomination, consisting mainly of assisted passages for agricultural workers and official sponsorship and government subsidies to encourage special programmes for juvenile immigrants. The resulting anachronistic dominance of domestic servants, followed by rural labourers, among the immigrants reflected neither the occupational structure or employment difficulties of inter-war Britain nor the changing occupational structure of New Zealand.

Australian settlement was also complicated by a disparity between rural myth and urban reality, but more particularly by domestic power struggles and Australian politicians' determination to use migration as a means of gaining access to British development capital. Under the ESA not only were approved migrants allowed a 33 per cent discount on the £33 passage; Wakefieldian-style schemes were also set on foot for settling 6,000 families in groups in Western Australia and New South Wales and 2,000 families in Victoria, with the imperial and commonwealth governments sharing the payment of interest on development loans. While Victoria and New South Wales hoped to recruit ex-officers with substantial capital, who would be given twelve months' training in an agricultural college or farm before being sold land of their own, the 75,000 migrants who were to be imported into Western Australia were to be people without capital or experience. After an initial learning period in farm service they were to compete for the 6,000 farms, which were to be cleared and developed as dairy enterprises, while it was hoped that the unsuccessful applicants would continue as agricultural labourers. Some of the state farm recruits came to Australia through 'selected' migration, a scheme whereby the state governments requested Australia House in London to recruit specified numbers and categories of settlers – which they did, uniquely among migrant-receiving countries, by enlisting the help of British employment exchanges. Most assisted migrants were nominated by individuals, however, and to a lesser extent by philanthropic organizations and employers, nominations being subject to the approval of the state governments and dependent on the provision of work and accommodation.

The disappointing results of assisted emigration to Australia were due to a combination of bad planning, Labour hostility and mutual suspicion about the motives of empire settlement. Western Australian land settlement was bedevilled by a shortage of farm labouring jobs, the determination of the migrants to stay together and go straight on to their land and the problems of inexperienced pioneers in ill-prepared territory. With nothing to lose, many abandoned their holdings, and by 1936 only 390 migrant families remained on farms. The expensive failure of the Western Australian scheme, combined with Labour opposition, prevented the implementation of the parallel scheme in New South Wales, while in Victoria, of 814 settlers approved, only 361 took up land, and only 50 succeeded. Complaints of misrepresentation and poor-quality land were corroborated by a royal commission appointed by the state government, resulting in *ex gratia* payments being made to 284 complainants, 116 of whom returned to Britain. Australia House found it difficult to fill the quotas for selected migrants, partly because of their damaging association with labour exchanges and unemployment, while from the British perspective there was resentment at restrictive bureaucracy, unscrupulous targeting of juveniles and inadequate aftercare. The £34 Million Agreement – an experiment introduced in 1924 with the aim of introducing 450,000 settlers in ten years conditional on the receipt of British development capital – failed either to induce mass settlement or to finance the infrastructure of roads, irrigation and industry envisaged. The Australian states were suspicious of the Development and Migration Commission, the commonwealth agency responsible for implementing the scheme, and manipulated the Agreement to obtain the maximum amount of loan funding in return for the minimum introduction of selected migrants.[44]

Even Canada was a somewhat ambivalent participant in sponsored colonization programmes as a continuing hunger for British farmers for the prairies was tempered by a tendency to equate assisted immigration with incompetent or impecunious settlers. Antagonism was fuelled as early as 1920 by bad publicity about British war veterans who emigrated to Canada under the auspices of the Canadian Soldier Settlement Board (SSB). Despite stringent selection by Canadian officials stationed in Britain, too few of these recruits were the physically fit, well-endowed agriculturists desired by the Canadians; many were men from urban-industrial backgrounds who remained in the cities and often became destitute, while two-thirds of the recruits were women and children – most of them war widows and orphans.[45]

The Liberal government of Canada also initially fought shy of subsidizing British settlers under the ESA, partly for fear that such selective assistance would upset the powerful western farming lobby and drive Canadians south to the USA. Images of remittance men and paupers died hard, and when in 1923 Canada did allocate $600,000 to empire settlement this limited sum was intended to assist only three categories of British settlers: domestic servants, agricultural workers nominated by Canadian farmers, and child migrants sponsored by private societies. The children were to be given a grant of $40 per head, but the agriculturists and domestics (or their nominators) were expected to find at least a quarter of the fare themselves, the Canadian government's contribution being to share with its British counterpart the remainder of this cost in the form of a passage loan.[46] But public and press criticism of such a parsimonious attitude was vociferous, focusing on the fear that Canada was losing out to the other dominions in the quest for desirable British settlers at the very time when an economic upturn seemed to give scope for a more expansive settlement policy. The Canadian government responded to this criticism – and to an influx of railway company-sponsored southern European immigrants – initially by introducing through the agency of the Canadian Pacific Railway (CPR) a £3 passage rebate for British settlers travelling third class after 1 March 1924 whether or not they were already receiving assisted passages under the ESA. This reduced the third-class steamship fare to £13, or £3 to those receiving ESA assistance, compared with a pre-war fare of £5, and an extension of the scheme in 1926 reduced the assisted passage for agriculturists and domestic servants to £2. Then in 1925 Canada promoted the 3,000 Families Scheme; land it had originally purchased for soldier settlement but which had been abandoned or never taken up was made available to 3,000 British families who, if they had £25 for immediate use on arrival, could receive advances of up to £300 each from the British government for the purchase of stock and equipment, while the Dominion government supplied the farms. The loans were repayable over 25 years at 5 per cent interest.

Subsequent collaborative ventures, in which the British and Canadian governments spent equal amounts of money on passage grants and aftercare, respectively, initially precipitated a doubling of assisted emigration, but by 1928 a Canadian reaction had set in against what was perceived as excessive expenditure on the importation of paupers and misfits. In yet another reflection of incompatible priorities Canada refused to countenance the British emigrationists' vision of a vastly expanded 3,000 Families Scheme, a revived Harvesters' Scheme for 10,000 unemployed miners who would be absorbed permanently into the Canadian labour market, and massive programmes for the settlement of domestic servants and juveniles. Agreeing only to proposals that involved no federal government financial commitment, Canada tightened up medical inspection of emigrants, forbade independent recruitment by provinces, railway companies and private organizations, withdrew passage assistance from single men and wound up the flagship 3,000 Families Scheme. All that the Oversea Settlement Department managed to salvage was a small-scale land settlement scheme which saw 349 families take up farms in New Brunswick, similar schemes involving the railway companies and the Hudson's Bay Company in western Canada, and a short-lived reduced transatlantic fare of £10 for all permanent British migrants. The reduced passage operated from December 1929 to October 1931 and was utilized by 56 per cent of the 104,252 emigrants to Canada in that period.[47] But from the wider perspective, although 107,084 assisted emigrants came to Canada between 1922 and 1935 – including over 20,000 female domestics, almost 10,000 juveniles pursuing a farming career, and 3,500 farm families – British emigrationists remained disappointed that spending under the 1922 legislation never reached even half of the annual budget allocation.[48]

Although more than 405,000 emigrants took advantage of the ESA in its first fourteen years, the recurring message from all the dominions was one of reluctant and sporadic participation, which was shaped by domestic politics rather than by a vision for imperial unity and progress. The recruitment of unemployed victims of the depression confirmed entrenched colonial suspicions of the British government's motives in assisting emigration, and the OSC never managed to shake off the reputation of exporting paupers and misfits under the guise of mutual welfare programmes. Nor did it succeed in its aim of diverting a significant number of migrants from urban-industrial to rural occupations. High rates of return migration further eroded its credibility, and in the 1930s British apathy about emigration was eclipsed by outright opposition fuelled by concerns about falling birth rates and the loss of labour to countries that began to be perceived as competitors rather than partners.

The government acknowledged recruitment problems as early as 1928, when a report of the Industrial Transference Board expressed 'regret, and indeed astonishment … [at] the rate of settlement of British people in Australia and Canada, notwithstanding the passing in 1922 of the Empire Settlement Act for the express purpose of stimulating it.' While it blamed complex procedures and 'numerous and restrictive' formalities for discouraging potential recruits, G. F. Plant twenty-three years later criticized over-ambitious land settlement schemes, aggravated by unrealistic requirements for the repayment of loans, and a general tendency to seek scapegoats for failures which were due primarily to international economic depression.[49] Contemporary concern that the domestic security provided by social insurance schemes in Britain had eroded the adventurous spirit of would-be emigrants was supported to some extent by a parliamentary inquiry in 1926, which recommended reciprocal welfare programmes in the dominions but maintained that the main causes of decreased migration were depressed trade and dominion-imposed restrictions on assisted passages for families.[50] Since the early nineteenth century advocates of state-aided emigration had emphasized its value as a vehicle of social reform; late Victorian philanthropists such as William Quarrier and William Booth had integrated assisted emigration into wider social rehabilitation schemes; and in 1924 L. S. Amery described empire settlement as 'simply social reform writ large', to be implemented in tandem with domestic relief and employment strategies.[51] It is therefore ironic that at the very time the state wholeheartedly endorsed emigration as a safety valve, its attempts to give it large-scale practical effect were impeded, according to some commentators, by the simultaneous development of British state welfare provision in the form of unemployment and health insurance, pensions and council housing.[52]

Disappointing recruitment under the ESA in an era of substantial overall emigration suggests that, as in the nineteenth century, official policy was only part of the story, albeit a larger part than in the unfunded Victorian age. The Ministry of Labour itself acknowledged this in the 1928 Report of the Industrial Transference Board. While regretting the limited effects of the legislation, it admitted that

> Stimulated migration under the Empire Settlement Act or otherwise, and operating through Government departments and voluntary migration societies should be regarded as supplementary to natural migration. The majority of intending migrants do not demand or need elaborate supervision or help. They want an opportunity to go overseas, under conditions they are able to meet; they want to take their chance in countries which hold both risks and prospects of success; they want the knowledge that they will receive a welcome, not necessarily from Governments and organised bodies, but from the ordinary men and women among whom they will lead their lives in future.[53]

One of the major aims of this study is to assess whether the significant Scottish component of the inter-war exodus from Britain was a demonstration of 'stimulated migration' – undertaken primarily in response to government or charitable initiatives in the context of a severe economic downturn – or a continuation of the largely independent movement of individuals, families and community groups that had characterized much nineteenth-century emigration and which rose significantly in the pre-war decade. Unlike the piecemeal Victorian legislation, which had been largely a response to highland crises, the ESA applied to the whole of Scotland, but it had to put down roots in a society which for more than a century had organized a significant emigration through individual, community and charitable society initiatives and might well be suspicious of the possible penalties attached to such a sudden, unprecedented government bounty.

The Scottish dimension

Ironically, in an age of voluminous official reporting and detailed information-gathering, incomplete statistical records present a major problem in evaluating the impact of overseas settlement legislation on different parts of the United Kingdom. Migration and emigration reduced Scotland's actual population by almost 1 per cent in the 1920s, but it is impossible to determine what proportion of the emigrants went out under soldier settlement or the ESA. British sources disaggregated departures under the legislation only by destinations, rather than places of origin, and although the official statistics compiled by the Board of Trade give details of gender, age and occupation, they are infuriatingly silent on the national or regional composition of the emigrants. The Empire Settlement Warrants mentioned in Canadian Immigration Department correspondence – which would have given a detailed breakdown of the major transatlantic movement – have not survived,[54] and a more cursory investigation of antipodean archives has also proved disappointing. Scottish preferences therefore have to be deduced from indirect information contained in newspapers, civil service records and the emigrants' own observations.

Debates about empire settlement and the reports and policies of the OSC were regularly reported in the Scottish press, which also gave extensive coverage to advertisements for emigration within and outside the empire under official schemes or private arrangements. Opportunities for soldier settlement, however (as opposed to general statistical reports of its progress), were not particularly well publicized during the scheme's three years of operation, with only occasional reminders from the regional booking agencies which administered it that 'Military dependants' vouchers [were] exchanged (free of charge) for through steamer or rail tickets' at their offices.[55] In 1923, however, the Canadian government agreed to extend passage assistance to civilian agriculturists, using the facilities of the SSB as a colonizing agency to help those who were financially capable of land settlement, and, through the SSB, offering advice to settlers on the selection of suitable land and the purchase of stock and equipment. According to both the Scottish and English press the new arrangements aroused particular interest in Scotland, and in spring 1923 the Aberdeen branch of Mackay Brothers' agency organized a series of recruitment meetings for W. M. Jones, Director of Administration of the Canadian SSB, during a prolonged Scottish tour undertaken in response to this interest.[56]

Then, in July 1923, Mackay's in Aberdeen advertised two assisted-passage recruitment programmes under the auspices of the main Canadian railways: a visit by a female representative of the Canadian National Railway (CNR) to the Canadian government emigration office in the city to engage domestic servants, and a drive by the CPR to recruit large numbers of harvesters for three months' employment on the prairies.[57] The introduction of passage rebates and the establishment of the 3,000 Families Scheme in 1924 reinvigorated federal, provincial and railway company recruitment, and in December 1926 Mackay Brothers' Aberdeen office was again active in arranging for a Nova Scotia agent to interview farm labourers and experienced farmers, with and without capital, not only at their city office but also in the outlying centres of Dyce, Inverurie, Oldmeldrum, Fyvie, Culter, Banchory, Ballater, Lumphanan, Skene and Ellon.[58]

Promotion was by no means confined to Canada. In 1923 Aberdeenshire agriculturists and tradesmen were sought out by a New Zealand government agent at meetings in Inverurie, Turriff, Alford, Huntly, Banff and Banchory, as well as in Aberdeen, and later that year the long-established Longside agent, William Maitland, claiming the authority of the New Zealand High Commissioner, advertised for plasterers and and bricklayers for Auckland.[59] Mackay Brothers was probably the most assiduous of all Scottish regional booking offices in terms of hosting lecture campaigns and undertaking interviews on behalf of antipodean agents, particularly those from Australia. In January 1923 one of its Aberdeen representatives was sent thirty miles inland to Turriff to interview farm labourers for 'guaranteed work' in Australia under the ESA, and two months later similar guarantees were offered to suitable agriculturists who were to be interviewed in Aberdeen by an Australian commonwealth government representative. In August 1923 assisted passages and Group Settlement in Western Australia were explained in a lecture and interviews arranged by Mackay's at the Aberdeen Employment Exchange, and four months later an Australian government agent was sent out under Mackay's auspices to explain reduced passages and loans to land workers, farm apprentices and domestic servants in the rural communities of Alford, Inverurie, Maud, Peterhead, Turriff, Huntly, Rhynie, Ballater and Banchory, as well as Aberdeen.[60] In July and September 1924 it was the turn of Victoria and New South Wales to have their Group Settlement schemes explained to Aberdeen audiences by agents T. E. Wyatt and A. M. Allen, respectively, while William C. Stillman, who in 1922 had been sent to Britain on a three-year assignment as chief clerk of the Commonwealth Government's Migration and Settlement Office in London, also undertook a Scottish tour during 1924. In November he appeared at the Aberdeen YMCA, giving a lecture (illustrated with film) on farming opportunities across Australia and claiming that some of the Commonwealth's finest Scottish settlers had come from the Aberdeen area.[61] Several of these recruitment visits were repeated in subsequent years, and opportunities were also given to youths to emigrate under the Dreadnought and Big Brother schemes.[62]

Agents' propaganda was reinforced by the rhetoric of visiting and resident politicians. When New South Wales premier Sir George Fuller came to London in 1923 to inaugurate the 6,000 Farms Group Settlement Scheme, he noted the Scots' particular aptitude for land settlement. At the same time Aberdeenshire-born Western Australian politician and businessman, J. A. Thomson, on the eve of his sixth visit home, was advised to 'tell his countrymen, the Scots, that they wanted in Western Australia a much greater percentage of the solid, sound, successful Scots who in the past had done so much to pioneer the outposts of the British Empire'. Thomson did as requested, outlining his own contribution to Australian commerce during forty-one years in the Antipodes and endorsing Western Australia's part in group settlement.[63] Two years later, in an address to the Unionist Association in Ballater on the empire's need for 'men, money and markets', local MP C. M. Barclay-Harvey stressed the opportunities Canada offered to the emigrant who was 'willing to take off his coat and work' and reiterated the Dominion's preference for Scottish settlers.[64]

The appeals of professional agents and occasional commentators were sometimes corroborated by editorial endorsement, particularly in respect of assisted emigration to Canada, although the muted enthusiasm of the *Press & Journal* suggests that the editor was mindful of the needs of his rural readership:

'Empire settlement made easy' seems to be the ideal which has inspired the new migration scheme prepared by the British and Canadian governments. The details of the revised rates are certainly calculated to make Scottish youths with a practical knowledge of land work decide to pack their 'kists' and turn their wandering steps to Toronto or Calgary at once. The 'cut' in rates for emigrants is on a substantial scale. For the modest sum of £3 it is possible to ship from Scotland to Halifax, and for £9 the migrant will be taken right across the Dominion to Vancouver. The reduction in rates represented by the new charges is roughly equivalent to from 60 to 80 per cent.

This revision of rates, it may be assumed, is the first definitely practical step taken by the Government to ease the unemployment difficulties by means of Empire settlement. From the point of view of the agricultural community the one drawback to the plan is that the big cut in rates is specially designed to attract to the Dominion farm workers and men, whether single or married, who are willing to go on to the land and put their backs into the business of growing wheat or rearing cattle. Experienced agriculturists are just the type of men that we can least

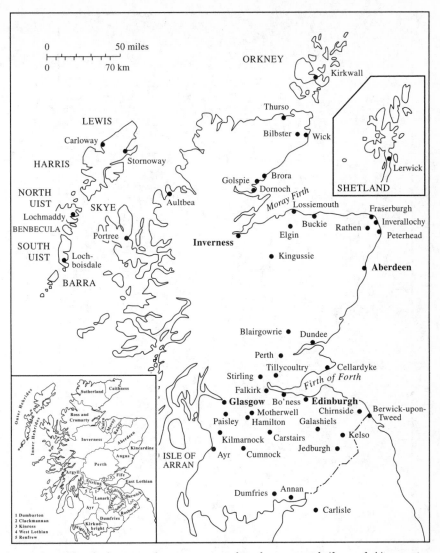

Map 1 Scotland, showing places mentioned in the text, with [*lower left*] counties

conveniently spare, but to the younger class of farm workers in the
North of Scotland Canada has always made a strong appeal, and the
lure of the Golden West has now a new and cheap attraction. Even in
our towns there are hundreds, indeed thousands, of able-bodied men
who have spent their early years on the land, but subsequently drifted
into casual labour in the large industrial centres, having their means of
living supplemented by the dole, and to this class the scheme offers
special inducements.[65]

[27]

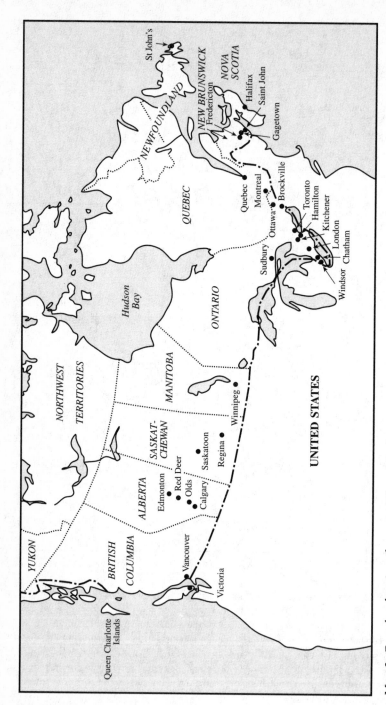

Map 2 Canada, showing places mentioned in the text

As in the nineteenth century, many emigrants continued to be recruited by private individuals or commercial agencies. The Maud-based agent of the Hudson's Bay Company regularly advertised through the *Press & Journal* for fit young men 'of good education and some business experience', and unaffiliated individuals sometimes came to Scotland to recruit domestic servants for themselves or others.[66] But most private recruitment was for destinations that did not fall within the orbit of the ESA. Ever since the 1830s planters from northeast Scotland had played a disproportionate part in the development of Ceylon's coffee and tea industries, and these 'old and numerous ties', as well as the largely informal methods of recruitment, were maintained into the 1920s. Retired planters' dinners continued to be held in Aberdeen, and on 6 May 1924 one of these men, Sir Leybourne Davidson of Huntly, advertised in the local press for an assistant for a rubber and tea estate, preferably a farmer's son or a man with banking and engineering expertise.[67] Wealthy intending investors in South Africa could respond to the frequent advertisements of the 1820 Memorial Settlers' Association, or to opportunities offered by enterprises such as the African Realty Trust Ltd and the African Irrigated Land Company Ltd, whose agents sometimes recruited through provincial booking offices.[68] Only a few openings in the United States, mainly for domestic employment, were advertised in the newspapers, so the large exodus which took place there was probably mainly a response to private encouragement from the large body of Scots who had previously emigrated there, many of them in the 1910s.

Evidence of emigrants' continuing interest in the USA is reflected in the regular press reports of substantial embarkations at Glasgow and Greenock. Between 1921 and 1923 about 100,000 emigrants, primarily from Lanarkshire and Renfrewshire, sailed from the Clyde, most to North America. The United States was fairly well represented, with thirty-four sailings in 1921 and thirty-seven in 1922, compared with twenty-seven sailings to Canada in 1921 and forty-five the following year. 1923 saw more emigrant departures from Scotland than any other year in the decade, the *Press & Journal* estimating that the period January to mid-September had seen 50,000 emigrants cross the Atlantic from Clyde ports, with a further 10,000 due to leave in 10 liners over the next fortnight, 600 of them for the USA.[69] Such was the demand that both the Canadian Pacific and White Star–Dominion lines regularly sent their Liverpool-based vessels to the Clyde to embark more passengers, and while large numbers of unemployed shipbuilding and engineering artisans came from central Scotland, the north, predictably, sent mainly agriculturists, as well as domestic servants.

Large numbers of people from the north of Scotland are making preparations to emigrate. Yesterday morning a party of 16 third class passengers for Glasgow left by the early morning train, and another party of 30

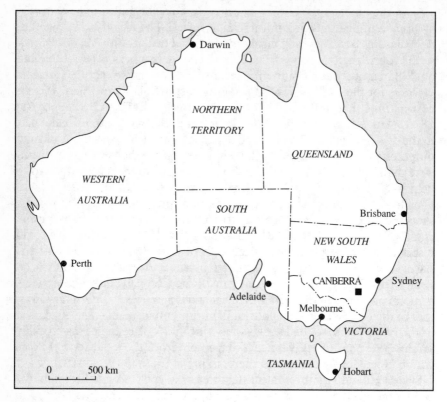

Map 3 Australia

second-class passengers by the 10.50 a.m. train. Both parties are bound for the United States, and consist mainly of young single men, while three of the number were three farmers who had given up their farms and are going out to join their sons.

There was a large crowd of relatives at the station. Every week from now to the end of July there will be conducted parties leaving Aberdeen for Canada and the United States. Special parties are being arranged for women and children who are going out to join their husbands, and also for single girls, who are emigrating in large numbers.

During this week a number of Canadian farmers have been in the locality selecting men for farm work in Western Canada, and some of these farmers are taking the men back to Canada with them.[70]

March and April were usually busy months for transatlantic crossings, but since Scotland had filled its quota by April 1923 bookings from the Clyde to the United States were suspended until 1 July, when there was an immediate upsurge in activity, with 4,000 leaving in one weekend.

Of 2,900 emigrants on two liners bound for Canada, more than 1,000 were continuing by rail to the USA, while a further 900 were sailing straight to New York. At the end of August there was another outflow of 6,000 emigrants from the Clyde to North America, 4,000 of them to the USA, including a large contingent of skilled workers from the lower Clyde on the White Star liner *Haverford*.[71] On 22 October 1923 the *Press & Journal* reported the unusual departure of a Sunday emigrant train from Aberdeen carrying the vanguard of the November quota of American settlers, with more to follow the next day. Sixty-eight young men and women, all from Aberdeen and Aberdeenshire, were to be joined at Perth by 130 emigrants from Dundee and Angus and, at Birmingham, by a separate contingent from Edinburgh and Glasgow before travelling on to Southampton to embark on the RMSP (Royal Mail Steam Packet) *Orea* for the USA. According to local booking agent Mackay, the Aberdeen area had even then almost completed its quota for the fiscal year ending on 30 June 1924, and two days later the *Press & Journal* reported the animated scenes that had attended the departure of eight special emigrant trains from Glasgow for Greenock, whose passengers were to form part of a 3,000-strong exodus on the last four liners taking emigrants to the USA before the opening of the new quota in July 1924.

Uncertainties and delays caused by quotas may well have caused many USA-bound emigrants to direct their steps to Canada instead. The waning of Clyde passages to the USA relative to those to Canada in 1922 was probably due to the impact of the previous year's legislation, just as on 19 April 1924 the *Press & Journal* reported an increased rush to Canada, particularly of skilled workers, because of a reduction in the American quota. Problems associated with the quota regulations included the last-minute prohibition of landings or diversion of vessels. In May 1923, for instance, the Anchor liner *Cameronia* was sent to Halifax instead of New York, with 399 emigrants, including 250 Scots, because the quota was apparently about to be filled. The passengers were then rushed to New York by special train to beat the arrival of another British ship, only to find it carried a mere seventeen British immigrants – small comfort to over 1,000 Scots who had abandoned sailing on the *Cameronia* because they had been told that the quota was virtually full.[72] Booking agencies predicted, rightly, that the revised American legislation in 1924 would wreak havoc with sailing arrangements and advised emigrants against making unalterable plans until they had been granted a visa certificate and arranged a firm sailing date. In February USA-bound Scots were warned that they might not be admitted until February 1925 under the new regulations, which had spread entry over twelve months and reduced the British quota from 77,342 to 62,500. In June 1924 7,000 emigrants were delayed at Glasgow because the consul, having received no instructions from the American immigration authorities, had been unable to issue visas, and four months later it was claimed that many of the 20,000 applicants for American visas from southwest and central Scotland would be unable to sail until late 1926 or early 1927. More than twenty applications were being received daily at the US consulate in Glasgow, over half of them from the wives, families and other near relatives of men already resident in the United States, but the quota for the Glasgow consular area had been exhausted for the next two and a half years.[73]

From time to time the Scottish press indicated that Canada's growing dominance was a result of the combination of American restrictions and the Dominion's own assisted settlement schemes. In April 1924, although 'the gateway to the United States is, it is true, closed for the moment', it was stated that over 2,000 people had just left Scotland for Canada and that bookings for the rest of the summer 'promise to be more than usually heavy'.[74] Later that year the inauguration of the 3,000 Families Scheme drew an editorial comment from the *Press & Journal* that, despite good openings in the Antipodes, South Africa and Rhodesia:

> The majority of intending emigrants will, however, probably bend their attention first to Canada, where a definite and not unattractive offer is made on behalf of the Government; and, in view of the severe restrictions placed on settlement in the United States, hundreds of Scottish families will almost certainly turn their footsteps towards the great open spaces of Canada before many months are over ... . The task of British statesmen is to get the thousands of surplus workers of this country into touch with those parts of the Commonwealth States which are starving for lack of population. To man the vacant spaces of the Empire is to strengthen the influence and the resources of the Motherland.[75]

Reports of emigrant shipping indicate a consistent – though not all-encompassing – Scottish interest in opportunities under the ESA. Since many of those leaving were artisans rather than agriculturists or domestic servants, they were unlikely to have qualified for assistance. In March 1923, for example, the *Metagama*, *Saturnia* and *Marloch* left the Clyde for Canada with 1,100, 450 and 300 emigrants, respectively. The *Marloch*, which usually sailed from Liverpool, had called at the Clyde in response to the keen Scottish demand and had embarked, among others, 'a party of 130 from Aberdeen, which is the largest to leave Aberdeen since the war. Many of the emigrants from Scotland are engineers, joiners, and brick-layers, and they are proceeding to America, where, it is reported, trade is brisk.' Transatlantic passages had been booked well into the season, with little third-class accommodation left on some steamers – particularly on the St Lawrence run.[76] Interest was still strong in December, when 900 emigrants, including a 'striking number' of domestics, left Greenock for

St John, New Brunswick, together with 15 Clydeside engineers, 13 clerks, 8 shop assistants, 3 masons, and several hundred labourers and miners 'of a very fine stamp'.[77] An even greater variety of tradesmen was represented, along with domestics and agriculturists, on another vessel bound for St John, the *Marburn*, which sailed in April 1924, while included among the 1,300 passengers on the *Metagama* in the same month were 105 domestic servants, 74 agriculturists, 64 engineers, 41 general labourers, 24 clerks, 20 joiners, 11 future brides, 11 miners and an elderly couple going to join a son, as well as 115 passengers travelling under the auspices of the Salvation Army. About 10 per cent of the party was going to take up farm work under the ESA.[78]

Assisted settlement was also popular among more than 600 emigrants who left the Clyde for Quebec and Montreal on the Anchor-Donaldson liner *Athenia* at the end of April 1924 in a youthful, rural-based exodus reminiscent of pre-war departures:

> An interesting feature of the Glasgow contingent was that about 120, or nearly one-fifth, of the passengers were girls and young women who are going out to Canada as domestic servants. Of this number half are travelling under the auspices of the Salvation Army, while most of the others are going under one or more of the various assisted passage schemes which are in operation. The girls came mainly from the sparsely populated districts in the North and North-East of Scotland and from the Islands. Among the male passengers were men of a great variety of occupations from many parts of the country, but, as usual, most of them were farm workers or general labourers in this country, and practically all are going to Canada with the intention of engaging in work on the land there. It was interesting to note that, taking the party as a whole, the younger elements predominated. Since the beginning of the emigrant season this year it has been noted that many of the men who are leaving Scotland are of middle age. Those on the *Athenia*, however, resembled as a class the typical emigrants of the pre-war days, when most of the men who went to Canada were between 20 and 30 years old. There were, however, a number of families, several of them including very young children. Most of yesterday's emigrants came from the country; Canadian emigration has not had any great effect on the population of the industrial areas since the rush of harvesters took place last summer.[79]

Emigrants on the *Cassandra* and the *Saturnia*, which followed the *Athenia* from the Clyde to Quebec and Montreal in succeeding weeks, also came mainly from rural areas and included large contingents of young, single men going out under the ESA to work on the land, as well as forty and fifty female domestics, respectively, 'numerous families' going to join relatives and a smattering of miners, engineers and mechanics.[80] Most of the 200 Scottish emigrants who sailed on the New York-bound *Tuscania* in May disembarked at Halifax, Nova Scotia, including a large number of assisted farm workers, labourers, domestics and tradesmen drawn from all over Scotland but particularly from northwestern farming districts.[81] On 23 May 1924 the *Glasgow Evening Times* confirmed that of more than 11,000 emigrants who had left Scotland for Canada since the beginning of March, a 'considerable number' had taken advantage of assisted passages under the ESA; and on 7 June *The Scotsman* explained that an upsurge in departures to Canada was due to large numbers of ploughmen leaving their situations at the May term, some of them emigrating with government assistance. The 3,000 Families Scheme was particularly popular with Scots throughout 1925, 1926 and 1927, with the *Stornoway Gazette* remarking on 21 August 1923 that the 950 emigrants who had just left the Clyde on the *Athenia* included not only miners and construction workers but also hundreds of agricultural workers and domestic servants going to 'try their luck on the land'.

Whereas emigration to Canada was conducted through a variety of private and official channels, the smaller number of Scots who went to Australia seem to have relied more fully on facilities offered under the ESA. This pattern conformed to nineteenth-century practice, when the greater cost involved in independent emigration to the Antipodes meant that those who went there were more likely to require subsidized passages than those who crossed the Atlantic. On 24 March 1923, in a footnote to a discussion of privately organized emigration to North America, the *Press & Journal* observed that 'parties are also leaving at intervals for Australia, facilities being provided under the Empire Settlement Act', and a year later, on 21 April 1924, in another article focused on the Canadian movement, it added that 'under the group migration scheme, which was initiated towards the end of January, a considerable number of families have also left for Australia'. As in the nineteenth century, an agent's visit sometimes stimulated a remarkable, if short-lived, interest in the Antipodes, illustrated by an upsurge in emigration to Australia from Lewis following W. C. Stillman's lecture tour in spring 1923.[82]

But just how significant was government-assisted emigration? Was the 10 per cent of funded agriculturists on the *Metagama* in April 1924 characteristic of the overall Scottish exodus between the wars? A Dominion Office claim in 1929 that Scotland was the easiest recruiting ground in the United Kingdom is brought into question by Canadian Immigration Department statistics of family settlement business generated by all the British agencies by the end of 1924. These records show, somewhat surprisingly, that most of the 259 cases submitted had come from the Bangor (Wales) agency, followed by Bristol, Glasgow, Southampton, Birmingham, Belfast, Aberdeen and Inverness (with equal numbers), Liverpool, London, Peterborough and York.[83] Although it could be argued that Scottish interest built up from a slow start to the enthusiasm implied by the Dominion Office report in 1929, Deputy Immigration Minister W. J. Egan's comparison of the activities of the Aberdeen and Inverness agencies in 1926 casts further doubt on the overall importance of emigration conducted through official channels. While the Inverness office had generated more nominations than its Aberdeen counterpart, the 363 Aberdeen nominations should be set alongside a total of 2,241 emigrants to Canada booking steamship passages through that agency, the vast majority paying their full fare.[84] When we add to this information the statement of the *Stornoway Gazette*, also in 1926, that highland emigrants were more reluctant than their city counterparts to participate in official migration programmes for fear of falling into debt, we have to explain the paradox of an area which was apparently loath to involve itself in official migration schemes producing more official recruits (and fewer private ones) than the much more heavily populated area covered by the Aberdeen agency.[85] Although the reduction of the Canadian assisted passage to £2 had produced a number of applications from families and single men in Lewis, islanders suspected that such a major financial concession was likely to have unacceptable hidden strings attached, but it is likely that the weight of poverty in the Hebrides made participation in government-funded schemes the only option for many highland emigrants.

There also seems to have been a more general Scottish reluctance to participate in official migration programmes for fear of falling into debt. In 1925 the Winnipeg immigration authorities, disappointed that relatively few Scottish families were coming to western Canada under the new empire settlement arrangements, questioned recent Scottish agricultural settlers about this trend. They were told that:

> Scots generally did not favour Government aided colonisation schemes. Many Scots families will come to Canada directly funds permit. There is no doubt at all of this. In the meantime the majority of prospective settlers, with families, would rather save up the necessary money than come on borrowed money, however easy the system of repayment.[86]

A distaste for bureaucracy was another deterrent – at least among domestic servants, who, according to the Dominion Office investigation in 1929, preferred to pay the (by then) £10 transatlantic fare rather than seek empire settlement funding 'to avoid the red tape of an assisted passage'.[87] Some press articles also expressed concern about state involvement in emigration. While accepting that restless farm workers could legitimately seek better prospects in Australia in response to government encouragement, the *Press & Journal* in 1922 still hoped that 'if it can be fostered and carried out without too much State aid, so much the better', and seven weeks later Esther Mackie of Montreal, in the course of a CPR-sponsored lecture in Aberdeen on opportunities for domestic servants in Canada, advised girls who could pay their own way to do so on the grounds that they were freer to choose their own work and seek the best situations.[88]

As in previous generations, personal encouragement probably remained the key factor in stimulating emigration. Nearly all the shipping reports mentioned emigrants going out to join relatives, while twenty Scottish women who in 1923 sailed from London to New Zealand in a party of thirty-eight domestics under the free-passage scheme were confident not only of guaranteed employment but of meeting 'plenty of their own folk over there'.[89] Also mindful of the importance of the personal touch was a group of Scottish businessmen in Winnipeg who, in the same year, formed the Caledonian Society to encourage Scottish farmers to settle in western Canada, not by supplanting the work of the migration authorities but by supplementing it with 'information and direction of a more personal nature than can be given by official bodies'.[90] The effect of private encouragement is, of course, impossible to quantify, but occasional snapshots – real and figurative – in contemporary commentaries and correspondence reveal the persisting significance of the well-established practice of chain migration. In 1922 the *Press & Journal* commended Canada to emigrants on the strength of the experiences of W. L. Henderson who, having left Aberdeen for Macklin, Saskatchewan, seventeen months earlier had, at the age of twenty and with no agricultural knowledge, proved his competence, improved his health and bank balance and was about to remit money to enable his widowed mother and two younger brothers to join him.[91] Henderson's experience was by no means unique but conformed to a pattern that was rooted in a century and more of Scottish emigration. For such emigrants, the novelty of government-funded emigration schemes might be an irrelevance if they had access to the means and mechanisms for making their own arrangements; for others, it might be a welcome addition, facilitating or expediting a decision that they would probably have reached anyway; for others still – particularly the poorly endowed and those bound for the Antipodes – it may have been the essential catalyst in bringing about the decision to emigrate. Official sources, and even press advertisements, may persuade us that emigration in the 1920s and 1930s revolved largely, or even exclusively, around government-driven schemes; but just as nineteenth-century emigration viewed through the Colonial Office window presents a distorted image of the exodus, so in the inter-war years the schemes spawned by the ESA seem mainly to have provided the framework for a movement which should be viewed in a much wider context, acknowledging the interaction of individual decision and statutory direction in all corners of the British Isles. Key aspects of that interaction are examined, in a Scottish context, in the following chapters.

Notes

1 N. H. Carrier and J. R. Jeffery, *External Migration. A Study of the Available Statistics 1815–1950* (London, HMSO, 1953), pp. 95–6. All figures are taken from this source unless otherwise stated.

2 Margaret Adam, 'The Highland emigration of 1770', *Scottish Historical Review (SHR)*, 16 (1919), pp. 280–93; 'The causes of the Highland emigrations of 1783–1803', *SHR*, 17 (1920), pp. 73–89; 'The eighteenth-century Highland landlords and the poverty problem', *SHR*, 19 (1921), pp. 1–20 and 161–79.

3 Gordon Donaldson, 'Scottish history and the Scottish nation' (University of Edinburgh, inaugural lecture no. 20, 4 May 1964), pp. 14–15.

4 For further discussion of the historiography of British and European emigration, see Dudley Baines, *Migration in a Mature Economy. Emigration and Internal Migration in England and Wales, 1861–1900* (Cambridge, Cambridge University Press, 1985), pp. 1–9, and Charlotte Erickson, *Leaving England. Essays on British Emigration in the Nineteenth Century* (Ithaca and London, Cornell University Press, 1994), Introduction, pp. 1–33.

5 Dudley Baines, *Emigration from Europe 1815–1930* (Basingstoke, Macmillan, 1991), p. 7.

6 Baines, *Migration in a Mature Economy*, p. 62.

7 *Ibid.*, pp. 60–1, 302–5. For example, net emigration from England and Wales was only 21.3 per cent of natural increase at its peak in 1911–20 and 16.5 per cent in the 1880s, another decade of heavy outflow; the corresponding figures in Scotland were 57.2 per cent and 42.7 per cent.

8 *Ibid.*, p. 60.

9 In 1854, 1855, 1861, 1862, 1907 and 1908 (Carrier and Jeffery, *External Migration*, pp. 95–6).

10 From 1 April 1912 the Board of Trade returns refer to permanent migrants in both directions rather than to passengers (*ibid.*, pp. 93, 140).

11 The combined figures for Great Britain and Ireland indicate a return movement of 49 per cent from the United States, 34 per cent from Australasia and 27 per cent from British North America (*ibid.*, p. 93).

12 Parliamentary Papers (PP) 1890–91 152 XI 586, Report from the Select Committee on Colonisation. For further details of the campaign for state-funded emigration in the 1880s, see Howard Malchow, *Population Pressures. Emigration and Government in Nineteenth-Century Britain* (Palo Alto, CA, Society for the Promotion of Science and Scholarship, 1979).

13 Baines, *Emigration from Europe*, p. 50.

14 The Emigration Advances Act, which allowed landlords to borrow from public money set aside under the Drainage Act to assist the emigration of their tenants (PP 1851 579 III, 77, Bill to authorise the application of advances to facilitate emigration from the distressed districts of Scotland).

15 The federal immigration budget escalated from Can$400,000 in 1896 to Can$4,000,000 in 1906 (R. G. Moyles and D. Owram, *Imperial Dreams and Colonial Realities. British Views of Canada, 1880–1914* (Toronto, University of Toronto Press, 1988), p. 116).

16 A. C. Buchanan, the chief Canadian immigration agent, often commented on the arrival of affluent Scots from the highlands as well as the lowlands – as in August 1840, for instance, when he commended the passengers on the *British King* from Cromarty, who 'bring out capital to the amount of from £7000 to £8000' (PP 1841 298 XV 369, Correspondence relative to emigration to Canada, p. 22).

17 Baines, *Emigration from Europe*, pp. 71–2.

18 Census of Scotland, 1931; Michael Flinn, *Scottish Population History from the Seventeenth Century to the 1930s* (Cambridge, Cambridge University Press, 1977), pp. 304–5. According to Flinn, the population of Scotland in 1930 was 4,842,554.

19 Andrew Marr, *The Battle for Scotland* (London, Penguin, 1992), p. 55; *Census of England and Wales, 1931, vol. I, General Report*, Preliminary Report, General Tables (London, HMSO, 1950), pp. 21–2, 32–61. With the exception of the City of London, it was the rural areas of England that lost population – Cornwall, Cumberland, Hereford, Rutland, Westmorland and the Isle of Wight.

20 There was no census of Ireland in 1921. After the Partition a census was taken on both sides of the border in 1926 and 1937. In 1926 the population of the entire island was 4,228,553 and by 1937 it had risen to 4,247,753.

21 The net loss of population from Scotland in the 1920s was 385,979, with only 108,754 arrivals from non-European locations.

22 *Census of England and Wales, 1931, vol. I*, pp. 168–70. Between 1921 and 1931 the number of persons of Scottish birth enumerated in Durham, Northumberland, Cumberland and Westmorland decreased by 13 per cent, while those in London and the five surrounding counties rose by 26 per cent. The Lancashire town of Barrow-in-Furness had a surprisingly large number of Scots-born (2,355) compared with other towns in the county.

23 G. M. Thomson, *Scotland: That Distressed Area* (Edinburgh, Porpoise Press, 1935), p. 5.

24 Elizabeth Kibblewhite, 'The impact of unemployment on the development of trade unions in Scotland 1918–1939: some aspects' (unpublished Ph.D. thesis, University of Aberdeen, 1979), pp. 21, 22–3.

25 *Ibid.*, p. 24.

26 Thomson, *Scotland: That Distressed Area*, pp. 26–46.

27 Kibblewhite, 'The impact of unemployment', p. 15.

28 PP 1928 Cmd 3156 X 55–6, Industrial Transference Board Report.

29 E. A. Belcher and J. A. Williamson, *Migration within the Empire* (London, Collins, 1924), pp. xiv, 137, 140.

30 J. W. Gregory, *Human Migration and the Future. A Study of the Causes, Effects and Control of Emigration* (London, Seeley, Service & Co., 1928), pp. 9–12, 197–8, 201–5.

31 W. A. Carrothers, *Emigration from the British Isles, with Special Reference to the Development of the Overseas Dominions* (London, Cass, 1929), pp. viii, 273, 287–304.

32 A. G. Scholes, *Education for Empire Settlement. A Study of Juvenile Migration* (London, Longman, 1932), p. vii.

33 G. F. Plant, *Oversea Settlement. Migration from the United Kingdom to the Dominions* (Oxford, Oxford University Press, 1951), p. 163.

34 Concessions included the Unemployed Workmen's Act of 1905 (which allowed local authorities to draw on local rates to subsidize emigration) and the Colonial Office's commissioning of Rider Haggard to report on Salvation Army colonies in the USA with a view to establishing similar settlements in the empire. Haggard's trip was financed by the Rhodes Trustees and his report, *The Poor and the Land*, published in 1905, was in turn considered by a committee under the chairmanship of Lord Tennyson, which recommended further discussion of the issues at the 1907 Colonial Conference (PP 1906 Cd 2978 LXXVI 533).

35 PP 1917–18 Cd 8462 X 83 paras 420, 421, Final Report of the Royal Commission on the Natural Resources, Trade, and Legislation of Certain Portions of His Majesty's Dominions (Dominions Royal Commission).

36 Keith Williams, '"A way out of our troubles": the politics of empire settlement, 1900–1922' in Stephen Constantine (ed.), *Emigrants and Empire. British Settlement in the Dominions Between the Wars* (Manchester, Manchester University Press, 1990), p. 32.

37 PP 1918 Cd 30 I 361, Bill to improve the existing organisation for affording information and assistance to those who wish to emigrate from the British Islands and to provide for the establishment of a Central Emigration Authority, and for the supervision and control of Passage Brokers and Passage Brokers' Agents, and Emigration Societies, and for purposes in connection therewith.

38 Kent Fedorowich, 'The assisted emigration of British ex-servicemen to the dominions, 1914–1922' in Constantine (ed.), *Emigrants and Empire*, pp. 45–71; Plant, *Oversea Settlement*, pp. 75–7. For statistics, see PP 1923 Cmd 1804 XII Part 2, 29. The scheme cost £2,418,263.

39 R. A. Divine, *American Immigration Policy, 1924–1952* (New Haven, Yale Historical Publications Miscellany 66, 1957); M. A. Jones, *American Immigration* (Chicago, University of Chicago Press, 1960).

40 Stephen Constantine, 'Empire migration and imperial harmony' in Constantine (ed.), *Emigrants and Empire*, p. 16. The legislation was renewed for a further fifteen years in 1937, even though emigration levels had been negligible since the early 1930s.

41 Janice Gothard, '"The healthy, wholesome British domestic girl": single female migration and the Empire Settlement Act, 1922–1930' in *ibid.*, pp. 79–80, 89.

42 Edna Bradlow, 'Empire settlement and South African immigration policy, 1910–1948' in *ibid.*, pp. 174–201. Although the decision by the imperial government in 1923 to make a per capita grant to every emigrant recruited by the 1820 Memorial Settlers' Association conferred an official stamp of approval, the links between the official British emigration scheme and the 1820 Association remained ambivalent.

43 Stephen Constantine, 'Immigration and the making of New Zealand, 1918–1939' in *ibid.*, pp. 121–49.

44 Plant, *Oversea Settlement*, pp. 98–106, 121–3. The £34 Million Agreement ended in 1932, by which time it had approved schemes estimated to cost £8,731,000, of which almost £1.5 million was payable by the imperial government. See also Michael Roe, '"We can die just as easy out here": Australia and British migration, 1916–1939' in Constantine (ed.), *Emigrants and Empire*, pp. 96–120.

45 Fedorowich, 'The assisted emigration of British ex-servicemen', pp. 60–4.

46 John A. Schulz, '"Leaven for the lump": Canada and empire settlement, 1918–1939' in Constantine (ed.), *Emigrants and Empire*, pp. 155–6. By the end of 1923 just over a third of the $600,000 had been spent.

47 Plant, *Oversea Settlement*, p. 95.

48 Schulz, '"Leaven for the lump"', p. 168.

49 PP 1928 Cmd 3156 X 783, pp. 55–6, Report of the Industrial Transference Board; Plant, *Oversea Settlement*, pp. 113–14, 151–4.

50 PP 1926 Cmd 2608 X 389, Report to the Secretary of State for Dominion Affairs of the Inter-Departmental Committee appointed to consider the effect on migration of schemes of social insurance.

51 *Hansard*, 5th series, vol. 174, 28 May 1924, cols 570, 63.

52 Stephen Constantine, 'Empire migration and social reform, 1880–1950' in C. G. Pooley and I. Whyte (eds), *Migrants, Emigrants and Immigrants. A Social History of Migration* (London, Routledge, 1991), pp. 62–83.

53 Report of the Industrial Transference Board, p. 49.

54 National Archives of Canada (NAC), RG76, C-4661, vol. 5, file 41, part 3, 'Emigration from Britain, 1918–52', W. J. Egan, Deputy Minister, Department of Immigration and Colonization, to J. B. Walker, Director of Emigration, London, 28 Aug. 1926.

55 *Aberdeen Journal*, 14 Jan. 1920. The *Press & Journal* was created in 1922 by the amalgamation of the *Aberdeen Daily Free Press* and the *Aberdeen Journal*.

56 *Press & Journal* (*P&J*), 28 Mar., 6 Apr., 3 May 1923; *Stornoway Gazette* (*SG*), 19 Apr. 1923; *The Times*, 5 Apr. 1923. In an interview with *The Scotsman* on 9 April 1923 W. M. Jones reported both the widespread national interest in Canadian land settlement and the fact that in Dundee alone he had received applications from fifteen men with substantial capital.

57 *P&J*, 20, 23, 26 July 1923.

58 *P&J*, 25 Feb., 22 Mar., 9 Apr., 11, 26, 30 Dec. 1926.

59 *P&J*, 28, 30 Apr., 11 Oct. 1923.

60 *P&J*, 30 Jan., 13 Mar., 15, 23 Aug., 15 Nov. 1923.

61 *P&J*, 2 July, 10 Sept., 11 Nov. 1924. For discussion of Stillman's career, see Australian Archives, CP 268/3/1. Stillman was a permanent civil servant in the Finance Department of the Commonwealth Public Service, but at the time he was loaned to the newly established Commonwealth Immigration Office in November 1920 as an immigration agent for Victoria he was working with the Defence Department.

62 *P&J*, 24 June, 17 July, 18 Aug. 1925; 26 Sept. 1926; *Highland News* (*HN*), 10 Jan. 1925.

63 *P&J*, 16 Mar., 21 Apr., 15 June 1923.

64 *P&J*, 30 Dec. 1925.

65 *P&J*, 17 Dec. 1925, 'Canada's Call'.

66 *P&J*, 31 Jan. 1923, 6 Mar. 1925, 17 Mar., 5 July 1926. Unaffiliated recruiters included one Mrs Scott of Toronto, who came to Aberdeen in July 1926 to recruit domestic servants for Ontario.

67 *P&J*, 19 Sept. 1925. For Davidson's involvement with assisted juvenile emigration, see chapter 5, pp. 170, 175.

68 *P&J*, 24 Feb. 1923, 25 June, 18 July 1924.
69 *P&J*, 2, 14 Sept. 1923.
70 *P&J*, 24 Mar. 1923. See also 2 Apr., 1 May 1923.
71 *P&J*, 23 June, 27 Aug. 1923.
72 *P&J*, 19, 21, 22 May 1923; *Glasgow Evening News*, 18 Apr. 1923. The latter newspaper claimed there were 347 Scottish emigrants on the *Cameronia*.
73 *P&J*, 8, 9 Jan. 3, 14 June, 6 Sept., 7 Oct. 1924; *The Citizen*, 23 Apr. 1924.
74 *P&J*, 21 Apr. 1924.
75 *P&J*, 22 Aug. 1924.
76 *P&J*, 19 Mar. 1923.
77 *P&J*, 18 Dec. 1923.
78 *P&J*, 5, 19 Apr. 1924.
79 *Glasgow Herald* (*GH*), 25 Apr. 1924.
80 *Glasgow Evening Times*, 29 Apr. 1924; *The Scotsman*, 9 May 1924.
81 *SG*, 22 May 1924.
82 See chapter 3, pp. 94–7.
83 NAC, RG76, vol. 248, file 179046, part 1, Table of Family Settlement Scheme, 31 Dec. 1924. Out of 259 cases submitted, 120 had been approved, 21 rejected, 6 withdrawn, 3 deferred and 109 referred back.
84 Walker to Egan, 30 July 1926; Egan to Walker, 28 Aug. 1926.
85 *SG*, 11 Feb. 1926.
86 *P&J*, 2 May 1925.
87 Public Record Office (PRO), Dominions Office (DO) 57/118/0164/2, Lindsay's report.
88 *P&J*, 26 Dec. 1922, 9 Feb. 1923.
89 *P&J*, 12 Oct. 1923.
90 *P&J*, 30 Apr. 1923.
91 *P&J*, 12 Dec. 1922.

CHAPTER TWO

Agents and activists

Although personal persuasion remained the key factor in stimulating emigration, professional and semi-professional agents also played a vital part in generating and directing the exodus between the wars. Their significance had increased steadily during the nineteenth century as overseas governments and commercial concerns began to send representatives to the British Isles to promote settlement through lecture tours, personal interviews, exhibitions and publications, liaising with an army of shipping agents who arranged their itineraries as well as earning a commission on the booking of passages. That agents exercised a considerable influence had been obvious well before the war, and the enforced lull in their activities between 1914 and 1918 did not dilute either their enthusiasm or their impact when emigration resumed. The more interventionist post-war approach adopted by the British and dominion governments clearly increased the scope and complexity of the agents' work as they integrated the new subsidized schemes into their existing promotional work and vetted applicants for assisted passage or settlement, but these were extensions of their pre-war functions rather than a radical new departure, and they continued to advise and help independent emigrants as well as those who took advantage of official initiatives. The following analysis is based primarily on the voluminous records of the Canadian Department of Immigration and Colonization (DIC) since, although antipodean agents also came to Britain, they have left remarkably little evidence of their presence apart from newspaper advertisements and Canadian references to the activities of rivals.

Reputations and rivalries

The recruitment of emigrants by agents and contractors had a long and controversial history. The efforts of land speculators like the Earl of Selkirk and Hugh Dunoon to entice highlanders to British North America around

1800 were equated with the nefarious activities of the military press gang, and pressure from the mercantilist landlord lobby gave rise to the first Passenger Act, which was passed without debate by parliament in 1803 in an ill-disguised but unsuccessful attempt to curtail emigration by making it prohibitively expensive. Subsequent passenger vessel legislation between 1823 and 1855 reflects a more genuine, but largely futile, effort to regulate transatlantic emigrant transportation, particularly after the appearance of a new, often more irresponsible, breed of shipping agent who had no stake in settlement but exported emigrants in much the same way as he imported timber from Lower Canada and the Maritimes. Although bounty emigration to the Antipodes was subject to stricter control, the government's selecting agents were accused of creaming off the flower of the population, particularly from the highlands, while, despite a licensing system, the activities of private operators under the colonial bounty system were not as closely monitored as those of their Colonial Office counterparts.

In the second half of the nineteenth century, as the antipodean colonies appointed recruitment agents in Britain to implement policies of assisted passage and settlement and as Canada developed sophisticated immigration strategies to combat American propaganda, charges of poaching brawn and brains were frequently made against professional agents by opponents of emigration. At the same time the government became increasingly uneasy at the unregulated activities of a vast regiment of several thousand amateur agents throughout Britain. These were the men at the sharp end, who were responsible both for selling tickets and for arranging public lectures and private interviews on behalf of the professional recruiters. The part-time ticket agents were generally appointed and licensed by the steamship companies, making their money from commissions and bonuses paid by those companies and the receiving countries, respectively. Concern that unsuitable emigrants were being recruited indiscriminately or even fraudulently by passage brokers' agents over whom the Board of Trade had only titular control emerged in the report of the Dominions Royal Commission, which recommended the licensing of passage brokers and their agents by a central emigration authority. Each agent was to pay an annual licence fee, submit detailed accounts and records of bookings, and publicize up-to-date information issued by the central authority, but the demise of the 1918 Emigration Bill prevented these recommendations being put into effect, so that in the inter-war period booking agents and steamship companies continued to operate under the same conditions as they had before 1918.

From time to time the DIC complained about the failure of the North Atlantic Passenger Conference (the cartel of steamship companies) to ensure that booking agents complied with changing immigration regulations in the uncertain economic climate after the war and tried to sideline the shipping companies by conducting business directly with the agents.[1] By 1920 all the dominions agreed that bonuses should be abolished, and, although no legislation was passed to that effect, their increasingly rigorous entrance qualifications ultimately brought the system to an end. While good booking agents were an undoubted asset to their professional counter-parts, Dominion immigration officials clearly regarded some as a liability. They might be dormant, which was the complaint of one Canadian agent for southern Scotland, who claimed in 1909 that of 241 ticket agencies on his books only 20 per cent were really active, 50 per cent being 'fair', and the remainder 'quite indifferent or useless'. They were also allegedly reluctant to shoulder any of the expenses of a lecture, even though they stood to benefit from bonuses arising from suitable recruits.[2]

The ignorance of booking agents was criticized by James Moir, a former booking agent and librarian from Bo'Ness, West Lothian, in a letter to Robert Forke, the Canadian Minister of Immigration, in 1927. After emi-grating to Alberta in 1909 Moir had kept abreast of immigration policy and, after the war, served on the advisory committee of the SSB. In his opinion the problem of ill-trained, wrongly placed professional agents was compounded by the attitude of many ticket agents:

> They are generally small store keepers, rental agents etc, and they carry these agencies as a sideline, but they do not care whether one wants to go to Africa or America, what concerns them wholly is the commission they earn. They know little of Canada, and that little they may have secured from 'steamship' literature, but generally they do not study that, reserving it for enquiries about berths. I venture to say Mr Forke that 95% of these sub-agents have never seen Canada, and many have lived their lives in these small hamlets and will die there, yet it is a fact that we today in Canada depend largely on such people for settlers. I know these things, because I was one of them, but I realised my ignorance and came, saw and learned.[3]

Ignorance could fuel excessive enthusiasm as well as dormancy, and booking agents were sometimes accused of issuing inaccurate information and recruiting unsuitable settlers. Both before and after the war disputed bonus claims formed a major part of the correspondence between ticket agents and the DIC, which also received periodic complaints from dissatis-fied settlers about ticket agents who had painted 'too bright a picture of good times in Canada'.[4] In 1914 the Canadian press launched a stinging attack on Andrew Spalding, a booking agent in Blairgowrie:

> The immigration agents, who have been accustomed to make their money easily in the old country, have been heavily hit by the campaign carried on

by ourselves and other papers during the winter with the view of restricting the flow of immigration for the next year or so. We have no regrets for having taken a very active part in that campaign, nor are we dissatisfied with the results produced. Our only regret is that the Government did not see fit to cut off the commission paid to unscrupulous agents scouring the old country, in order to put an end to the gross misrepresentation that has been and is still going on. It is that bonus system which is responsible for such scoundrelly work as is being performed in the rural districts of England and Scotland by such men as Andrew Spalding whose damnable lies, in the Blairgowrie press, we hope, Mayor Allan, of Hamilton, will be able to counteract with a true statement as to the condition of affairs. Spalding and his brethren, who are engaged in this mean and despicable method of making a fat living out of lean and poor people, should not be left outside prison walls. Theirs is a most heartless form of deception, and in addition, it is a criminal attempt to make money by false pretences.[5]

In the fragile post-war labour market booking agents were even more severely criticized for issuing misleading information and recruiting emigrants for urban-industrial, rather than agricultural, employment. Glasgow agent A. Warrick was a particular thorn in the flesh of the Canadian immigration authorities and even the shipping companies, which ultimately withdrew their licences from the Union Transit Company, which he managed. Described by the Glasgow representative of the CPR as an incompetent speculator whose experiences were 'more calculated to arouse our pity than to draw down our censure', Warrick canvassed Canadian employers to predict industrial vacancies, place recruitment orders with his firm and assist with the cost of passage. Despite repeated warnings about the lack of industrial openings, he flagrantly misrepresented Canadian labour requirements, and artisans and labourers were sent out to unapproved situations or in the hope, rather than the assurance, of employment, with predictably negative results.[6] More reprehensible still were the bogus agents such as James Mincher of Glasgow, who in 1923 was jailed for three months for obtaining money on the fraudulent promise of securing employment in America for his recruits.[7]

Accusations of deception were also made against professional agents, both by disgruntled emigrants and by a hostile British press, much of which echoed the nineteenth-century refrain that the flower of the population was being exported. In 1908 John MacLennan, Canadian government agent at the recently opened Aberdeen office, complained that as a result of the local press having 'poisoned the public mind' against prospects in Canada, business at both his premises and the booking agencies had decreased considerably. The newspapers were in the pocket of the farmers, who objected to what they perceived as the abduction of the cream of the farm servant community, producing a further observation from MacLennan in 1910 about the importance of not antagonizing unduly this 'powerful force' in the northeastern community.[8] One farmer, who complained to MacLennan's successor at Aberdeen in 1925, sent a copy of his letter to the *Scottish Farmer* to alert his peers to the seductive activities of agents.

> Sir, I have received your letters asking various questions with reference to two of my farm hands who you say are applicants for farm work in Canada. Some time ago I happened one afternoon to return to my farm earlier than usual, and found an empty motor car standing at my steading. My employees happened to be engaged in threshing operations upon that occasion, and, on going to the cornyard, I found an emissary from your office interviewing some of my younger ploughmen, apparently with a view to getting them to desert their service and emigrate to Canada. I suggested to your agent that, instead of trying to seduce ploughmen to leave their present employment, in which they were perfectly contented, he might find in Canada some work for a few of the million unemployed. But he said quite frankly that it was only the best ploughmen that they wished to take away from this country. I think it was most improper for your agent to visit my farm for such a purpose without my knowledge and consent, and I have given my grieve [foreman] instructions summarily to eject any such intruders from my premises in future.[9]

The subsequent decision to close the Aberdeen office in 1926 was prompted partly by the 'hostility which has been manifested by the President of the National Farmers' Union of Scotland and by other agriculturists against our Agent, and indirectly the Agency, at Aberdeen'.[10] Four years earlier the proposal to open a third Scottish office in Edinburgh had been shelved partly on the grounds that 'While the Scotch settler is a real acquisition to Canada, we do not always get the warmest reception when we are found trying to get the Scotch agriculturists out of the country and there is a danger of over-doing this along this line.'[11] In 1928 similar problems were being encountered in the five-year-old Inverness agency, which reported antagonism from employers and general public alike. While recognizing that employers opposed the loss of the best of the agricultural population, the Director of Canadian Emigration in London suggested that the system of recruitment was excessively bureaucratic and multilayered, involving two interviews, a medical and endless correspondence, so that 'the applicants get confused and they feel they are being sought after too eagerly. The uneducated mind cannot realize that all this propaganda work and expense may be worth while to the British and Canadian Governments. They judge only the obvious, with the result that all over the country there is a growing suspicion against Canada and her schemes.'[12]

Australian agents were also vilified by Scottish agricultural commentators for the 'specious promises' with which they enticed young men to the other side of the world, only to expose them to such 'rotten conditions' on farms that they preferred to move to a life of unemployment and semi-starvation in the cities and towns.[13] Then, towards the end of the 1920s the onset of the depression brought the agents' work into even greater disrepute on the grounds that they, as well as the ticket agents, were knowingly making fraudulent promises about better prospects. One Canadian correspondent of the *John O'Groat Journal* was unequivocal in his condemnation:

> I see by the old country papers that the immigration agents are still endeavouring to get men to go over to do farm work in Canada. With all the unemployed in Canada there are enough people here to do all the farm work and the other work too without taking over more to be stranded in a country with six months of winter and no work at all.
>
> May I ask these immigration agents, what has Canada got to offer any ordinary immigrant in farm work or any other work? She has got nothing to offer but very hard work and long hours and little pay. A farm worker in the Old Country has a nine-hour day, with a half holiday on Saturday. He comes to Canada thinking he will better himself, but when he finds he has to work from daylight to dark he soon realises he has got out of the frying pan into the fire. The fact is the immigration agents are telling people about a country they know nothing about from actual experience. So my advice is: stay in the Old Country if you have a job at all.[14]

Since the emigrant market was a competitive one, field agents and their policy-making superiors were always anxious to emphasize their probity and extend their influence. Canadian inter-provincial rivalries sometimes provoked federal reminders that provincial agents should co-operate and avoid an 'overdose of energy' since 'an emigrant for any Province is an emigrant for Canada',[15] but most concern was reserved for external challenges. Before the war Canada was fairly confident that antipodean competition could be contained. The challenge had been growing since the 1880s, when New Zealand, New South Wales and (especially) Queensland had begun to offer commissions and bonuses to booking agents who recruited agriculturists and domestic servants for free and assisted passages. Although Queensland's Dundee-based Scottish representative, Peter Fleming, was active in Aberdeenshire, Banffshire, east Sutherland and Caithness in the 1880s, he did not attempt to challenge Canadian dominance of west highland agency work, and in 1891 he transferred his loyalties to Canada, becoming the Dominion government's sub-agent for the lowlands.[16] The Australian Commonwealth Act of 1901, which made immigration a federal responsibility, introduced a much more centralized and consistent approach, although most of the individual states continued to employ agents-general in London. In 1910 Australian recruitment was stepped up in the British Isles, Europe and America, and by the time the war broke out most states' agents-general presided over vigorous advertising, publishing and lecturing campaigns, offering assisted passages to eligible settlers and to individuals who were nominated by relatives or friends. While the states concentrated on filling specific openings, an injection of £20,000 of Commonwealth government funding in 1912 reinforced the general targeting of both emigrants and tourists through guidebooks, posters and 'landseekers' excursions'. Booking agents could claim a bonus of £1 per head on adults and half that amount on children, with an additional bonus of 1 per cent on the capital deposited by recruits who possessed £200 or more.[17]

Despite these advances and the almost exclusive promotion of Australia by some booking agents, John MacLennan did not find in his Aberdeen district in 1909 'that the emigrating public are seriously considering the competition of Australia and other Colonies with Canada', while Malcolm MacIntyre claimed that Canada's weekly recruitment from his Glasgow area was equivalent to Australia's annual recruitment from that territory.[18] Although Canada did not offer assisted passages to its pre-war settlers, it claimed that growing antipodean success in all other aspects of recruitment by 1912 was simply the result of copying Canadian practices, not least the state-sponsored visit in 1910 by part of the Scottish Agricultural Commission that had toured Canada to good effect two years earlier.[19] Meanwhile, E. B. Robertson, the Assistant Superintendent of Immigration in Ottawa, favoured healthy competition, likening Australian–Canadian rivalry to that of the agents of rival life insurance companies canvassing the same town: 'each gets more business than he would were the other not there. If Canadian and Australian agents succeed in awakening the industrious desirable workers living hand to mouth existences in the United Kingdom to the advantages offered by emigration to the colonies, each country will get more settlers than would be obtained were the other not in the field.'[20]

Throughout the war Robertson's superior, W. D. Scott, remained confident of Canada's reputation being such that 'we need not fear the competition of either the other British Dominions or any country looking for an increase in its population',[21] and in 1917 he was particularly disparaging about Australian propaganda:

> The problem of returned soldier settlement will engage all our attention and offer problems enough for our efforts for the first couple of years after the War is over. With 300,000 Canadians at the Front whose presence there appears to be generally known, I take it that Canada is not likely to be completely overshadowed and forgotten by the frantic efforts of Australia to impress upon Imperial or overseas soldiers the merits of her offer to settlers. By virtue of our geographical position we, perhaps, have an advantage over Australia in the matter of securing immigrants. It is much better to build wisely than hurriedly, and I cannot see that the Department, even yet, should make an immediate move to advertise herself in the Mother Country.[22]

By the end of the war, however, the policy-makers' confidence was not shared by field officers on the other side of the Atlantic, and throughout the 1910s and 1920s there was constant friction within the Canadian immigration service over the best way to outstrip competitors and promote Canada against a changing economic, social and political backdrop. J. O. Smith, who had overall charge of agency work in Britain and Europe, was a constant thorn in the flesh of his superiors in Ottawa. Even in 1912 he had recommended that booking agents should be given the benefit of the doubt in disputed bonus cases to woo them away from Australian rivals and thus secure the loyalty of a 'body of men who can make or mar the emigration movement to our Dominion'.[23] His proposal in 1914 to tackle a shortage of farming recruits by canvassing first-generation town dwellers was resisted by Scott on the grounds that only capitalist farmers should be encouraged, since 'more strongly than ever before "Quality" rather than "Quantity" must be the watchword'.[24] The further loss of a reservoir of straightforward farming emigrants during the war led Smith to repeat his proposal in 1915, and also to suggest that the agents capitalize on the dislocating experience of the conflict by canvassing men in the various barracks and training camps, but his arguments fell on deaf ears.[25]

J. B. Walker, Smith's predecessor in the London post and formerly the agent at Glasgow, was equally concerned about the complacency of the Ottawa office in the face of aggressive antipodean propaganda during the war. After a visit to London in summer 1917, he wrote confidentially to Scott about the danger of Canada being 'permanently relegated to a subordinate position in the work of British emigration'. Although he acknowledged the need for financial retrenchment in the wartime climate, the success of rival destinations in stealing a march on Canada – particularly in London advertising and in canvassing among soldiers – had created a need to resume recruitment 'persistently and courageously'.[26] Two months later Smith reinforced the message in a hard-hitting letter to Scott, drawing his attention to American as well as antipodean competition. The decision to discontinue the distribution of school atlases was particularly unfortunate in the light of American plans to adopt a similar tactic, as well as other Canadian techniques:

> as the days go by the decisions of the Department become all the more regrettable to those of us who have spent the best years of our life in the service of Canada, and have seen the Government of Canada spend millions of dollars in bringing to perfection a propaganda which has now ceased, and which cannot be resuscitated and recovered except after a long lapse of time and expenditure of thousands of pounds, and the consequent loss in the interim of a large number of desirable British people.[27]

The divergence between London and Ottawa became even greater after the war. While balancing the books continued to be the priority of Superintendent Scott and Canadian Department of Immigration and Colonization Minister J. A. Calder, the agents in Britain felt they needed to redouble their efforts in the light of the opportunities opened up first by soldier settlement schemes and later by the ESA. Smith continued to remind his counterparts in Ottawa of competition from New Zealand, Australia and even South Africa, accusing them of favouring American farmers over British land seekers and neglecting British agencies, so that 'We are not doing Canada justice and the fault lies on your side of the Atlantic.'[28] Ottawa's response was to reiterate the importance of economy and careful selection, to curtail advertising expenditure, to accuse Smith of mischief-making and obsolete methods, and to compare Canadian procedures favourably with those of other countries:

> If the South African, Australian and New Zealand Governments prefer, figuratively speaking, to put all their eggs in one basket and spend huge sums of money on large central exhibitions, I do not see why we should make the same mistake. The same is true about agencies. All the other Overseas Dominions centralize in London and by the expenditure of huge sums of money on offices or office buildings in London, they apparently hope to accomplish their purpose. It was not even enough for the Australian Commonwealth to have one central building in which the various Australian States would find accommodation, – each State was running a separate show of its own. They have, I believe, recently combined their efforts, but they are all in London. Our method is decentralisation and while it is no concern of ours how other Overseas Dominions do their work, I cannot see that we should follow their example. Canada may (as Mr. Smith suggests …) be obliged to take the second or third place to South Africa or Australia, but I am quite sure that it will only be in the matter of expenditure. We have no difficulty in getting far more people than we can absorb. Our difficulty is not to make Canada better known in the Mother Country, but rather to make an intelligent selection of those who are anxious to emigrate.[29]

In 1925 the Canadian press entered the fray, claiming that Australia, New Zealand and South Africa were 'securing the cream of the British agricultural population' as a result both of better incentives and the negative legacy of pre-war Canadian propaganda, which had consisted mainly of 'lavish promises and tempting expectations' held out by over-enthusiastic agents.[30]

What was the effect of all this friction on territorial agency work, particularly in Scotland? From time to time Ottawa accused its field representatives of apathy, poor record-keeping and even sharp practice. In January 1925 an inspection of the Glasgow office found not only that the Prospect Book, in which the agent was supposed to record all contacts made and followed up, was out of date, but also that the office was claiming credit for generating business which was in fact almost totally stimulated by local booking agents. Territorial officers were therefore warned sharply 'that the future of their career as agents of the Department of Immigration and Colonization and possibly the future of the offices themselves, will depend on the business generated, as we do not propose to maintain quarters to serve merely as clearing houses for anything and everything that is offered to them by booking agents. If necessary, we will close most of the offices rather than carry on in this way.'[31] Sometimes, however, agents were misled into pursuing fictitious prospects, as W. R. Little, the London-based Director of European Emigration for Canada, found when he visited Glasgow and Aberdeen in February 1925 as part of his investigation into the causes of a 50 per cent drop in British bookings. While this was due primarily to expectations of better conditions in Britain, along with warnings about unemployment in Canada, erroneous lists of likely emigrants had also been compiled by representatives of the CPR and CNR. During a recent lecture tour of Scotland these men had passed on to the government agents details of numerous 'good prospects', most of whom, it was later discovered, had never expressed any intention of going to Canada.[32]

Ottawa's obsession with cost-cutting also hampered the transmission of information to would-be emigrants. The lack of written advice for married women emigrants was a particular concern of Inverness agent Anne MacDonald, and there is more than a hint of frustration in an internal memorandum which she submitted to Ottawa in autumn 1924.

> During my lecture tour in Caithness the only literature I had dealing with the women's side of emigration, was 30 copies of 'Women's Work' which does not give much information for the settler's wife. I have two families at the present time where the husband and children are anxious to go forward and are most suitable, but the wife in each case is holding back, not because she does not realise the prospects held out, but because she has a doubt in her mind as to whether she will be able to fall into the Canadian ways, and if any real practical assistance will be given to her when she reaches the other side. With regard to the receiving and after-care of the menfolk, I have, in addition to the information which I give verbally, printed leaflets giving full information, but from the women's side, I can depend only on the verbal information which I give personally from my own practical experience of Canada. The women are anxious to go in many cases and all that is required is some practical information in black and white to show that the officials on the other side realise and appreciate that they also must be helped and encouraged when they arrive in a new country as settlers. It is difficult enough to convince the women that they will receive all possible kindness and at the same time have to admit that I have no literature showing details of the Women's Organisations which are going to take a special interest in the new settlers.

On the 31st October after holding a Lecture at Bilbster, I motored over nine miles to interview a prospective family and after leaving the car walked three quarters of a mile over a moor to the croft. There was no road across the moor and the last three miles I travelled by car was merely a cart track. During my interview with the wife, she expressed herself most anxious to go to Canada with her family but pointed out that she might find it difficult to render all assistance to her husband because of the strange and new ways which she would require to meet in Canada. She stated that she did not mind the loneliness because her present home was most isolated, but she wondered if there would be anyone on the other side who would be available to give her information and help during the first few months. I explained about the Women's Institutes and Red Cross Outposts showing her the typewritten list in respect of the Red Cross Organisation, but whereas I was able to give her husband printed matter regarding his side, I could give her nothing, which is apt to convey the impression that the women's side is not treated with great importance ... I give the above details of typical cases which I shall meet over and over again in this area, to show that the women have been brought up under loneliness and hard conditions in this country and are most suitable as settlers and are anxious to go forward, but at the same time they realise fully that the woman's part of a settler's life, if they are going to be real helpmeets to their husbands, must necessarily entail difficulties which they cannot satisfactorily cope with, however willing, unless some practical assistance be given. I wish to be able to reassure them on this point.[33]

Financial stringency meant, moreover, that pleas for additional offices were generally ignored. Although a new highland sub-office was opened experimentally in Inverness in 1923, suggestions in 1913 and 1928 that representation be increased further down the east coast by establishing a Dundee office were unsuccessful, as were negotiations to create an agency in Edinburgh in 1921–22 and to transfer the Aberdeen office to Perth in 1924.[34] More seriously, in 1926 the Aberdeen office fell victim to Ottawa's cost-cutting measures despite trenchant opposition by J. B. Walker. Six years earlier Smith had argued unsuccessfully for a reorganization of Scottish agencies involving an Edinburgh office, the transfer of the inefficient Aberdeen agent Major Murphy elsewhere and the promotion of assistant agent Murray. Ottawa's negative response was based on cost and a preference for Murphy on the grounds that he had agricultural experience and a good knowledge of Canada whereas Murray had visited the Dominion only once.[35]

But Murphy's experience was of no avail when Ottawa decided to close the Aberdeen office on 30 September 1926 and centralize its northern Scottish activities in Inverness. While admitting that the Aberdeen personnel left 'much to be desired', Walker made a strong case for the retention of the office, suggesting that the axe should fall instead on the smaller, less strategically important Inverness agency, which generated fewer suitable recruits.

> Aberdeen is the centre of the greatest agricultural districts in central Eastern and Eastern Scotland, and the area tributary to the Aberdeen office has a population of 1,179,548, whereas the Inverness area, which is not a farming area but rather an area of pasturage for sheep and cattle, has a population of only 249,671.
>
> Aberdeen is a great railroad centre, with lines running in all directions except North-East. It has direct short lines with frequent services through the rich agricultural Counties of Aberdeenshire, Banffshire, and Forfarshire, and towards Fife and Perth and Glasgow, while Inverness is out of the way in a sparsely populated district.
>
> The Aberdeen area is, and always has been, a prolific producer of first-class immigrants, and is capable, I think, of even greater development ... .
>
> The Steamship Companies, between January 1st and June 30th this year, took out of the Aberdeen office area 2,241 immigrants, and from the Inverness office area in the same period 446. The County of Aberdeen alone produced 800 immigrants, while the whole of the Inverness area produced 446.
>
> The more distant the living centre of a movement is from its circumference, the greater the cost of time and money to reach it. The proposed move does not make it any easier for the anxious enquirer to see and talk to the Agent.
>
> It seems to me a doubtful experiment to place this fruitful territory in the hands of an Agent who has no practical farming experience in Canada, who is not a Canadian resident, and who is to be represented in the actual field of operations by an Assistant who has not only no farming experience but whose knowledge of Canada generally is confined to a brief visit and a run through the country in a train some years ago.
>
> Miss MacDonald will doubtless bring to this extended work her rather vivid personality, her keen interest and enthusiasm, but it should not be forgotten that different methods and very different peoples obtain South of the Grampians from those North thereof.[36]

Walker's prediction, which he claimed was echoed by several booking agents, was that among the douce farmers of northeast Scotland Anne MacDonald's 'personality and her sex would not have the same appeal as would that of a competent male Officer' and valuable business would be lost as a result.[37]

W. J. Egan, Deputy Minister of Immigration in Ottawa, responded to this lobbying by defending Anne MacDonald's credentials and reminding Walker of the northeastern farming sector's entrenched antagonism to agency work. He also contradicted Walker's claims about the strategic location and economic significance of the Aberdeen office, challenged his recruitment statistics and claimed that his London-based director of emigration was 'surveying the north of Scotland through the distant end of a telescope'. He further justified the Aberdeen closure as a cost-cutting measure that would not only save rent and travelling expenses but would also allow Anne MacDonald to combine the two functions of agent and woman officer.[38] Walker remained unconvinced, however, not least because he believed that the reduction of agency coverage to ten offices had given a considerable advantage to Australia, which not only recruited settlers through 2,000 employment exchanges – a device never employed by Canada – but had also created thirty special agencies among booking agents throughout the British Isles. Ticket agents such as Mackay Brothers of Edinburgh and Moses Buchanan of Glasgow received advertising allowances and a commission of thirty-three shillings on each migrant recruited for Australia from the several lowland counties they covered, while in 1926 the Australian Commonwealth was allegedly considering extending its agency work even further by copying the Canadian practice of operating provincial offices across the country.

Tactics and achievements

Yet, despite budgetary constraints, internal tensions, external criticism and inter-provincial and inter-dominion rivalries, professional agents continued to play a key part in stimulating and directing emigration throughout the 1920s, as they had done since at least the late nineteenth century. The high-profile, decentralized Canadian agency activity was co-ordinated by the DIC in Ottawa and funded from the federal budget. A London office, managed until 1924 by a Superintendent and thereafter by a Director of European Emigration for Canada, supervised the work of the vital territorial agents, most of whom were stationed at up to fourteen key locations throughout the British Isles and on whose regular reports and recommendations the Ottawa authorities based overall strategy.[39] For half a century these agents were responsible for encouraging the emigration of farmers with capital, farm labourers and female domestics, for discouraging undesirable settlers and for inspecting all emigrants, as well as liaising with ticket agents, visiting delegates and railway company representatives. Whereas the first generation of agents was appointed largely through political patronage, in the 1920s the service was professionalized through the introduction of competitive civil service examinations and training programmes, as well as pre-embarkation medicals to replace the unsatisfactory inspection of immigrants on arrival in Canada.[40]

In their battle for recruits the agents exploited every promotional tool available to them, updating their methods in response to changing conditions. Their activities are recorded in the published annual reports of the DIC and in unpublished correspondence. Both before and after the war written advertising was the easiest method of blanket publicity and was generally the first step in alerting public interest. In the 1920s the Department supplied weekly news items to as many as 1,000 British newspapers, but pamphlet compilations of letters from successful settlers, often with a regional focus, continued to be particularly popular. The written word was reinforced by visual promotions, involving not just eye-catching posters in libraries, post offices and railway stations but also static displays of produce and, as technology improved, cinematographic presentations. Many lecturers continued to favour lantern slides, which allowed them to comment at length on each picture, and slides were also frequently borrowed by schoolteachers and other 'unofficial friends of Canada', being used on 1,301 occasions in 1923.[41] Agents regularly rubbed shoulders with the farming community at weekly markets and summer shows, assisted in their travelling and propaganda by a growing fleet of horse-drawn exhibition wagons and motorized 'missionary cars'.

The agents set a particular premium on lecture tours, usually undertaken in winter and encompassing not only urban areas but also the most remote parts of their districts. These public lectures, together with private interviews, allowed the agents to make personal contact with interested parties. Having been alerted to a forthcoming lecture by press publicity, would-be emigrants were subsequently invited to arrange a private interview with the lecturer at a local booking agent's office the next day, and sometimes over 100 interviews had to be slotted into a single day. In 1914 737 free public lectures were delivered by the Department's officers, and when this method was resumed fully in 1921 354 lectures were given, rising to a peak of 435 in 1925, then dropping to as few as 9 in 1932 before being discontinued altogether.[42] Federal agents were joined on the lecturing circuit by temporary assistants, provincial agents and representatives of the transcontinental railway companies. Some of these men took the personal touch even further by accompanying their recruits across the Atlantic, securing jobs for them and helping them to settle in, at the same time collecting fresh propaganda for their winter campaigns. Particularly in the pre-war period, delegations of journalists and tenant farmers were also invited to tour Canada at the goverment's expense, and successful settlers were brought back to Britain, in the hope that their favourable impressions would be transmitted through promotional lectures and private conversations at fairs and booking agencies. From 1925, however, the farmer delegates were phased out, replaced by trained Canadian assistants who were required to have a practical knowledge of farming, public-speaking skills and good business sense.[43]

Even before the war the increasing sophistication of enquiries had begun to demand a more focused and professional response. In 1911 Smith alleged that the basic printed literature was no longer meeting the needs of a new generation of informed questioners, whose enquiries should be followed up by customized letters offering specific, relevant information. A year later E. B. Robertson suggested that a press agent should be appointed to revise literature and advertising, a smaller number of more competent farm delegates should be sent to Britain to lecture for five-month periods, the obsolete lantern slides should be replaced with motion pictures, and three new offices should be opened, including one at Dundee.[44] These concerns were reiterated after the war by R. J. C. Stead, the DIC's director of publicity; in 1920 he recommended improvements to office window displays and posters as well as press advertising and publications, including compilations of the ever-popular settlers' letters, and a schoolchildren's excursion to Canada, which would not only attract press publicity but would lead to the children becoming 'apostles of Canada in their home localities'.[45] In the same year Smith reiterated and enlarged on his pre-war observations, complaining that recruitment tactics had not been modernized in response to the increasing sophistication of potential emigrants.

> I should point out that the class of person seeking to go to Canada in these days in no sense is the same as in the early days of emigration. In the days of steerage passage on a passenger liner, sleeping and eating among the anchor chains and bilge water, the emigrant of those days sought relief and a living overseas as a forlorn hope. The reverse is now the case. Times have changed. Children have been educated and people live well in the British Isles, and, there being little or no destitution, Canada has to make her appeal to the best blood and sinew of the homeland in the cradle of the British race.
>
> An inquirer now is one who asks fifty questions, whereas an emigrant of years ago asked only one, and that was probably how much his ticket would cost ... .
>
> Financially and industrially the conditions in the British Isles show a remarkable recovery from the after effects of the war, so much so that were it not for the energetic propaganda work of the Canadian Government, ably seconded by the unofficial emigration efforts of hundreds of thousands of patriotic Canadian officers and soldiers, we should not be able to induce many persons to leave the established comforts of the homeland, even for the advantages and prospective financial prosperity of some other part of the Empire.[46]

Scotland was well integrated into the agency network. A resident Canadian agent had been employed north of the border since 1869, when an office was established at Glasgow, and for most of the period up to 1907 that office represented Canadian interests throughout the whole of Scotland and northern England.[47] An increase in federal funding and commitment at the turn of the century allowed the opening of the Aberdeen agency in 1907 to cover northern Scotland, and in his first week of operations the new agent conducted 258 interviews, 114 of them in a single day. In 1908 the Aberdeen office – with opening hours of 8.15 a.m. to 9.30 or even 10.30 p.m., six days a week – dispatched 7,650 school atlases and maps, as well as 45,000 general and specialist pamphlets to many of the 190 booking agents throughout the region.[48] In 1923 the volume of highland business led to the creation of the experimental sub-office in Church Street, Inverness, under Anne MacDonald, an individual whose robust approach soon established her agency as 'most successful in maintaining a good publicity for Canada and a well-selected lot of immigrants who were a real asset to Canada', contributing to the closure of the Aberdeen office in 1926.[49] While post-war agents tended to be war veterans or career civil servants, their pre-war counterparts were chosen with reference to local needs and conditions, generally being either emigrants themselves, first-generation Canadians with roots in the areas to which they were sent, or men with specialist knowledge of emigration procedures. For instance, H. M. Murray, appointed to Glasgow in 1897, had previously been a purser with the Henderson Line, John MacLennan, the first agent for northern Scotland, was a Gaelic-speaking Canadian of highland descent, and MacLennan's successor, W. B. Cumming, was the grandson of an emigrant from Elgin.

One of the Department's most successful assistant agents both before and after the war, Hugh McKerracher of Paisley, Ontario, was a Gaelic-speaking Ontarian whose parents came from Glenlyon and Rannoch while his wife was from Aberdeenshire. He was first appointed to the Aberdeen office in 1907, taking charge of the horse-drawn travelling exhibition wagon throughout the north. After resigning briefly in March 1910 because of his wife's illness, he was reappointed later in the year and continued to canvass the highlands until the war broke out, when his horses were commandeered and McKerracher, being too old for active service, returned to Canada in 1915. When at the end of 1920 the Immigration Department wished to appoint a travelling agent in the Scottish highlands, McKerracher was the obvious choice, having been commended frequently by his employers and booking agents alike as an 'enthusiastic Canadian' with a 'free and easy manner' who drew crowds around him in a 'simply amazing' way.[50] Although the following press account of his visit to Carloway in Lewis is from 1911, the methods employed, and the response elicited, were the same in the 1920s and reinforced the foundation for post-war work.

> Behind and on either side of the waggon was emblazoned in golden letters the inspiring and much-favoured name 'Canada'. It was readily recognised as the Canadian Government waggon, and this happy discovery was sufficient to enkindle to the highest pitch the people's interest and enthusiasm, and secure for the gentleman in charge ... a warm, whole-hearted Highland welcome. The horses were pulled up in front of the

Public School, and as the afternoon was one of bright sunshine and the occasion most opportune for exhibiting the young people's interest in Canada, all the senior classes were allowed outside, and with gladsome shout they soon arranged themselves around the waggon ... . Mr Mackerracher [sic], in his capacity as Dominion Government emigration agent, gave a short spirited address, and when he intimated that he would give a lecture in the evening on Canada, illustrated with magic lantern views, the announcement was greeted with loud hurrahs for Canada and the maple leaf for ever by the boys and girls as they rushed back to resume work in school. It was felt that the evening meeting would soon be widely advertised and the issue of bills for that purpose superfluous. Before eight o'clock the accommodation of the school, large and commodious as it was, was taxed to its utmost capacity, extra seats having had to be arranged along the whole available floor space. When Mr Mackerracher appeared he found himself face to face with a large and intelligent gathering ... . Mr Ranald Macdonald, J.P., headmaster, who presided, briefly introduced the lecturer, proclaiming his own partiality for Canada and his strong faith in its unlimited possibilities and high destiny. His preference for Canada was enhanced, too, by the fact that many of the choicest young men and young women who had passed through his hands as pupils in the school were today scattered all over Canada, and all doing well as was evidenced by their occasional ample remittances to their parents at home. Mr Mackerracher spoke first in Gaelic and afterwards in English. He undoubtedly had a good subject in Canada, and while he dealt with it in all its aspects, forcefully and eloquently describing it as an unrivalled field for emigration, a country of vast extent and inexhaustible resources and of great potentialities for the future, it was felt, as view after view of scenes throughout the Dominion appeared on the screen, that with all his praise of the country in no instance did Mr Mackerracher exaggerate or overstate the case for Canada.[51]

Another, rather less glamorous, insider's snapshot of Hebridean agency work twelve years later is given in Aberdeen agent D. J. Murphy's account of a lecture tour in Skye in January 1923. It was forwarded to Ottawa by J. O. Smith as an example of 'the enthusiasm and also the difficulties' under which field representatives worked, and – in response to Smith's plea for support – may have precipitated the opening of the Inverness office eight months later.

Arriving at Portree, Skye, at 6.30 p.m. 16/1/23, where our outfit (sent on ahead) was already loaded and car waiting, we promptly set out for Staffin, 18 miles distant, under typical Hebrides weather. Gales, mists and mountainous roads made progress slow. Staffin was reached at 8.20 p.m. where an audience of 131 (all figures actual, no guesses) drawn from miles around awaited our arrival. They were worth the effort. No finer type have I seen anywhere, and as you may believe all had ancestors who had helped to develop Canada. Our address closed at 10.0 p.m. when we had to go on to Uig, 10 miles distant, through a gorge and around a headland thrilling even in day travel. Midnight brought us to one of these abominations called Inns. Although advised ahead, no provision was made, and I got a bed last slept in in September. I gave an address at Uig next night (17th) and had six splendid and refined girls call and fill in 'E' form to sail in April. Men also very anxious to go, but as in Staffin, they have only what they earn, from day to day, which is all absorbed in living. (Attendance 117).

After the Uig lecture on the 17th, I had to drive on to Portree (15 miles) to get new driver, since the previous night had been too much for the native. Leaving Portree in daylight with gale and snow, we made slow progress to Colbost, via Dunvegan, 29 1/2 miles distant. Here in a great saucer-shaped amphitheatre of gorse and moor with crofts scattered widely separated, we had the largest audience of our tour. I stood between men sprawled on the floor or sitting on their shins, so packed was every corner of a good-size school, while without howled one of the worst sleet storms I have ever seen in this country. We were late leaving here owing to so many enquiries, but again few were able to pay all their fare. Girls we can get, because loans are made by certain Provinces. (Attendance 147).

We called at Edenbain [sic] School on way, and gave talk to students, also distributing 'Atlases', 'Women's Work' and 'Canada, Where When & How'. We requested children to take these books to their brothers and sisters at home.

After Colbost lecture we had to drive seven miles to Dunvegan for lodging. Here, next day, we visited Higher Grade School and repeated Edenbain method. In this way our literature was very widely and wisely distributed. The Atlases and Wall Maps won the heart of the Headmaster every time.

Our next call for lecture was at Bernisdale School, 14 miles from Dunvegan, which was reached in fair weather and by day travel. As our lecture was not until 8.0 p.m. we had the novelty to us, of attending a Gaelic Service in the same school, which lasted from 6.0 p.m. to 7.30 p.m ... . Contrasting his congregation of 11 people with the audience of 128 that swarmed in to hear about Canada, it was painfully evident to all that this is a materialistic age. Maybe the collection plate was the deterrent cause in the first instance.

Again we had to drive on eight miles to get shelter at Portree. Here on Saturday we met the different Clergy and business men who all seemed very cordial to Canada. Indeed Mr. MacDonald and Mr. McLean, two large land proprietors, were even enthusiastic. The latter is to visit the Dominion this summer and may take up property, so he stated.

Saturday afternoon we moved on to Breakish, 25 miles distant, along roads truly picturesque. Through the defiles of the Cuillian [sic] range, where for over 3 miles you descend at a grade of 1 ft. in 8, with many acute angle turns. This road is seldom made by night trip. This village was the last of our series, and again we had an audience to capacity of school (127).

After lecture and various interviews we drove on to Broadford for hotel, remaining over Sunday for first boat 8.0 a.m. Monday to mainland.

Summing up, I feel sure we will get a fair migration from the class who have the money to pay their fares. The great majority are of those who only can pay a portion, say 50%, as money on these Isles is very scarce. In no way would farmer delegates or others overcome this money shortage, and I feel certain from what I have experienced that now is not the time for delegates, but instead if the agent has latitude to hire help as occasion demands, so that he may do the lecturing and outside work, in that way will best results be obtained.[52]

Murphy was also active as a lecturer in and around Aberdeen, where in 1923 he was introduced to an audience at the Chamber of Commerce as one of the most popular Canadian government agents ever based in the north.[53] The work of Murphy and other federal agents was supplemented by a host of other professional and amateur emigration agents promoting a range of enterprises and destinations. During a tour of Scotland and England made – somewhat surprisingly – in the early months of the war, Nova Scotia provincial agent E. B. Elderkin reported back to his employer on his dealings with booking agents and gave his views on the potential for highland settlement in the Maritimes. While he admitted that crofters from the mainland around Inverness would do well in Cape Breton and southwest Nova Scotia, this was not true of those from the Western Isles, whose ancestors had pioneered settlement in the province a century earlier:

From my observations I would say that the Hebrides are the most hopeless places that I have ever seen in which to secure suitable emigrants for Nova Scotia … . I did not meet a single individual whom I would have felt justified in recommending, even had they been willing to go. However we only met a very small percentage, and there may be those who would be desirable, but I did not come across any such.

At Loch Maddy I met a Mr. Ferguson who was a Shipping Agent for North Uist, and he informed me that he knew a man who would have between £100 and £200, who was desirous of going abroad, and that there were a number of others in like condition. I gave him full information in regard to Nova Scotia and had a full supply of literature, and a map for each school house sent to him. He agreed to communicate with me in London with regard to this man and the others, but although I have written to him since, I have not yet heard from him … . The wants of these people are few, and easily supplied, and I cannot help but say that in my judgment it would be next to a crime to put forward an organised effort to transplant them into a different climate and conditions.[54]

Unlike Elderkin, Canadian railway company agents who toured Scotland after the war were unequivocally positive about the benefits of the Dominion. The CPR was particularly well represented in word, picture and action. In

February 1923 Esther Mackie of Montreal delivered an illustrated lecture in Aberdeen with the aim of attracting farm workers and domestics, particularly to CPR lands in the west.[55] Just over a year later emigrants from Inverness-shire, Aberdeenshire, Perthshire and the lowlands were reported to comprise a 'large party' of farm labourers recruited for Canada under the auspices of former Tillycoultry man and CPR agent J. Millar. He was to accompany them across the Atlantic, with a second party due to follow in June under T. H. Scotland, the CPR's Scottish district representative, who also regularly interviewed would-be emigrants at booking agents' offices.[56] Promotional work across Scotland was spearheaded by John Cameron, a Winnipeg farmer and lawyer of Scottish parentage, who in 1924 addressed an audience of 500 in Aberdeen and packed halls in the surrounding rural hinterland. With the aid of seven promotional films, he assured agriculturists who settled near the railway that Canada offered them a cordial welcome and good opportunities on small mixed farms of their own, free of the hardships suffered by the pioneers. By the time he returned a year later he had adopted the Federal Immigration Department's prop of a travelling exhibition wagon to reinforce the message of movie film and verbal encouragement.[57] More potent than Cameron's occasional visits, however, were the ongoing efforts of local CPR colonization agents – men such as James Hogg, who in 1929 was singled out for particular praise by J. W. Stewart, an emigrant correspondent of the *Fraserburgh Herald*. Eighteen months earlier Stewart had moved from Rathen, Aberdeenshire, to Birtle, Manitoba, with his wife and twelve children, not without reservations, for 'it was no small undertaking to uproot myself from the old places and ways of living and come away with such a large family'. But thanks to Hogg, who had accompanied the emigrant party and subsequently visited Stewart on several occasions, he had made a successful settlement, and he therefore advised any farmers with thoughts of emigrating to consult Lossiemouth-born Hogg during his winter recruitment drive in Aberdeenshire, 'for they could not find a man better suited to advise them on all matters related to farming and settlement in Western Canada'.[58]

The Colonization and Development Department of the CNR responded to the CPR's challenge by sending Falkirk-born George Adam from Montreal on a lecture tour of Scotland in March 1924 and appointing Scottish emigrant Alexander McOwan as its District Superintendent for Scotland four months later. Farmer and journalist McOwan, who had already gained considerable experience as a federal agent in the Canadian government's Glasgow and Bristol offices, subsequently toured Scotland with the CNR's three-reel promotional film *The High Road to Independence*, and his work, like Cameron's, was underpinned by the dogged canvassing of local CNR agents.[59] It was further reinforced by the immensely popular *People's*

Journal when CNR Vice-President William Robb commissioned a special reporter from the newspaper to tour Canada at his company's expense and prepare a series of seven promotional articles, which appeared in the late summer and autumn of 1924. Robb, who was in charge of the CNR's Colonization and Development Department, had a particular interest in Scottish recruits, his parents having emigrated from Angus just before he was born.[60]

The role of the booking agents

Since most lectures and interviews were organized by local booking agents, it was vital for dominion officials to cultivate the loyalty of these legions of amateur, usually part-time, agents. In the absence of resident territorial representatives, the antipodean states and provinces operated exclusively through ticket agencies and employment exchanges. As previously noted, the bulk of Australian business was cornered by Mackay Brothers, based in Edinburgh and Aberdeen, which orchestrated most of W. C. Stillman's mainland Scottish lecture tours, hosted numerous interviewing sessions conducted by visiting female agents and also liaised with trades unions and the New South Wales government in the recruitment of Scottish masons to work on Sydney Harbour bridge in 1926. The masons, many of whom took their families with them, were recruited on five-year, passage-paid contracts by bridge-builders Dorman & Long of Middlesbrough and sailed from Liverpool in two parties to work in quarries at Moruya, 200 miles south of Sydney.[61] Canadian recruiters too often relied on local booking agents, not only to organize their itineraries and sell tickets for the steamship lines they represented but also to overcome the natural conservatism and suspicion of the farming constituency the dominions sought to recruit. The lack of booking agents in northwest Scotland may have been one reason for the creation of a highland-based Canadian government office, where most of the business had to be generated by the government officials themselves through posters, school packs, the publication of selected emigrant correspondence and meetings which they organized themselves, often after Anne MacDonald had made use of the electoral roll to circularize agricultural workers.

In other parts of Scotland, however, local ticket agents could play a key collaborative part in the recruitment process, delivering lectures on their own initiative, liaising with Canadian employment registries and chaperoning parties of emigrants, as well as selling tickets and managing the professional agency network. In the largely rural northern territory the Canadian government office in Aberdeen liaised with about 100 ticket agents, the most active of whom – both before and after the war – were John Sinclair in Elgin, Andrew Spalding in Blairgowrie and John Wood in

Kirkwall, as well as the larger-scale Mackay Brothers. No records survive for at least one other active agent, Murdo Maclean of Stornoway. Sinclair, an accountant and the manager of Miltonduff distillery near Elgin, was described on his appointment in 1908 as 'energetic and pushing', and in 1923 as 'one of the best if not the best agent in this territory … thoroughly reliable in every way'. His clients were also noteworthy for having more means than their west coast counterparts, generally being able to pay their own way, and often emigrating to join friends. Despite being vilified in the Toronto press in 1914, Spalding, an ex-provost of Blairgowrie, was commended in 1923 as 'a very active Agent [who] has a good knowledge of Canada'. And Wood, who was a farmer and later a cycle merchant as well as a booking agent, was classified as a good appointee with very few disputed bonus claims. He was 'active and energetic, travelling from place to place on bicycle soliciting business' – a practice which did not, however, meet with the approval of the more sedentary ticket agents in Kirkwall.[62]

The rural emphasis of the northern agencies was echoed at the other end of Scotland, as reflected in the surviving papers of two Border booking agents. J. & J. H. Rutherford of Kelso were classified by the Canadian government office in Glasgow as long-established businessmen but only mediocre agents, for whom promoting emigration was secondary to their main business as stationers and booksellers.[63] Walter Easton of Jedburgh, on the other hand, was highly commended as 'without doubt the best booking agent in the South of Scotland. He is very energetic, and in consequence he practically controls the whole of the shipping for quite an area around Jedburgh. A first-class agent.'[64] Easton combined his ticket agency with running a bookselling, printing and newsagency business and managing the *Jedburgh Gazette*, through which he frequently promoted emigration. After spending two months touring Canada in 1906, he published an account of his trip in the *Gazette* and subsequently in an illustrated booklet. In that publication he highlighted encounters with settlers from the Borders, offered observations on farming opportunities, and concluded with the observation that 'Having seen so much of the country and interviewed so many of the representatives of the Government and other gentlemen we are in the position, unequalled by any other emigration agent in this district, of giving reliable and trustworthy information direct from the spot from personal observation and official sources.'[65] Like Sinclair, Easton found that his clients were often men of means, but, despite considerable family assets, he himself was advised against emigrating when in 1919 he tried unsuccessfully to capitalize on his good standing as an agent to secure preferential treatment in Canada. Easton's desire to emigrate was prompted by his expectation of post-war dislocation at home, concern for his son's career prospects and the interest of other family members in relocating in Canada.

I forsee [sic] nothing but industrial troubles and unrest for a considerable time ahead, and having had my full share of worries since the war began, I think this is now the time to make a clean end. I am not 'bare' by any means … as I would have between £2,000 and £3,000 clean to invest after coming out. With interest on this capital and an appointment of some kind connected with emigration, shipping interests or railways … I would have a much easier mind than I have at present. I have one son, 18 years of age, who is at present on the staff of this newspaper.… He means to push ahead and will have a much better chance of doing so in Canada than here. Do you consider I would [stand] any chance of such a job as I have indicated? For a start I would accept any kind of responsible work (clerical or of an organising nature) but do not know how to set about it, so perhaps you could give me a wrinkle or two. My brother … has been so overworked during the war, and so closely confined that he has been recommended by his doctor to sell off and take up a fruit farm in the Niagara Peninsula which he intends doing as soon as circumstances permit if I agree to go out and settle somewhere in Ontario. The capital will be somewhere between £1,000 and £2,000 … . Further – should my brother and I decide to go, two unmarried sisters with a capital of £1,000–£1,500 between them, will come also. This money too would be put into some industry, such as poultry farming.[66]

As in the northern agency, no papers survive for most of the booking offices visited by the Glasgow-based Canadian agent in places as far apart as Campbeltown and Carnoustie, Coldstream and Jura, Annan and Auchtermuchty, in addition to the industrial conurbations.[67] Ayrshire, however, did boast two ticket agents whose skills and enthusiasm are recorded in surviving correspondence with Ottawa. James Scott of Ayr was appointed by J. B. Walker shortly after he took over the Glasgow office in 1903 because the existing agents 'were a sleepy and indifferent lot'. As a result of Scott's appointment, business increased by leaps and bounds, soon bringing Ayrshire to 'the forefront of the Scottish counties'. Like Easton, Scott visited Canada in 1906 in order 'to further increase his force and influence', and in 1923, having relinquished employment as a house agent to concentrate exclusively on his shipping business, he was still commended as 'one of the most active Agents in Scotland' who attracted 'a splendid type of agricultural class'.[68] Printer and guidebook author James Ballantine of nearby Cumnock, who represented the Allan, Donaldson, Canadian Pacific and White Star–Dominion lines, was even more highly commended as 'certainly one of the best Booking Agents in the Kingdom' who operated almost entirely on behalf of Canada and showed some individual initiative.[69] Before the war his good reputation earned him an expenses-paid transatlantic trip to cultivate links with employment agents in Ontario and the west, and he continued to advertise widely in southern Scotland during the 1920s, making use of his Canadian contacts to secure situations at high wages for hand-picked recruits, whom he recommended only if they could produce satisfactory testimonials from former employers. In 1920, recognizing that many good farm labourers could not afford the high transportation costs after the war, Ballantine even persuaded a few Saskatchewan farmers to advance employees' fares through the Royal Bank of Scotland in Cumnock, securing written agreements from recruits and their parents regarding the full repayment of these loans.[70]

While complying with the regulations, Ballantine was not slow to upbraid the Ontario immigration authorities for impeding effective recruitment by booking agents through excessive bureaucracy and an unrealistically high loan limit of £16 in place of the pre-war ceiling of £4.

> Look at the matter from the agent's point of view. Say I am sending 20 farm hands into Ontario. I have to get the Information sheet … and references of the 20 sent for approval to London. Ten are paying their own passages, and beyond the shipping and the Declaration Forms there is no trouble. The other ten require assistance. I have to notify London, get the loan document and guarantees filled up. For my own protection I have to make enquiries if possible, about the guarantors to learn if they are respectable, causing anything from six to ten additional letters from first to last in each case, for which not one penny is allowed, and in the end I find that I am held as guarantee for the repayment of £160 to the Ontario Government.
>
> To follow the position further – the ten young farm hands go out and are placed at work. Nine make good with the result that the Province of Ontario derives rich benefit as the fruit of their work. The tenth, for good or bad reason, fails. I am called on to make good the loss. The parents are perhaps a married ploughman or decent labouring man with the usual large young family. With your knowledge of Dumfries-shire conditions, what are my chances of recovery, unless extreme measures are resorted to, and that I would not do.
>
> Why should the agent be asked to shoulder all the responsibility? In the former days with a £4 limit we did it and out of dozens I sent this way I had practically no trouble. With the larger sum and greater risk it is a different proposition.[71]

The most common complaint levelled against the Canadian immigration authorities by urban booking agents in central Scotland, however, was the unjustified rejection of bonuses on recruits who had only recently moved from country to town prior to emigrating and whose urban occupations obscured their farming experience and intentions. Glasgow agents David Cumming and George McFarlane both suggested that inspectors at landing ports should take more account of emigrants' *primary* occupations and skills since 'they would very often find that men who have served the best part of a lifetime on farms are often induced to come into the towns'.

Their complaints were echoed by Falkirk agent Mary Farnon, who was also penalized for claiming bonuses on 'ineligible' urban recruits whose backgrounds often fitted them perfectly for the farming careers they intended to pursue as emigrants.[72]

The demise of agency activity

The reduction of emigration to a trickle as a consequence of worldwide depression brought agency activity to a standstill. After the staff of Australia House was reduced in 1928, the Wall Street crash in 1929 spelled the virtual end of assistance and the £34 Million Agreement. New Canadian regulations in March 1931 permitted entry only to British subjects and American citizens who had the means to support themselves, to dependents of Canadian residents who could maintain them, and to agriculturists with the means to begin farming. During 1930–31 advertising and publications were discontinued, the few lectures that survived became educational rather than promotional, booking agents were ordered to discourage even those with capital from emigrating, and the number of British offices was reduced to three – at London, Liverpool and Glasgow.[73] Some agents anticipated recovery. In 1932 James Ballantine wrote to Immigration Department Secretary F. C. Blair of his son Duncan's forthcoming visit to Canada to gain first-hand information 'that will be of use in our shipping business once normal conditions are restored', and in 1936 John Bridges of the Overseas League (which had almost 9,000 members in Edinburgh and Glasgow) liaised with Blair and Glasgow's Canadian government agent J. G. Perdue to promote Canada among Scottish tourists and educationists. This was achieved through the establishment of a Canadian film library in Edinburgh for the distribution of up-to-date productions and by arranging for 180 Scottish secondary school teachers and 200 pupils to tour the Dominion in 1937.[74] But agency recruitment of emigrants never really had the opportunity to revive before the curtain descended once again in 1939, and its resumption after 1945 was not characterized by the same seamlessness that had marked the agents' activities during the transition from war to peace in 1918.

Although professional agents had played a part in shaping emigrants' decisions since the early days of mass emigration, it was not until the second half of the nineteenth century that they became an integral and ubiquitous component of the recruitment process. As a variety of states, dominions and provinces competed for agriculturists, domestic servants and, of course, settlers with capital, increasingly sophisticated techniques and incentives were employed to entice the undecided emigrant. Scotland, like the rest of the British Isles, experienced an influx of agents that probably reached a peak of volume and commitment in the two decades before the First World War. After the enforced mothballing of activities between 1914 and 1918 techniques and personnel changed little during the 1920s, although schemes promoted under the ESA enlarged both the responsibilities and the opportunities of agents. Paradoxically, however, the 1920s saw a growing divergence between the agents' continuing enthusiasm and determination to capitalize on unprecedented public funding and the parsimony of policy-makers in the destination countries, who sometimes seemed to be more concerned with balancing the books than facilitating the recruitment of colonists, even before the depression. Professional agents had to steer a difficult course between antagonizing their employers by excessive expenditure and arousing dominion hostility by careless selection, while simultaneously avoiding accusations of capitulating to competition. Along with the booking agents, they also had to counter criticism from disgruntled emigrants and armchair opponents of emigration in Britain, who accused them of making fraudulent promises and abducting the flower of the population. While most recruiters acted responsibly, a few maverick operators could do serious damage to the reputation of established agents, and Scottish emigration, both before and after the First World War, was punctuated by examples of controversial agency activity. In the Hebrides in particular, where the legacy of enforced emigration cast a long shadow, paid agents were held accountable for the success or failure of many of those who constituted the haemorrhage of the 1920s.

Notes

1 NAC, RG76, C-4661, vol. 5, file 41, part 3, memorandum to booking agents issued by the London office of the DIC, 29 Nov. 1919.
2 *Ibid.*, C-10294, vol. 405, file 590687, part 1, J. O. Smith, Assistant Superintendent of Emigration, London, to W. D. Scott, Superintendent of Immigration, Ottawa, 'Report on British Agencies', 15 Mar. 1909, evidence from Malcolm MacIntyre, Glasgow office.
3 *Ibid.*, C-10612, vol. 514, file 800180, J. M. Moir to R. Forke, 6 Jan. 1927.
4 *Ibid.*, C-4661, vol. 6, file 41, part 3, Assistant Deputy Minister, Ottawa, to W. R. Little, Director of European Emigration, London, 18 Dec. 1930.
5 *Ibid.*, C-10325, vol. 450, file 686431, Andrew Spalding, Blairgowrie, quoting unnamed Toronto newspaper, 9 May 1914, 'Immigration agent who should be in jail'. See also p. 62.
6 *Ibid.*, C-10275, vol. 378, file 524037, A. Warrick, Glasgow. J. D. Cameron, Glasgow District Representative of CPR, quoted in J. N. K. Macalister, Assistant Commissioner of CPR, to DIC, 15 Feb. 1927; G. E. Corbett, Montreal Society for the Protection of Women and Children, to the DIC, 27 Mar. 1924.
7 *P&J*, 15 June 1923.
8 NAC, RG76, C-10294, vol. 405, file 590687, part 1, John MacLennan, reports for weeks ending 22 Feb. 1908 and 16 Oct. 1910.
9 Letter from J. L. Anderson, Pittornie, Dairsie, to the *Scottish Farmer* (*SF*), 28 Feb. 1925, p. 265.
10 NAC, RG76, C-4661, vol. 5, file 41, part 3, W. R. Little to J. B. Walker, 28 Aug. 1926.
11 *Ibid.*, vol. 6, file 41, part 2, F. C. Blair, Secretary, DIC, to W. J. Black, Deputy Minister, DIC, internal memorandum, 20 Feb. 1922.

12 Annual Report of the DIC for year ended 31 March 1928, Report of Inverness agency, contained in the Report of J. B. Walker (Canadian Sessional Papers, Annual Departmental Reports, 1927–28, vol. 2).

13 *SF*, 6 Mar. 1926, p. 299.

14 *John O'Groat Journal*, 3 Aug. 1930.

15 NAC, RG76, C-10644, vol. 564, file 808836, J. O. Smith to W. D. Scott, 15 Mar. 1909.

16 Marjory Harper, *Emigration from North-East Scotland*, vol. 2. *Beyond the Broad Atlantic* (Aberdeen, Aberdeen University Press, 1988), p. 23. For details of the upsurge of Queensland emigration agency activity in the 1880s, see J. C. R. Camm, 'The hunt for muscle and bone: emigration agents and their role in migration to Queensland during the 1880s', *Australian Historical Geography, Bulletin*, 2 (Feb. 1981), pp. 6–29 and Camm, 'The origins of assisted British migrants to Queensland, 1871–1892', *Australian Geographical Studies*, 23 (Apr. 1985), pp. 87–104.

17 NAC, RG76, C-10644, vol. 564, file 808836, part 3, W. D. Scott to W. W. Cory, Acting Deputy Minister, DIC, 11 Dec. 1911, quoting extracts from *The Year Book of the Commonwealth of Australia*.

18 NAC, RG76, C-10294, vol. 405, file 590687, part 1, J. O. Smith to W. D. Scott, 'Report on British Agencies', 15 Mar. 1909. By 1912, however, McIntyre was complaining that Australian competition was becoming more effective (*ibid.*, C-10324, vol. 449, file 682150, part 1, weekly reports, 27 Jan., 3 Feb. 1912).

19 NAC, RG76, C-4661, vol. 5, file 41, part 3, E. B. Robertson to Cory, 12 Sept. 1912.

20 *Ibid.*

21 *Ibid.*, Scott to Smith, 21 Nov. 1916.

22 *Ibid.*, Scott to Cory, 22 Mar. 1917.

23 *Ibid.*, Smith to Scott, 5 Sept 1912.

24 *Ibid.*, Scott to Cory, 13 Jan. 1914; Smith to regional agents, 9 July 1914; Scott to Smith, 23 July 1914. Smith's idea was subsequently reinforced by an article in the (Vancouver) *Daily Province* of 19 July 1923, which urged Canada to modify the doctrine that it always needed farmers more than people of any other class, pointing out that wealth-creating urban dwellers were the 'best friends of the farmer'.

25 NAC, RG76, C-4661, vol. 5, file 41, part 3, Smith to Scott, 6 Mar. 1915.

26 *Ibid.*, Walker to Scott, 7 June 1917. By this time Walker was Superintendent of Immigration at Winnipeg. (In the 1920s he was appointed Director of Emigration for Canada in Europe.)

27 *Ibid.*, Smith to Scott, 8 Aug. 1917.

28 *Ibid.*, Smith to J. A. Calder, 22 Apr. 1919; Smith to Scott, 17 June 1919; Smith to F. C. Blair, 11 Feb., 2 Mar. 1920, 21 June 1921.

29 *Ibid.*, Blair to Cory, 21 June 1921. See also criticism of Smith in Blair to Black, 9 Jan. 1923; Little to Egan, 19 Aug. 1924; Little to Egan, 6 Mar. 1925.

30 NAC, RG76, C-4661, vol. 5, file 41, part 3, 'Immigration or stagnation' in *Winnipeg Tribune*, n.d., quoted in letter from R. J. C. Stead, Director of Publicity, to Little, 28 Dec. 1925.

31 NAC, RG76, C-4661, vol. 5, file 41, part 3, Egan to Little, 19 Jan. 1925.

32 *Ibid.*, Little to Egan, 6 Mar. 1925.

33 *Ibid.*, C-7396-7, vol. 248, file 179046, part 1, 'Scheme between British and Canadian governments, settlement of British families on land, 1924–5', undated memorandum from Anne MacDonald to the DIC, Oct. or Nov. 1924. Little replied somewhat complacently on 11 Nov. 1924.

34 *Ibid.*, C-4661, vol. 5, file 41, part 1, Walker to Scott, 1 Dec. 1913; vol. 6, part 3, Walker to Egan, 9 Nov. 1928; vol. 6, part 2, Smith to Blair, 15 Dec. 1921; Blair to Egan, 2 Apr. 1924.

35 *Ibid.*, vol. 5, file 41, part 1, Smith to Calder, 15 Sept. 1920; vol. 6, file 41, part 2, Smith to Blair, 15 Dec. 1921; Blair to Black, 20 Feb. 1922.

36 *Ibid.*, file 41, part 3, Walker to Egan, 30 July 1926.

37 *Ibid.*, Walker to Egan, 19 Oct. 1926.

38 *Ibid.*, Egan to Walker, 28 Aug. 1926. See also chapter 1, p. 35.

39 Four federal departments supervised immigration work at different times: the Department of Agriculture (1867–92), the Department of the Interior (1893–1917), the Department of Immigration and Colonization (1917–36) and the Department of Mines and Resources (from 1936). The Director of European Emigration, appointed in 1924, and his assistant were responsible to the Deputy Minister of the DIC in Ottawa. H. Gordon Skilling discusses the agency structure in detail in his book *Canadian Representation Abroad. From Agency to Embassy* (Toronto, Ryerson Press, 1945), pp. 1–34. See also *Annual Report* of the DIC, 31 Mar. 1925.

40 Skilling, *Canadian Representation Abroad*, p. 30. Medical examinations in Britain were initially carried out, for a fee, by 1,750 British 'roster' doctors, but in 1928 the latter were replaced by 20 Canadian doctors who conducted free medicals at the territorial agents' offices and at 300 other centres throughout the British Isles.

41 J. O. Smith's report, in *Annual Reports* of the DIC, 31 Mar. 1922, 31 Mar. 1923.

42 *Annual Reports* of the DIC, 1914, 1921–32.

43 *Annual Report* of the DIC, 1925.

44 NAC, RG76, C-4661, vol. 5, file 41, part 3, Smith to Scott, 28 July 1911; Robertson to Cory, 12 Sept. 1912.

45 *Ibid.*, part 1, Stead to Cory, 5 Nov. 1920.

46 *Annual Report* of the DIC, 31 Mar. 1920, pp. 37, 40.

47 The Scottish agency functioned from 1869 to 1876 and after 1880. Briefly located at Carlisle, it was moved to Glasgow because of the latter's importance as a shipping port for Canada, and was soon reckoned to be the most important regional office after Liverpool (see NAC, RG76, C-4660, vol. 5, file 41, part 1, report of 10 Aug. 1892 from Sir Charles Tupper, High Commissioner, to E. Dewdney, Minister of the Interior).

48 *Annual Report* of the DIC, 1907; MacLennan's weekly reports for weeks ending 2 and 9 Mar. 1907; NAC, RG76, C-10294, vol. 405, file 590687, part 1, Smith to Scott, report on British agencies, 15 Mar. 1909.

49 NAC, RG76, C-7401, vol. 252, file 186833, 'Inverness office, 1923–36', T. A. Russell, Toronto, to Hon. Wesley Gordon, Minister of Immigration, Ontario, 23 Dec. 1932. The Inverness office moved to more convenient premises at 33 Academy Street in 1926.

50 *Ibid.*, C-10318, vol. 440, file 662655, 'Hugh McKerracher, Paisley, exhibition wagon, 1907–21', Hon. W. Gibson to W. D. Scott, 22 Dec. 1908, undated extract from the *Oban Times* (1908), D. L. Edward, Emigration and Shipping Agent, Perth, to W. D. Scott, 10 June 1910.

51 *HN*, 8 Apr. 1911.

52 NAC, RG76, C-4660, vol. 5, file 41, part 3, Smith to Blair, 25 Jan. 1923; D. J. Murphy to Smith, 25 Jan. 1923.

53 *P&J*, 17 Feb. 1923.

54 Public Archives of Nova Scotia (PANS), MFM 3614, pp. 32–3, Elderkin's Report (1914) in Report of the Secretary of Industries and Immigration, Journals of the House (1915).

55 *P&J*, 9 Feb. 1923.

56 *Ibid.*, 20 Feb. 1924, 6 Jan. 1926.

57 *Ibid.*, 12 Feb., 1, 7 Apr. 1924; 22 Jan. 1925. See also *SF*, 26 Jan. 1924, p. 110.

58 *Fraserburgh Herald*, 31 Dec., 1929. Hogg, who farmed in northern Saskatchewan, also advertised on behalf of the Hudson's Bay Company (*ibid.*, 4 Mar. 1930).

59 *SF*, 8 Mar. 1924, p. 296; *P&J*, 31 July 1924, 2 Feb., 4 Dec. 1925.

60 *People's Journal*, 23, 30 Aug., 6, 13, 20, 27 Sept., 4 Oct. 1924. See also chapter 4, pp. 148–50, for the activities of female travelling agents of the CPR and CNR.

61 *P&J*, 24 July, 11 Nov. 1924; 25 Feb. 1926. Further information on the recruitment of masons for Sydney Harbour bridge was kindly supplied by Mrs Norah Berry, whose father accompanied his parents to Australia at the age of five, returning with them to Aberdeen in 1930.

62 Northern territorial agent's reports in NAC, RG76, C-10644, vol. 564, file 809010 (Mackay Brothers); C-10315, vol. 435, file 652801 (Sinclair), C-10325, vol. 450, file 686431 (Spalding), C-10269, vol. 369, file 493191 (Wood). See also chapter 2, pp. 43–4.

63 NAC, RG76, C-10311, vol. 429, file 635503.

64 *Ibid.*, C-10269, vol. 369, file 497599, report on Easton by James Miller, Canadian government agent, Glasgow, 22 Apr. 1913.

65 *Notes and Observations of a Visit to Canada* (Jedburgh, n.p., 1906), p. 41.
66 NAC, RG76, C-10269, vol. 369, file 497599, Easton to Scott, 10 Mar. 1919. Easton's italics.
67 *Ibid.*, C-10324, vol. 450, file 682150, weekly reports of Malcolm MacIntyre, Glasgow agent, 1909–12, 1922–23.
68 *Ibid.*, C-10261, vol. 358, file 410827, Walker to Scott, 8 Aug. 1906; Andrew O'Kelly, report on James Scott, 31 Jan. 1923.
69 *Ibid.*, C-10260, vol. 356, file 402561, Little to Cory, 11 Dec. 1920; Blair to Thomas Molloy, Superintendent of Employment Service, Regina, 20 Jan. 1921. Ballantine was allegedly the author of *The Golden West: or Canada at Closest Quarters* (n.p., n.d.), which he described on his headed notepaper as 'the best book published for the intending emigrant'.
70 NAC, RG76, C-10260, vol. 356, file 402561, Blair to T. Molloy, 20 Jan. 1921.
71 *Ibid.*, Ballantine to Little, n.d. but probably late 1920.
72 NAC, RG76, C-10309, vol. 426, file 629453 (Cumming, 1907–15, 1918); C-10315, vol. 435, file 652806 (McFarlane, 1907–9, 1909–10, 1910–13, 1923); C-10311, vol. 430, file 636689 (Farnon, 1907–21).
73 *Ibid.*, C-4661, vol. 5, file 41, part 3, Little to Deputy Minister, 3 Nov. 1931. The agencies at Bristol, Cardiff, Dublin, Inverness and York were effectively mothballed on 31 December 1931.
74 *Ibid.*, C-10260, vol. 356, file 402561, Ballantine to Blair; C-10303, vol. 148, file 608438, Overseas League, Scotland, 1936–37. The teachers' party travelled under the auspices of Bridges' Overseas League and the schoolboys, accompanied by their teachers, went out with the Scottish Secondary Schools Travel Trust, Edinburgh.

CHAPTER THREE

Highland problems and solutions

Throughout and beyond the nineteenth century Scottish emigration was, in the public mind and public print, largely synonymous with an unwilling exodus from the highlands and islands. The reshaping of the region's demographic, social and economic map during a century and a half of estate reorganization and clearance fuelled a negative, pejorative and enduring historiography of enforced diaspora, which distorted the diversity of the movement, obscured the significant outflow from other areas and suffused Scottish emigration as a whole with the symbolism of the highland exodus. In the 1920s the imagery of banishment was adopted by socialist and nationalist critics of urban-industrial emigration at the same time as a renewed outflow from the Hebrides – reminiscent of the mass departures of the mid-nineteenth century – reignited the smouldering debate over emigration as exile or opportunity. The debate was all the more intense in northwest Scotland not only because of the long and bitter legacy of clearance and landlord-aided emigration but also because that was the area which had felt the impact of the government's first tentative experiments in imperial colonization in the 1880s. This chapter investigates the extent to which attitudes towards state-aided colonization from the highlands in the 1920s were shaped by the earlier experiences of highlanders and governments alike, with particular emphasis on changing and continuing perceptions of overseas settlement, the influence of agents and disparities between expectations and experiences.

Initiatives and images in the nineteenth century

The first stirrings of mass emigration from northwest Scotland in the second half of the eighteenth century had been accompanied by strident protests from landlords and government, reinforced periodically by legislative attempts to sabotage a movement that was perceived as economically and militarily damaging. In the nineteenth century, however, the alarm of landlords gave way first to acquiescence and then to approbation as much-vaunted schemes of estate development began to crumble in the face of recession and recurring subsistence crises. In an attempt to tackle chronic problems of poverty, overpopulation and land hunger, proprietors began to encourage and even subsidize emigration from their estates, often replacing people with sheep and, later, deer, the only profitable commodities in the highlands' marginal economy. Their attempts to persuade the government to finance emigration elicited the appointment of a select committee but no tangible assistance in that age of *laissez-faire* economics; although the committee reported unequivocally in 1841 that extensive state-subsidized emigration was an essential preliminary to effective relief measures for the region in the aftermath of the 1830s famine, it took the more devastating famine of 1846 before the government responded, and even then the Emigration Advances Act of 1851 only allowed landlords to borrow from public funds to assist tenants who wished to emigrate.

It was in this era that the already negative definition of highland emigration as enforced exile became firmly embedded in the psyche of emigrants and commentators alike. Perhaps the state's failure to become financially involved aggravated the parsimony of impecunious landlords and overburdened emigration societies in their attempts to despatch maximum numbers of emigrants at minimum cost. Certainly the chief Canadian immigration agent was scathing in his condemnation of the inadequate provision made by some landlords who, having chosen Canada for its proximity and relative cheapness of passage, expected the Immigration Department to foot the bill for onward travel from port of landing. But far greater notoriety was attached to the brutal manner in which many landlords, particularly in the Outer Hebrides, recruited emigrants. Numerous episodes of enforced removal were brought to public notice by commentators, journalists and bards, whose graphic descriptions helped to create a powerful image of the highland exodus, in all eras and all circumstances, as an unreservedly negative experience.

By the time the government came to play a more active part in highland emigration in the late nineteenth century, crofting opinion in the region was firmly set against further removals. Grasping the unprecedented opportunity of the Napier Commission to express their grievances, crofter witnesses inveighed against the injustice of earlier emigration and urged on the commissioners the need to address the highlanders' problems through positive rather than negative policies, through a redistribution of land rather than an expulsive redistribution of population. The commissioners, while acknowledging the need to establish crofting tenure on a more secure basis, thought that enlargement of holdings could best be achieved in conjunction with a measure of 'properly conducted' state-aided emigration, which, they declared, was an indispensable remedy for the condition of parts of the northwest.

On the basis of Napier's recommendation, and galvanized by the unsettled condition of the Hebrides, the government took uncharacteristic action in 1888, advancing £10,000 towards the settlement of 100 families from Lewis, Harris and North Uist on prairie homesteads in Manitoba and the Northwest Territories. The financial and organizational difficulties which plagued this unprecedented experiment in state-directed colonization did nothing to inspire confidence among the crofting population that relocation overseas, however constituted, was the answer to land congestion and continuing poverty at home. Throughout the rest of the pre-war period the government retained, but did not further engage, the emigration option, concentrating instead on a variety of investigations and state-funded expedients designed to redistribute land and strengthen the economic and social infrastructure of the highlands. While such a policy turned the spotlight of state intervention on the region in a manner that was both unprecedented and unparalleled in any other part of the British Isles, the government's efforts were costly and inappropriate – criticisms expressed in J. P Day's shrewd evaluation of public administration in the highlands and islands, published in 1918. Although he attributed the failure of the prairie colonization scheme of 1888 to the enervating effect of state subsidies on the colonists' self-reliance, he still claimed that state-aided migration or emigration schemes were the only remedies for persistent problems that more than a quarter-century of legislation had failed to solve. He painted a particularly pessimistic picture of the Hebrides.

> Today (1914) rates are higher than they have ever been and continue to increase; the fishing industry of the western coast has ... stagnated and, if anything, declined. More serious still, the inadequate minute holdings, from which the Napier Commissioners hoped to have the people 'firmly but gently' withdrawn, still exist in very large numbers and the population remains congested. Arrears of rent, both on private and State-owned property, continue to accumulate, though the Land Court is busy cancelling them and reducing and re-reducing the rents. The crofters refuse to purchase their holdings, and State purchase has not been a success. Meantime the owners have their income reduced on the one hand by the Land Court and on the other by the increasing rates. Some, at least, are finding it impossible to afford to live on their estates, nor can they get rid of them by selling, since none, not even the State, is willing to buy. There are more landless cottars and squatters in Lewis to-day than ever before, and the population continues to increase.[1]

The reign of the Congested Districts Board (1897–1912) was rendered ineffective by inadequate funding and the absence of compulsory purchase powers; the greater authority given to its successor, the Board of Agriculture for Scotland (BOAS), under the Small Landholders (Scotland) Act of 1911 was vitiated by bureaucracy and continuing landlord recalcitrance; and although the Land Settlement (Scotland) Act of 1919 provided improved procedures, it was only partially successful in its efforts to satisfy war veterans, retain the rural population on the land across Scotland and meet the clamour for holdings in congested districts.[2]

Despite these problems, the BOAS did not share Day's support for emigration from the highlands and islands. In August 1916, anticipating post-war reconstruction, it sent a memorandum to the Local Government Board, the first point of which declared that there was 'emphatically no need for emigration from the north of Scotland' on the grounds that, at least on the mainland and in the Northern Isles, any expansion of resources or industries was impossible without an increased population. It went on to deplore the way in which internal and external migration, by siphoning off the flower of the population, had created 'decadent and spiritless communities' in a region which had rich, but untapped, natural resources of water power and timber. The highlands had been 'artificially wasted' by short-sighted landlord policies that had removed the population and created agricultural deserts, abetted by the state's tendency simply to police rather than actively to develop the region. The pro-emigration policies of the proprietors of Lewis had been both economically and socially catastrophic – a point that was endorsed by the Local Government Board respondent to the memorandum, who confirmed that any further attempt to encourage emigration would be opposed by the islanders. Experiments in assisted emigration undertaken by Distress Committees under the Unemployed Workmen Act of 1905 had been discouraging, most emigrants having returned home after a short time, and instances of congestion in western Lewis and eastern Harris should, said the local government board spokesman, be dealt with either locally or by assisted migration to sparsely populated mainland areas.[3]

The Hebrides in the 1920s: economic crisis and attitudes to emigration

The cataclysmic events of 1914–18 set a more urgent and radical context for debate in the ensuing decade, prompted by the failure of land settle-ment policies, deepening depression and the activities of emigration agents. Popular opposition to any policy that smacked of enforced removal was bolstered by recollections of the nineteenth-century clearances and rein-forced by the polemic of writers, poets and politicians. Such sentiments were particularly acute in the Outer Hebrides, which was not only the scene of some of the most notorious evictions, but also the area where – despite the Board of Agriculture's wartime claims – chronic overcrowding and poverty in many townships gave particular poignancy to Lloyd George's promise to provide 'homes fit for heroes'. Highland regiments had played a distinguished part in the Great War, as they had in many earlier conflicts, and Hebridean war veterans seemed especially qualified for government assistance to reinvigorate their island communities.

The government, however, found itself on the horns of a dilemma. On the one hand it was anxious to do all it could to placate and retain a stratum of British society whose military potential it had long recognized. On the other hand pre-war experience, summarized in Day's gloomy observations, had already shown the difficulty of financing meaningful schemes of social and economic improvement in an area that generated almost no wealth of its own but, rather, imposed a severe drain on local and national authorities. These problems became more acute in the straitened economic circumstances of the early 1920s, when they were further compounded by the renewed militancy of tenants disappointed at the failure of the BOAS to tackle problems of landlessness and congestion effectively. Land raids took place throughout and beyond the Hebrides, with particularly bitter incidents – both before and after the war – on the South Uist and Benbecula estates of Lady Gordon Cathcart, a notoriously implacable proprietrix. Lewis also saw land raids in protest against the development plans of the new proprietor, Lord Leverhulme, and, as economic conditions worsened in 1922–23, war veterans in particular lost patience with the apparently dilatory bureaucracy of the BOAS and the pettifogging recalcitrance of landlords and simply took possession of the farms they claimed.

The serious deterioration in the economy was the catalyst for much of this unrest. Not only was agriculture in crisis, with low prices for livestock once wartime protection was removed; fishing was also in the doldrums, the loss of the German and Russian markets having dealt a hammer blow to the herring industry and curtailed a vital source of supplementary seasonal employment for crofters. In 1923 penniless hired workers had difficulty paying their fares back from the east coast fishings to Lewis, at the same time as the once-prosperous inshore line fishings around the island were 'completely ruined by the depredations of trawlers, and there is absolutely no employment of any kind for the thousands of men who are involuntarily idle'.[4] Furthermore, the failure of the potato crop and a wet summer, which prevented the gathering of hay and peats, led to the institution of local distress committees in Lewis before the year was over, and on 14 December an entry in the Cromore school log book recorded that it had received four pounds from the Lord Lieutenant's fund to provide a midday meal for the children, 'many of whom are starving for want of food'.[5]

On 20 December an editorial in the *Stornoway Gazette* declared:

> The greatest distress exists in those places, especially in Lewis, Harris, the Uists, Barra, and Benbecula, and on the west coast of Ross-shire, where there has been the double failure of the land and sea harvests, with the addition of lack of peats. Peats are scarce for the same reason that has

caused the failure of the corn and potato crops – the consistently wet weather throughout this year's summer and autumn. Taking the country all over, there has been no rainier year within the memory of those living, and the result has been, as we have stated, in addition again to a famine of hay which it was impossible to get dried at all. In many places the cut hay lies black on the ground. In many more places ... fields of potatoes (this refers more particularly to the mainland) are still to 'lift' while it is not an uncommon sight to see stooks of corn standing where they were placed after the cutting, with patches of corn still unmown. These failures, along with the lean fishing years since the war, have together produced in many parts of the Highlands a state of matters as serious, if not more grave, than were experienced during the Hungry Forties.

Matters did not improve greatly the following year, and on 1 February 1924 the seventy inhabitants of Soay appealed to the Scottish Secretary to send them immediate aid in the form of potatoes, coal, employment and better communications with the mainland. A *Press & Journal* editorial on 24 March 1925 blamed highland poverty and depopulation on unfavourable topography and altitude, rather than 'the iron hand of the landowner or the encroachments of the sportsman', and in a subsequent attack on the Scottish Liberal Federation's radical land policies it declared that

> The decline of life and industry is due not to original sin on the part of the landowners, but to the low productivity of the land, the disinclination of the younger generation to rough it as their fathers did, and the concentration of the fishing and other industries in the larger centres of population. That is the real explanation of the desolation of the Highlands, and the disease will not be cured by nationalisation pills prescribed by political quack doctors.[6]

Against such a background of increasing political radicalism, coupled with partially fulfilled promises, crofter penury and frustration, the climate did not seem propitious for encouraging emigration. With rather different sympathies from the *Press & Journal*, the *Stornoway Gazette*'s plaintive editorials throughout the 1920s maintained a consistent attack on the government's preference for empire settlement over investment in the promotion of forestry, fishing and hydro schemes, harnessed to crofting, which it claimed could turn the region into a 'prospering paradise'.[7] Reflecting on 15 February 1923 on the 'invasion' of the islands by Canadian agents and their alluring promises of 'work, wages, and independence', the *Gazette* expressed simultaneous pride and sadness in the identification of young islanders as the pick of British emigrants, and berated the government for its failure to stem the tide of human exports. It returned to the same theme on 3 May, in the aftermath of mass departures from Lochboisdale and Stornoway, and on 7 February 1924 it likened the ongoing emigration to a criminal attempt to extinguish the highland race and termed it a 'wholesale clearance of the people even more extensive than took place when straths and glens were turned into solitudes of sheep or deer'. Editorials throughout the spring and summer of 1924 repeatedly emphasized the images of exile and betrayal of unwilling emigrants whose native land had 'neither room nor use for them' and warned that if the government took no remedial action by spending money on the development of domestic, rather than imperial, resources, both the empire and southern industrial centres would within a few years be bereft of 'the finest bone and sinew' on which they were accustomed to draw.[8]

Nothing in recent years has been more deplorable – or depressing – than the streams of emigrants leaving the Highlands for the Colonies. It is pathetic to hear of shiploads of able-bodied men and young women sailing away from their homeland for life and labour under other skies. There are those, we are sorry to think, who are glad – or profess to be so – at the prospect of a greatly reduced population in the Highlands in the coming years. We do not know how to characterise such strange patriotism, especially on the part of Highlanders ... . Too many do not seem to realize that this year's emigration means not merely an immediate decrease in the population, but will mean a more tragic decrease in years to come ... . We sometimes read some fine words about emigration in the London and other southern papers that profess, not only to have the monopoly of wisdom, but to speak the national mind on this as on every other subject. In one of them last week – a prominent London daily – we were told, with an Imperial gesture and in language no less expansive than it was generous, that we should not look upon emigration as a thing to be discouraged or deplored. After all, said its writer, dictating no doubt between the puffs on a mighty cigar as he reclined in the recesses of a richly upholstered armchair, our emigrants are only quitting one part of their homeland for another, for are not our Colonies part of the one Great Empire and peopled by ourselves? Should we not be proud to replenish the stock of our kinsmen across the seas with the brain, blood and bone that are the finest in the world? And so on – in similar patriotically-Imperial vein. We should not object if the emigrants left from those densely-populated centres where they are so largely a nuisance to themselves and the rest of us. But we do feel that it is unfair – and a national loss – that so much attention should be paid to the Highlands, which can ill spare their stock of the 'best brains, blood, and bone.' No doubt there are emigrants leaving from the populous centres, but their numbers are practically negligible in relation to the millions available as compared with the very large numbers (in relation to the population) which have been leaving from the Highlands. The slum-lands of Glasgow, Liverpool, and similar large centres, could well have their thousands shipped in bulk to the virgin lands of Canada and Australia where, for their own good, they ought to be set to work for a livelihood and the development of those lands as the Creator intended.[9]

Editorial disapproval of emigration was reinforced by occasional letters from like-minded readers, warnings from discontented emigrants, and disapproving reports of the activities of men like Angus Robertson, President of An Comunn Gàidhealach, who in 1923 called for the transfer of 200,000 highlanders to uninhabited parts of Canada.[10] On 14 February 1924 a correspondent of the *Stornoway Gazette* tried to discourage further Hebridean emigration to Canada by warning of out-of-date literature, onerous and ill-paid farm work, and worsening unemployment – particularly in Winnipeg, where hundreds of emigrants had been left destitute as a result of believing the false promises of fraudulent agents. Nine months later another emigrant painted a similar picture of Ontario:

> Canada is an awful place – nothing doing of any kind. If we could get to the Bush it wouldn't be so bad, but they only want experienced men. There are about 20,000 idle in Toronto in the meantime. They are talking about Relief Works – what we were so used to in Lewis before we left. They are just the same out here, promising but nothing coming off. I hear there is another ship leaving Stornoway next Spring, but anybody that hasn't got a job or a very close friend to come to out here, he had better stay at home. It's easy enough coming out, but it's not so easy getting back. If it was I would be back long ago, and not only me but thousands more. So I am telling you it is pretty hard out here when you are out of work.[11]

Yet, despite these examples, the 1920s were not characterized by the universal public hostility to emigration which had marked the nineteenth century. Warning letters were countered by encouraging correspondence, disapproving reports by persuasive propaganda and attractive job advertisements. Promotional lectures were well attended, and agents found it worthwhile making regular recruitment trips to the highlands. On 1 July 1924 the *Press & Journal* – admittedly more favourably disposed to selective empire emigration than the *Stornoway Gazette* – commemorated Canada Day by portraying the Dominion as 'a land of prosperous communities, of well-established cities, with all the amenities of modern civilisation, and with boundless opportunities for youth and ambition', at least for the surplus population of the barren and overcrowded Hebrides. But even the critical *Gazette* publicized overseas opportunities, such as the agreement with the Ontario government that assisted around 300 islanders to emigrate to the province in April 1923, the recommendations of emigrants to Western Australia under the Group Settlement Scheme, and the offer of the Lewis-born chairman of the St Andrew's Society of Richmond County, Quebec, to assist unemployed islanders (to be selected by Stornoway's Free Church minister) to find work in and around the town of Richmond.[12] Its correspondents occasionally advocated emigration,[13] and on 1 November 1923 it reported the result of a debate in

Stornoway on the motion 'Is emigration a solution of the unemployment problem?', in which the motion had been carried by twenty-two votes to eleven. A similar debate just over a year later on the motion that emigration was a 'good thing for Lewis' was lost by only a narrow margin, it being argued that not only did the emigrants themselves enjoy higher living standards, reflected in their ability to spend holidays at home (whereas their stay-at-home counterparts could never hope to holiday in America), but their parents also lived more comfortably as a result of remittances from overseas, which sometimes amounted to as much as £60 per year.[14]

There is also evidence of a softening in official attitudes to emigration. By 1921 the BOAS was beginning to acknowledge its validity, although it defended the earlier work of the Congested Districts Board and claimed that land redistribution had created enough smallholdings in North Uist to obviate the need for emigration. In Barra, South Uist, Harris and Lewis, however, where all suitable land had been allocated but more than 1,300 applications remained outstanding, it now maintained that only migration or emigration could reduce overpopulation and create acceptable living standards.[15] On 8 May 1924 the *Stornoway Gazette* reported a resolution adopted at a meeting of the General Committee of the Highlands and Islands Distress Fund in Edinburgh the previous week that, 'while refraining from expressing an opinion upon emigration as a means of solution of existing conditions in the Highlands and Islands', grants might be made on an individual basis to needy applicants who had 'decided to emigrate of their own free will'.

Increasing ambiguity in press and public statements on emigration was to some extent a reflection of a more conciliatory popular attitude, of which *The Scotsman* remarked on 2 September 1922:

> Although nothing of it has been reported in connection with the Secretary for Scotland's visit to the Hebrides, there has been lately a distinct change of feeling in the Islands regarding emigration. It is not suggested that this movement has made itself an active rival of land settlement schemes, to which the lifelong habits of the islanders naturally tend. But unquestionably emigration is not now regarded with the extreme distaste that was almost everywhere found a few years ago. This change is largely to be attributed to two causes; one the encouraging reports which are being received from crofter families who have gone out from Barra and South Uist, if not from other islands, and the other a new readiness on the part of some of the priests to consider emigration as a means of improving the condition of the people. In these circumstances it is most desirable that the Government authorities at the Scottish Office should not overlook the ideas of land settlement in the Dominions as well as in the Islands themselves.

The Canadian government, the article continued, was currently financing a fact-finding visit by three crofters and a priest, who were to select suitable areas for Hebridean settlement, and *The Scotsman* concluded:

> Although it would be misleading to represent these incidents as indicating a widespread impulse, they are sufficiently significant to warrant the belief that the prejudice against the transfer of the home from the Hebrides to the prairies is becoming less stiff. If the Scottish Office and the Government here were willing to lend financial assistance the necessary money might readily be saved in the curtailment of smallholding development which can never lead to industrial prosperity, and an emigration policy, administered in conjunction with the Dominion authorities, might at last have a fair chance of a thoroughly adequate trial.

The Scotsman's impressions were confirmed two years later by James Wood, fishery officer in Stornoway. Replying to an enquiry by the Scottish Fisheries Board about Hebridean attitudes to emigration, he alleged that while it was still bitterly opposed by clergymen, it was openly advocated by teachers, merchants and parents, and by the emigrants themselves, as 'the only real solution to the problem' and 'not such a bad evil after all', the rapid erosion of prejudice being helped by the regular receipt of large remittances from recent emigrants.[16]

Entrenched popular opposition to emigration was eroded not only by agency activity, enthusiastic correspondence and remittances, but by a number of external factors that made the early 1920s something of a turning point in highland history. Paradoxically, as they began to achieve the tenurial security and redistribution of land so long denied them, crofters became more aware of the insurmountable physical limitations, meagre economic returns and health hazards of their environment. Ex-servicemen were probably best able to compare the subsistence lifestyle of parts of the highlands more fully with the rest of Britain. Family and community self-sufficiency were eroded by the steady encroachment of a money economy, which in turn meant that the croft came to be seen primarily as the provider of an income sufficient to sustain a reasonable standard of living. That was barely possible even in good years, and the depression of the early 1920s raised serious questions about the economic future of crofting at the same time as its social viability was also being challenged. Lord Leverhulme's 'abandonment' of Lewis emphasized the intractability of the island's problems and led the *Stornoway Gazette* to predict an emigration 'greater than at any time in its history'.[17] As tuberculosis reached almost epidemic proportions – particularly in the Hebrides, which had a record worse than some of the most overcrowded Glasgow slums – emigration also seemed to offer better physical, as well as economic, guarantees. Furthermore, as crofting legislation and state pensions promised a measure of security to elderly parents, young people were released to 'seek their fortunes in lands more richly endowed with natural resources',[18] and emigration could sometimes be viewed as a stepping stone to advancement rather than a punishment. When some proprietors, discouraged by high rates and low rents and frightened by the spectre of bolshevik socialism among their tenantry, began willingly to relinquish lands to the BOAS the crofters perceived that the traditional enforcers of emigration had capitulated. But even on estates where land raids had taken place, crofters might use emigration as an economic expedient. Some tenants on the farm of Eoligarry in Barra, for example, who went to Canada in the early 1920s, retained their crofts either as insurance against failure overseas or as a base to which they fully intended to return once they had earned enough money abroad to cushion them against the hardships of crofting.[19]

But what part did imperial settlement strategies play in effecting such a change of heart in an area where emigration had long been an emotive issue? Was the British government's more proactive stance on emigration the key factor in persuading the Scottish Office of its acceptability? Were impecunious and hostile crofters converted into relatively willing exiles simply by expediency, arising from the unprecedented financial assistance provided under the ESA, or by a new conviction that emigration was a good option? The evidence seems contradictory. According to a BOAS memorandum of 3 February 1922, many applicants for smallholdings in Lewis and Harris lived in conditions 'so uneconomic that it would be of benefit to them and also to the State if they could be induced to migrate or to emigrate. ... It was for many years difficult to induce people from the islands to migrate but that feeling is now much less strong, and, given reasonable prospects and State-aided passages, it is believed that a large number would take advantage of the opportunity of bettering their position.'[20] Although that prediction was not borne out in the *Stornoway Gazette*'s statement in 1926 that highland emigrants were much more likely than their city counterparts to shun official migration schemes for fear of falling into debt,[21] Canadian immigration returns show the opposite trend; as we have seen, the highland area produced more official recruits for Canada, and fewer private ones, than the much more populous Aberdeen agency area, a paradox surely explained by the poverty which made enrolment in government-funded schemes the only option for many highland emigrants. It might therefore be argued that the 1920s exodus was simply a continuation of a long-standing highland tradition of emigrating only under pressure and in response to external remedial initiatives, and that the ESA should be evaluated simply in terms of its negative effectiveness as a safety valve, implemented on a more extensive scale than the experimental palliatives of the 1880s. On the other hand, the highlanders' apparent enthusiasm for emigration may have arisen not simply from a desire to cut their losses but from a new confidence in the imperial rhetoric, bolstered by a growing tide of encouraging correspondence and a more positive public attitude – influences which combined to erode the traditional images of guilt and betrayal that had long marked highland emigration.

British Columbian fisheries schemes

A new confidence in the post-war imperial rhetoric on the other side of the Atlantic may also have persuaded the provincial government of British Columbia to reactivate a scheme for the importation of Hebridean crofter-fishermen which it had first mooted in the 1880s. The original ambitious proposal was the brainchild of Alexander Begg, a native of Caithness, who in 1887 was appointed as an unpaid emigration commissioner of the British Columbian provincial government, and by 1892 had finalized a colonization plan that would have seen up to 1,250 Scottish fisher families settled on the coast of Vancouver Island. The scheme was to be funded by a £150,000 loan from the British government and administered by the British Columbian authorities, who were to provide the settlers with land, work and houses and guarantee the repayment of advances made to them. The proposal was defeated partly by a loss of interest on the British side after Gladstone's return to power in summer 1892, but mainly by British Columbia's reluctance to undertake financial commitments which it feared it might not be able to honour. The provincial government feared not only that the impecunious settlers would be unable to repay their advances but also that they would become a public charge on the province. These fears were not alleviated even after the scheme was reinforced by the formation of a London-based investment syndicate to institute a deep-sea fisheries company to acquire and distribute public land and employ colonists in catching, curing and exporting halibut to eastern American markets. The Canadians' desire to reduce the financial risk further by recruiting lowland as well as highland fishermen was firmly opposed by the British government, so after six years of fraught negotiations and increasingly negative – including misleading – press coverage, Begg's idea was abandoned in 1893.[22]

When the scheme was resurrected in 1924, in response to both the ESA and earlier experiments in crofter colonization on the prairies, it bore several of the hallmarks of Begg's prototype. Once again the initiative was taken by British Columbia. The OSC was given no advance notification of the new proposals, which were intimated in the provincial press in February 1924, having probably been initiated by Duff Pattullo, the British Columbian Minister of Lands. Hebridean settlers, who were offered off-shore fishing employment as well as a small piece of agricultural land on which to build a house, grow vegetables and keep poultry, were to become transatlantic crofters, nominated by the British Columbian Agent-General in Britain and sent out at the joint expense of the imperial and provincial governments under the ESA. They could fish independently for commercial companies or even, if they preferred, seek opportunities in the logging industry, and were to be given instruction and supervision in respect of agricultural and fishing operations, location of fishing grounds, disposal of catches and purchase of equipment. As Pattullo saw it:

> The settler leaves the Hebrides with his passage paid either by himself or by the Imperial and Dominion Governments to British Columbia. On his arrival in British Columbia he has a credit of $600 to be advanced as required. He will be placed on a suitable piece of agricultural land, either on the Coast islands or the Coast mainland, of an area from five to twenty acres; or if desired by the settler further inland, 160 acres. He will be charged the current prices for the land, which on 160 acre blocks will run from $2.50 to $5.00 per acre, and on the smaller tracts according to location not to exceed $25.00 per acre, with a rebate of $10.00 an acre for every acre put under cultivation within a period of five years.
>
> He will be provided with a tent so that he may have immediate covering until he can make provision himself to build a house. Every assistance will be rendered to him to secure immediate employment with the various fishing concerns; or it may be possible that the settler himself may be able to make arrangements to fish on his own account as there are numerous small boats operating on their own account, and who are making considerable sums of money.
>
> The Government will keep careful watch over the settler, but beyond this the settler will be expected to rely on his own energy and endeavour to get along; and the Government will not interfere any more than is absolutely necessary.
>
> The foregoing seems to me as simple as a-b-c. If these settlers cannot get along upon this basis it would seem that the only thing they can do is to stay where they are and either live off doles or eke out an existence from interstices in the rocks.[23]

Fishing colonization was already being recommended by Hebridean commentators, sometimes in preference to farming settlement. The minister of St Columba's, Oban, who had spent eighteen years in different parts of Canada and subsequently delivered lectures in Lewis for the CPR, wrote in 1923 to Sir John Gilmour, Secretary for Scotland, that while 'lack of energy' might prevent the Lewisman from being a successful arable farmer, 'a settlement along the coast where his natural bent for fishing might have scope would be the most successful form of settlement'.[24] A year later an emigrant farmer from Argyllshire, writing to the *Oban Times*, claimed, in similar vein, that while Hebrideans were temperamentally unsuited to prairie farming, they would thrive in the temperate, home-like environment of Canada's Pacific coast.

> British Columbia ... is a country most admirably adapted in every respect to suit all the requirements of the Hebrideans, and although appeal after appeal has been made for that class of settler, there has been no response whatsoever. As far as the coast fishing has been exploited, it has been found that the supply of marketable fish is practically inexhaustible. Thousands upon thousands of fishermen could find steady and profitable employment all the year round, but as yet the waters have only been tapped by Indians and Japanese, while the white man's efforts are too few and far between to be worthy of any mention. Beyond question the Japanese have reaped a splendid harvest for many years, and can in nowise be blamed for mono-polizing the industry to a limited degree, as the fault lies entirely in the lack of competent opposition.
>
> The most valuable asset of the province has been left untouched through lack of skilled workers; and as the Japanese fishing licences are being greatly curtailed, this prolific field will shortly depend almost entirely, on the half-hearted enterprise of white tyros and a few slothful Indians. So here is waiting the open gate to prosperity; and yet it is passed by in the sheep-like rush to acquire land on the prairie.[25]

After confirming the Dominion government's endorsement of Pattullo's scheme and consulting with the OSC and the Fishery Board for Scotland, the Scottish Office concluded that the proposal was 'generous in its terms and attractive in prospects'. The Secretary for Scotland believed that Lewis could 'spare many thousands for such a purpose', and the Board of Health was also supportive, its Under-Secretary having met a successful and enthusiastic fisher-emigrant to Prince Rupert during a recent visit to North Uist.[26] The Fishery Board supported the venture on the grounds that commercial fishing prospects were much healthier along the 7,000-mile coastline of British Columbia than in Scotland, where markets had become exhausted. With outlets for cured herring in China and Japan and a developing home market in fresh fish, the Board felt that Hebridean fishermen, if adequately instructed, would readily adapt to different fishing methods and would enjoy a higher standard of living than at home.[27]

Thus encouraged, the Scottish Office unilaterally submitted a draft agreement to Pattullo in summer 1924. The scheme's administration was to be in the hands of the provincial government, which was to select, receive, accommodate and supervise the colonists for at least twelve months, making every effort to find employment for them and ensuring both that their debts were repaid and that, as far as possible, they were settled in groups of families rather than in isolated locations on more adequate acreages than they had been used to in the Hebrides. In response, the British Columbian authorities – apparently on the erroneous assumption that the agreement had been fully accepted by the British government – proposed in September 1924 that an immediate experimental settlement of five Scottish families should be made on the Queen Charlotte Islands, the settlers taking up work offered by the Langara Fishing and Packing Company. The firm's credibility was attested by the provincial government, which was confident that adequate housing and fair wages would be provided, but the lateness of the season necessitated postponing the plan until the following spring.[28]

In the meantime the Fishery Board was anxious to verify Pattullo's claims in respect of the viability of the larger scheme, with particular reference to mechanisms for supervising and instructing the settlers during their first year in Canada. The OSC not only sought further assurances about the Queen Charlotte Islands proposal but also wanted to ascertain whether opportunities in British Columbia were sufficient to warrant the British government becoming involved in the scheme. Only two years earlier the Committee had warned against emigration to the thinly populated, inaccessible Queen Charlotte Islands, which it claimed were suitable only for stock-raising and dairying, undertaken by people with 'considerable capital'.[29] Government anxiety was then probably aggravated by the negative comments of the Scottish emigration agent Andrew MacDonell, who in July 1924 told the OSC that herring fishing was pursued in Alaska, not off the British Columbian coast, that salmon fishing offered only seasonal employment, that wage labour in canning factories was unsuitable for crofter-fishermen and that the cost of clearing land would be beyond the Hebrideans' means and capabilities.[30]

In an attempt to address these and other concerns, in December 1924 the OSC sent Fishery Board chairman David Jones to British Columbia on a two-month fact-finding mission. Jones was also well briefed by Inverness-based agent Anne MacDonald, who claimed that she could supply 'any number' of far more suitable fishing families from the highland mainland than from the Hebrides. She also urged him to impress on the provincial government the need both to tighten up their selection procedures and to supply specific information, well in advance, about fares, employment, accommodation, markets, schools and churches to avoid the disruption caused by postponing the Queen Charlotte Islands experiment.

> This Office was notified some time ago that five Fisher Families were required in November, and I secured the families for British Columbia, but was notified immediately afterwards that they were not wanted. You will understand that this action on the part of the British Columbia Government does a great deal of harm. If they want families, let them give us due notice and stick to their original requirements and, above all, impress on the Officials on the other side that such families must receive

absolutely fair treatment and be well looked after for the first year until they become used to the country.

You will appreciate that I cannot send out families unless I am definitely assured that the conditions on the other side are satisfactory. Any requirements must be notified here by January or February at latest in order to allow the people to make arrangements for the spring.[31]

Jones arrived in Vancouver on 18 December, two days after the Provincial Assembly had voted £4,000 to promote immigration. Although fishing operations were suspended for the season, he spent four weeks visiting coastal locations from Prince Rupert to Victoria, meeting fisheries officials, municipal authorities and settlers, and being lobbied by land speculators on the northern mainland coast. In his subsequent report he recommended that a small-scale experiment should be undertaken in the first instance at sites adjacent to the fishing grounds, where cleared, tillable land was readily available. As previously proposed, five families should be settled on Graham Island in the Queen Charlotte Islands group, where a living could be made fishing locally for clams and for halibut and salmon further afield, under the supervision of one Captain Babington, manager of the clam canning factory. Twenty families were to go to Alberni on the west coast of Vancouver Island, a site recommended by Andrew MacDonell's 1924 delegation, which had 'four churches, a High and a public school, and a hospital in the town, as well as a commodious harbour for fishing boats' and a population of 1,200.[32] Jones negotiated with Alberni Corporation to provide each family with a three-roomed wooden house and two acres of cleared town land at $50 per acre, along with basic supplies of food and livestock. Each family, which should preferably be composed of parents with children of working age, was to be guaranteed fishing employment with 'reputable firms' on arrival, and the joint loan to each family should be raised to $1,000, possibly with extra assistance provided by the Highlands and Islands Distress Committee.

I am convinced that a parsimonious policy would be fatal to the success of the experiment as it has been shown repeatedly that the success of most settlement schemes is dependent on the nature of the new[s] sent home by the settlers as to their treatment, and a good beginning is half the battle, as well as the best and most economical form of propaganda. There are many prominent citizens in Vancouver Island and Prince Rupert who would, I feel sure, take a keen interest in the welfare of any emigrants from Scotland and would do everything in their power to make the experiment a success.[33]

Having met some unsuitable and unsuccessful Hebridean settlers in Vancouver, Jones echoed Anne MacDonald's emphasis on the importance of rigorous selection; he feared that Hebridean crofters might lack 'the grit and staying power necessary to overcome the initial difficulties which have to be faced in a new country and under strange conditions', and recommended that selection be given over to the experienced Inverness agent.[34]

The scheme was thwarted not by unsuitable recruits but by an impasse in the negotiations between the provincial and imperial governments. Although Pattullo was willing to increase the loan to $1,000 per family, he refused to guarantee employment to the settlers on the grounds that this would defeat the objective of promoting independent fishing enterprises, and no welfare committee was to be established either. He was particularly adamant that the settlers should not be 'tied down to one locality nor to a piece of land until they had had opportunity to get their bearings and thereafter make decisions for themselves', rejecting Jones' claim that Hebridean crofters were not nomadic by nature and required firm inducements in terms of accommodation and employment. He was unwilling to supply wooden houses instead of 'tents' until the settlers were properly located, and refused to provide holdings at $50 per acre, claiming that the land in Alberni required further clearing at a cost of up to $100 per acre, while that adjacent to the fishing grounds was heavily timbered and would cost from $350 to $500 per acre to clear.[35] Although Pattullo had to some extent gambled his political future on the success of the scheme, it was he who proposed its abandonment in October 1925 – to the disappointment of the OSC and despite W. Bankes Amery's attempt to negotiate a compromise during a visit to Vancouver in August.

The 1924–25 proposal to export crofter-fishermen to British Columbia under joint imperial and colonial government auspices therefore suffered the same fate as its predecessor more than thirty years earlier. The vagueness of Canadian promises regarding supervision and their reluctance to guarantee the provision of houses and employment or the repayment of loans, along with administrative confusion and delays on the British side, probably contributed to the failure – as did a blindness to some of the problems experienced in the 1880s. In March 1924, shortly after the scheme was mooted, John Deacy of Massett, Graham Island, in the Queen Charlotte Islands group, wrote to Agent-General F. C. Wade expressing general approval of the scheme on both economic and defensive grounds but also voicing concern at the way in which history threatened to repeat itself. Drawing on sixty years' experience as a pioneer, he stressed the need for the preliminary development of a transportation and marketing infrastructure rather than 'bringing in hundreds of "settlers" and fishermen without the wherewithal to build up a "settlement" and expecting them to start fishing on small capital or without funds'.[36] Similar concerns were expressed by Anne MacDonald, who in June 1925 repeated her earlier advice on the importance of advance planning and careful supervision if the scheme was ever to get off the ground; it was already too late to recruit crofters that year as they had completed their spring sowing and taken up summer fishing work.[37]

A reluctance among highlanders to commit themselves to full-time fishing occupations also helped to defeat Pattullo's scheme. This reluctance was highlighted by James Wood, fishery officer at Stornoway, when he was asked in 1924 to report to the Scottish Fisheries Board on Hebridean attitudes to emigration, with particular reference to British Columbia. Although Lewis was losing almost 1,000 emigrants annually, 80 per cent of them young men, they invariably preferred farming to fishing, while Wood's belief that they enjoyed a reputation as successful agriculturists contradicted the claims made at the same time by the emigrant correspondent of the *Oban Times* and, a year earlier, by the Rev. M. McKerracher of Oban. A canning factory's advertisement for six families to take up salmon fishing in the Queen Charlotte Islands in 1923 attracted only one casual enquiry although all expenses were to be paid, accommodation provided, and a household with four working members could apparently earn £20 per week. In Wood's opinion:

> Probably better results would have been achieved in this direction say a matter of 15 years or so ago, when the average Lewisman was more of a fisherman than he is at the present day. Emigration to the Hebridean now means work on the land, whether it be farming or other labouring work, and he does not concern himself as to the possibilities of fishing in any of the Colonies which he may elect to select as his future home. Assuming that crofter fishermen could be induced to emigrate to British Columbia it would be wise if there is a livelihood to be obtained from fishing alone, to give them as little interest in soil cultivation as possible. An illustration of the evils of the two interests is only too evident in this island and elsewhere. By engaging in both crofting and fishing success is achieved in neither the one nor the other.[38]

But perhaps the major reason for the scheme's failure was that the objectives of the imperial and British Columbian governments were incompatible. From the British perspective, the Scottish Office and Fishery Board for Scotland saw a means of tackling the overwhelming poverty of the Hebrides, while the Colonial Office probably also sought to strengthen the imperial presence on the strategically vulnerable Pacific coast. For Pattullo and his colleagues, however, the primary aims were to counteract the growing influence of permanent settlements of Japanese inshore fishermen on the west coast, and to introduce an alternative source of cheap labour for the canneries, perhaps with the 1924 provincial election in mind. The Barra priest Donald McIntyre claimed that the farming emigrants who left on the *Marloch* in 1923 had originally been earmarked to go as 'fishermen settlers to Vancouver and district in order to try and wrest the fisheries of that coast from the yellow races'.[39] A year later J. A. Motherwell, Chief Inspector of Fisheries at Vancouver, sanctioned an attempt by the West Mildcure Salmon Company at Clayquot Sound to recruit twenty Stornoway families on these racist grounds, claiming that too much of the lucrative salmon business was concentrated in the hands of 'Orientals':

> My Department has been endeavouring to eliminate the Oriental and to replace him by Whites and Indians ... . Unfortunately the results have not been as hoped and taking last year for instance, although there was a reduction of 82 Japanese there were also fewer whites and Indians fishing although licences are not restricted in numbers to those in the two last categories. It is felt that Old Country white fishermen would have a good opportunity to make a reasonably good living in this method of fishing.[40]

The OSC, aware that the provincial government was, 'with incomplete success', trying to eliminate oriental fishermen, advised the Fishery Board for Scotland to take this into account when evaluating 'the possibility of Scottish fishermen making good on the fishing grounds of British Columbia in competition with other nationalities with a lower standard of living'.[41] David Jones' own prejudices were revealed by a reference in his draft report to 'the Oriental menace' – a description which, on Scottish Office instructions, was subsequently amended to the oriental 'problem'.[42] Jones discussed the recent legislation that aimed to eliminate the Japanese from the west coast fishery by reducing steadily the number of licences granted to them, an unpopular procedure with the commercial canning companies because it reduced their pool of skilled labour and forced up wages. Although the companies' difficulties made them 'very sympathetic to the idea of introducing Scottish crofter fishermen to make good the shortage', Jones was concerned that Hebridean immigrants might not adapt easily to unfamiliar Pacific conditions, and he was therefore not prepared to compromise when Pattullo refused to agree to his stipulations.[43] His concern was shared by Anne MacDonald, who claimed that British Columbia required full-time fishermen rather than crofter-fishermen, that the settlers would be isolated in Japanese and Indian communities, and that Hebrideans were not 'sufficiently good workers to make a satisfactory return under such a scheme'.[44]

The extra ingredient of empire settlement funding did not, therefore, prevent a second stillborn government attempt to introduce crofter-fishermen to the province. But the saga did not end completely in 1925. Just as in the 1880s the provincial government had tried to reactivate its moribund scheme by harnessing it to the activities of a commercial company, so in the 1920s and 1930s commercial interests attempted to compensate for the increasing elimination of Japanese licence holders by recruiting cheap crofting labour for fishing and canning. Pattullo's own proposal had involved the Langara Fishing Company of Queen Charlotte Islands, and another aborted scheme in 1924 concerned the proposal of Captain L. M. Vince, a Yarmouth seafarer and emigrant to Berkley Sound, to establish a model fishing village at Numukannis Bay with Scottish as well as English settlers.[45] In 1927, two years after Pattullo's idea had been abandoned, the British Settlement Society of Canada approached the OSC with a scheme to settle two or three Aberdeenshire families in Vancouver Island to work for the Broughton Straits Trading Company at fishing, salting and sawmilling. Failure to agree terms with the Dominion government on the provision of assisted passages prevented the venture going ahead, but in 1936–37 more detailed proposals, 'very similar to those which were made by the Government of British Columbia in 1924–25', were made by Robert Payne, production manager of the Canadian Fishing Company, Vancouver, to F. L. Floud, British High Commissioner in Ottawa.[46] Although he admitted that post-war Hebridean immigration had been largely unsuccessful, since 'a good many of the men were of mature years and found themselves unable to adapt themselves to the ways and methods employed in British Columbia', he still suggested the settlement of about 300 crofters around the Gulf of Georgia. In that well-populated area, between Vancouver Island and the mainland, there were markets for both fish and farm produce, along with off-season employment in the logging industry for carefully vetted recruits who showed no sign of 'Communistic and radical thought'.[47] Payne, who modelled his proposal partly on a successful settlement of Peterhead fishermen almost thirty years earlier, was motivated by a desire to secure cheap, submissive labour for an industry in which an increasing number of fishermen came from the Mediterranean, many of whom were poorly equipped, 'some are transients, and others stop work as soon as they have earned a few dollars'. Although he expected opposition from existing fishermen on the grounds that the industry was already oversupplied, he claimed this could be overcome by locating the settlers on 5–10 acre smallholdings as well as finding them employment with some of the larger salmon fishing companies. But Payne's optimism was not shared by the Scottish Fisheries Board and the OSC. Although Japanese fishermen were still being squeezed out of the west coast fishing, the impact of worldwide depression had cancelled out the argument for replacement labour, and Scots would have to sell their fish to the canneries at the same price as the Japanese, 'who have a much lower standard of living'.[48] In the *Glasgow Herald*'s opinion internal political as well as economic reasons militated against mass emigration, while the British High Commission in Ottawa thought Payne's scheme was 'merely designed for the benefit of his own company and the idea of bringing out Scottish fishermen to compete with Japanese, Indian and

Canadian fishermen on the spot would almost certainly prove a failure'.[49] Although the immigrants were to be employed by commercial concerns, Payne expected the financial arrangements to be 'handled entirely by Government', a proposal with which neither the provincial, dominion nor imperial authorities were willing to comply. The main recurring obstacle impeding attempts to introduce crofter-fishermen to British Columbia from 1888 to 1937 therefore seems to have been the inability of governments, at all levels, to make effective funding arrangements for every scheme proposed, a problem that was aggravated rather than resolved by the provision of empire settlement legislation.

Highlanders in the South Atlantic

By no means all highland emigration that did come to fruition was dependent on government funding, or even directed towards the empire. In addition to the statistically obvious, long-standing movement to the United States, the Outer Hebrides in particular developed remarkable links with the Falkland Islands and Patagonia in the late nineteenth century, with hundreds of islanders taking up employment on large estancias well into the inter-war period. Although the Falkland Islands had first come under titular British control in 1771, they were abandoned three years later, and it was only in the late 1820s that British traders began to press for their colonization. In 1841 a lieutenant-governor was duly appointed, and revenue from land sales began to be used to assist the passage of labourers under the auspices of the Colonial Land and Emigration Commission. Scottish settlement was advocated by the *Colonial Magazine*, which in 1842 recommended highland proprietors to form an association for the purchase of land, to which, in association with the government, they could send thousands of their famine-stricken tenants, to their mutual benefit. In one correspondent's opinion, although 'the native of the southern part of this empire will never be reconciled to the stormy, rainy, cold climate of the Falkland Islands ... the hardy inhabitant of the Hebrides, Orkneys, Shetlands, and northern coast of Scotland would find himself there on a soil and in a climate, and among productions, similar to those of his own country, only a better edition of them'.[50]

There was no such purchase, although Samuel Fisher Lafone, a British resident of Montevideo who bought over 600,000 acres on East Falkland in 1846, intended to have his brother Alexander in Scotland recruit suitable Scottish settlers – particularly from Shetland – to promote stock-breeding. In 1848 the Emigration Commissioners reported that steps were being taken to settle in the islands a small body of military pensioners and their families 'who will be judiciously selected from districts in Scotland, where their present habits and mode of life are likely to make them a valuable acquisition in this colony'.[51] Beset by financial problems, Lafone failed to introduce any settlers and, in 1851, he sold his interests to the newly formed Falkland Islands Company Limited. After it opened its first sheep station eight years later significant numbers of highlanders began to be recruited, and in 1860 a Free Church chapel was built at Darwin.[52] When William Halliday from Johnstone, Dumfriesshire, signed up as a Company shepherd in 1862, he found a significant highland presence in the Falklands:

> Indeed, to a Scotsman they were in many ways home from home. On an almost equivalent latitude, they bore a strong resemblance to the Outer Hebrides ... . The capital, Port Stanley, was like a new town of the Western Highlands with its rows of whitewashed cottages, and Government House resembled an Orkney manse. The main sheepstation of FIC at Darwin ... was simply a village of Scottish shepherds, some from the Western Islands, some from Ross and Sutherland, some from Inverness, and now joined by a sixteen-year-old from Dumfries.[53]

By the early twentieth century, however, however, the Falklands were overstocked with sheep and had lost their alternative source of income from ship-repairing. The governments of Chile and Argentina seized the opportunity to sell cheaply vast tracts of pasture in the arid, windswept southern wasteland of Patagonia to disgruntled 'kelpers' and to companies that advertised in the Scottish press for shepherds, foremen and managers for their farms, slaughterhouses and freezing plants. British concerns included the Estancia Brazo Norte, owned by the Mackay family from Achmore in Lewis, the Estancias Rinconada, Tipperaray (sic) and Flora-doras in the Santa Cruz region, owned by the Bain brothers from Wick, and the Estancia San Julian, established at the turn of the century by an Englishman and two Ross-shire Scots who left the Falklands with their stock of sheep and subsequently employed many Lewismen on its vast farmsteads. Spaniard José Menendez's Tierra del Fuego Development Company, the largest sheep-farming enterprise in the world, similarly recruited Lewismen, as well as Chileans, Argentinians and Europeans, including seven men from Keose in Lewis who in 1910 were employed on the 300,000-acre Estancia Menendez-Behety alongside four Welshmen who had survived the wrecking of their ship near Cape Horn. Patagonian emigration was not greatly disturbed by the First World War. Angus MacDonald from Habost, who arrived in 1915, was one of at least three wartime recruits from Lewis; he went back home to marry some years later, after which he returned to work on the Estancia San Sebastian in Chile, where he died in 1948.[54]

Impersonal press advertisements were not the only means of recruiting Scottish emigrants to South American sheep farms. Some estancias employed local agents in Scotland, such as Donald MacCallum, the Established Church minister in Keose from 1889 to 1920, who was active not only in the Lochs area but also in Harris and North Uist. His efforts contributed significantly to the emigration of thirty-two men from Keose's fifteen crofts between 1903 and 1928, including nine from a single household. MacCallum also played a part in the Patagonian settlement of fifty-six men from Balallan between 1899 and 1937, and twenty-two from Lochganvich, Achmore and Cleasacro, while others went from Uig, Carloway, Callanish, Bernera, Stornoway and Laxdale. The emigrants crossed the Minch to Kyle of Lochalsh, then travelled to Liverpool or Southampton by train, where they boarded ship for a minimum thirty-day passage to Argentina at a fare which in the early twentieth century was only £14 but had risen to £48 by the 1920s. Once on the estancias, they were sent with dogs, horses and supplies to isolated shanties, where they were responsible for several thousand sheep, meeting up with their fellow shepherds only at dipping and shearing times.

Although most recruits were Hebrideans, a few came from the lowlands. William Halliday, who had met and married into a Dumfriesshire family in the Falklands before moving to Patagonia in 1885, retained his Scottish links and numbered among his neighbours Scots from Berwickshire, Dumfriesshire and Aberdeenshire. At least one employee on his estancia also came from Aberdeenshire. Fintray-born John Gordon had, like his employer, first come to the South Atlantic on the books of the Falkland Islands Company – as had William Dickie of Oldmeldrum, who subsequently founded the Estancia Bon Accord in Patagonia, and other Patagonian property-owners, John Hamilton from Wick and John Scott from Loch Ettrick.[55]

Farm worker Bill Coupland from Annan in Dumfriesshire first went to Patagonia in 1913 at the age of 17 on the assumption that 'out there you got as much in a month as you would have in a year in this country'.[56] His passage was paid by his sister Jean and brother-in-law Peter Bell, with whom he travelled as they returned to Patagonia after an expenses-paid trip home. In or around 1906 an agent had recruited Bell for contract work as a groom and gardener, but by 1913 the halcyon days of contract labour had ended and, although living standards remained higher than in Scotland until 1929, Coupland had to seek work after he arrived. He found a position as a foreman with the Tierra del Fuego Development Company, later taking charge of farm sections on three different estancias, Cameron, Guido and Filaret. In 1924 and 1929 he came home on holiday, and in 1934 was joined by his fiancée Jan Morrison from Lochmaben, who took a £50 passage from Liverpool to Punta Arenas and was married the day after she arrived. The isolated life of the estancia, where neighbours were often twenty miles distant, was relieved by the annual visit of two woolclassers from Bradford and by the regular exchange of letters with home. By the time the Couplands returned to Scotland in 1951–52 oil had been discovered in Patagonia, rampant Chilean inflation had eroded their savings and the sheep economy was declining.

Many of the west highland and Hebridean emigrants to Patagonia and the Falklands also returned home eventually, perhaps as many as 50 per cent of them. Some, like Bill Coupland, spent almost their entire working lives there, including Calum Mackay of Achmore, who emigrated in 1914, came home in 1921 to marry, then returned with his wife to manage an estancia seventy miles north of Punta Arenas until they retired to Lewis in 1960. Although their four children were initially schooled in Lewis, two were brought back to Patagonia after a few years and are still there. Some returned to Scotland in unusual circumstances – such as nine-year-old Murdoch MacIntosh, who in 1914 was admitted on to the Applecross poor roll as a deserted child after his mother, Mary Macdonald, sent him home from his birthplace of Punta Arenas in the care of an Elgin woman whom she assured that the boy would be met by an uncle from Inverness. The uncle, who knew nothing of the arrangement, refused to have anything to do with Murdoch, while the boy's father, an erstwhile shepherd in Patagonia, was shortly to be admitted to the Applecross roll as a lunatic after a spell in a Liverpool workhouse.[57] Others came home sooner than they expected; Malcolm Smith, for instance, who had emigrated in 1921, came back to Achmore to marry with the intention of returning to South America, but was deterred by his wife. Some re-emigrated to other parts of South America, including a number who worked in the Cerro de Pasco area of Peru, either on haciendas or for the Cerro de Pasco Copper Corporation, while others laboured in copper mines on the Chilean–Bolivian border. British government incentives had nothing whatever to do with this notable stream of Scottish emigration to the southern tip of South America, in which permanent settlers and temporary sojourners alike responded primarily to private commercial incentives and word-of-mouth personal encouragement for almost half a century.

Highlanders in Australia

In other contexts, however, highland emigration in the 1920s was clearly related to the availability of government-funded passages and the expectation of permanent settlement. In common with other Scots, most highlanders who emigrated to the Antipodes in the 1920s appear to have been assisted under the terms of the ESA, just as their nineteenth-century predecessors had subscribed primarily to the schemes of the Colonial Office in the 1830s and the Highland and Island Emigration Society in the 1850s. While the cost of going so far away precluded privately funded antipodean emigration for most highlanders, W. C. Stillman managed to persuade significant numbers of Hebrideans to apply for government subsidies in the early 1920s. Stillman first visited Lewis in spring 1923, when, at a series of meetings in and around Stornoway, he focused on the benefits to crofters of group settlement in Western Australia at £22 per head, expressing satisfaction with the calibre of applicants who responded to his propaganda. On a follow-up visit in July he gave particular encouragement to artisans and female household workers to go to 'this new country of such wonderful possibilities', and during subsequent visits at the beginning and end of 1924 he held well-attended illustrated lectures which he targeted at boys, youths and young women, assuring parents that their offspring were offered guaranteed apprenticeships and would be well cared for by the Caledonian clubs, which were especially interested in highlanders.

Stillman's visits bore surprisingly good fruit. In 1923 – a year dominated by the departure of the *Metagama* to Canada – the Stornoway booking agent Murdo Maclean also persuaded several 'splendid families' to take up blocks of land under the Western Australia Group Settlement Scheme and a contingent of young single men and women to emigrate to Victoria. On 30 August 1923 the *Bendigo* sailed from London with 1,000 passengers, including 99 from Lewis, their fares of £22 per head being advanced by the Australian government for repayment over two years. All the married men were would-be farmers, who were to be settled under the block system in Western Australia, while the single men were going in for sheep farming. Stillman's description of the scale and modernity of farming methods had made a special appeal to young Lewismen, and a year later the *Stornoway Gazette* commented on the remarkable transformation that had taken place in islanders' attitudes since the Australian agent's first visit. Until then very few Hebrideans had thought seriously about emigrating to the Antipodes, but his recommendations on repeated occasions, coupled with encouragement from pioneer emigrants to their friends and relatives, had resulted in an exodus of more than 250 in December 1924, with more to follow.[58]

The traditionally anti-emigration *Stornoway Gazette* was convinced that group settlement was a viable imperial cement, and in 1923 and 1924 it paid unprecedented (if still limited) attention to opportunities in Australia.

> This, we feel sure, is one of the soundest and most liberal schemes of Empire Settlement yet undertaken, and the Australian Government is to be congratulated on its courageous and statesmanlike action. Such schemes as these not only assist in the development of our great outposts of Empire, but offer good prospects of a comfortable living to many who, through the congestion and overcrowding of the Homeland, have had such a right denied them. It is to be hoped that the opportunities offered by the

Australian Government will be seriously considered by many in the Island of Lewis who have not had a chance in the past of taking up agricultural pursuits under such good conditions. In Australia they will be assured of a warm welcome from people of their own kith and kin. They will still be within the same Empire and under the same old flag, and whilst helping themselves they will at the same time be assisting in the development of our great southern continent, the resources and wealth of which have as yet been scarcely touched.[59]

Ninety-nine islanders, mainly from Lochs and Shawbost, did not merely 'seriously consider' group settlement; in July 1923, under Stillman's superintendence, they left for London to board the SS *Bendigo* for Western Australia, followed by a second party in September. One Lochs crofter-fisherman, who left with his wife and eleven children, told the *Stornoway Gazette* that 'he had become tired waiting for a holding, for which he had made application as an ex-Service man. He felt that he could put in a hard day's work for many years to come, and he added that all his family were glad to go to Australia because they saw no prospect of any improvement in their condition in the Hebrides.'[60] The *Stornoway Gazette* followed the experiences of the *Bendigo* pioneers with some interest, and on 10 January 1924 published a photograph of eight Lewismen who were part of a Scottish group settlement on the Peel estate near Fremantle, along with a letter from John Maciver, one of the settlers, to Murdo Maclean, the Stornoway shipping agent and local inspector of poor. Writing in November, Maciver reported that

we are all well and got on our land here. We have our huts up now since three weeks. We sure got a welcome from the people here, and we like the place all right. We are clearing now since a month … . We didn't get the full Group yet. We have 13 now, one from Glasgow, and one from Sutherland – a pipe-major – so we have lots of music. We were expecting some from Stornoway, but they have not come so far, but I hope they will. They won't let anybody in our Group except Scotchmen.

Further observations on the Peel settlement were made by one of the women emigrants to her father-in-law. Although she confirmed that there were thirteen Scots in the group, there were also seven Englishmen and one Yugoslavian.

Foodstuffs are cheaper than at home … . We were speaking to a man from Dingwall who came out here two years ago and his land is partly cleared. He told us that he got £340 for his potatoes alone and that he is almost clear with the Government, but you are liable to success or failure here at any time … . I am sure I will never see you again but I would not go home now for anything. This place is so lovely and the trees are green all the year round.[61]

Another Lewisman in Albany, Western Australia, was 'thankful that we got away from that place' to a land of plentiful employment and good prospects, to which he wished his father had come fifteen years earlier. Meanwhile a fellow islander, writing from Victoria, endorsed Western Australia but suggested that the next party should go to Victoria, which was 'the best place for young strong lads who are not afraid of hard work' and where, thanks to the efforts of Murdo Maclean, all the Scots were placed, at good wages, as near to their relatives as possible.[62]

The Metagama *and the* Marloch

Not surprisingly, however, Hebridean emigration to Australia in the 1920s – as in the nineteenth century – was an intermittent sideshow compared with the movement to Canada, while New Zealand seems to have aroused almost no interest among highlanders. The allocation of substantial government funding to assist emigration to the highlanders' traditional destination reinforced established catalysts and increased the outflow, but it also introduced new controversies and tensions which were not so apparent in the smaller Australian movement. Public and press attention focused primarily on two major embarkations that seemed to symbolize – for contemporaries and later commentators alike – all the paradoxes of generations of highland emigration.

April 1923 was a remarkable month in the demographic history of the Outer Hebrides. Within little more than a week the Canadian Pacific liners *Marloch* and *Metagama*, calling at Lochboisdale and Stornoway, respectively, embarked a total of around 600 emigrants from the Long Island and took them across the Atlantic to new homes in Alberta and Ontario. The colonization schemes had many similarities, were exten-sively documented on both sides of the Atlantic and are still remembered in the islands. There were, however, significant and unexplored differences between the experiences of the two parties, particularly in the way the exodus was promoted, supervised, and subsequently perceived. Although both enterprises clearly came under the ESA umbrella, can it be claimed that the Presbyterian exodus from the northern Hebrides to Ontario on the *Metagama* and its sister ships was a government agent-inspired conspiracy that largely succeeded, while the Catholic exodus from the southern Hebrides to Alberta was a private agent-inspired conspiracy which, for the most part, failed?[63]

The exodus from the northern Hebrides was orchestrated by William Noxon, the Agent-General for Ontario, after one Major Goodliff, also representing the Ontario government, had aroused public interest with a series of lectures in and around Stornoway in the early weeks of 1923 and Murdo Maclean had placed an eight-inch advertisement in the *Stornoway*

Gazette on and after 25 January. Anticipating a leakage of rural workers to better-paid work in American car factories, the Ontario government had ordered Noxon to step up the recruitment of agricultural settlers, who, if they could raise 25 per cent of the fare themselves, were promised assisted passages and a year's farm employment at £5–£6 a month in southern Ontario in relatively close proximity to each other. Successful recruits were then to be offered uncolonized soldier settlement lands further north, near Sudbury. The Ontarian initiative was welcomed by the Scottish Office and the BOAS on the grounds that dangerous tensions might be defused if impatient applicants for domestic land settlement were successfully apprised of overseas opportunities. Although cautious civil servants refused to canvass applicants for smallholdings directly, they were justifiably confident that newspaper advertising by the imperial and colonial governments would attract recruits while deflecting any charge that the BOAS was expediently substituting emigration for failed land-settlement policies.[64]

The emigrants' departure on 21 April was extensively publicized locally, nationally and internationally, and remains the best-known example of inter-war Scottish emigration. While the *Stornoway Gazette* hoped that Canada would prove to be 'not only a land of promise but a land of performance', it also craved effective government intervention in the islands to prevent a repetition of the events of April 1923. The more optimistic *Press & Journal*, meanwhile, focused on the abundant employment, high wages and good prospects in Ontario, where the advent of the motor car and the telephone at almost every farm was guaranteed to dispel 'the bogey of loneliness'.[65] Of the 315 passengers who embarked, 260 came from Lewis – primarily young, single men with an average age of 22. Some had recently finished working for Lord Leverhulme on the construction of the Ness–Tolsta road, which perhaps gave them the wherewithal – and the incentive – to emigrate. According to one recruit, Donald MacLeod of Ness, emigration was the only alternative to unemployment for the post-war generation of islanders, since traditional outlets in the army and naval reserve had been closed off and the few industrial openings available in mainland Britain had been reserved for ex-servicemen.[66] North Uist emigrant John MacLeod, too, found that the casual labour he could pick up in the islands paid far less – '£16 every six months' – than he had been able to earn on minesweepers just after the war, while his father and two colleagues were earning barely £1 per week fishing lobsters for shipment to Billingsgate.[67] MacLeod, like many other passengers on the *Metagama*, already had acquaintances in Canada, which he also preferred to Australia on the grounds that greater proximity and cheapness of passage would facilitate any subsequent trip home, whether temporary or permanent.

The *Stornoway Gazette*'s hopes that the 1923 exodus would put an end to emigration were vain, for 1924 saw further mass departures from the islands as the Ontario government endeavoured to consolidate and extend Hebridean recruitment. In April the *Marloch*, having already taken 198 islanders from the southern Hebrides a month earlier, returned to embark 290 passengers at Stornoway, mainly young men and a larger contingent of women than had sailed on the *Metagama* the year before. Although penury obliged most of them to take assisted passages and employment as labourers and domestics until they could repay their loans, several had been sent remittances by siblings who had emigrated in 1923. Similar circumstances characterized the 270 Lewis emigrants who embarked at Stornoway on the White Star liner *Canada* on 19 May and, according to the *Press & Journal*, their departure attracted relatively little display of feeling, so used had the islanders become to such events.[68] Deepening public indifference grieved the *Stornoway Gazette*, which on 10 July 1925 complained that 'perhaps nothing so proves the apparent hopelessness of conditions in the Highlands and Islands as the unconcern with which the general public regards the continued flow of young life for other shores' and claimed there was not a parish in the region that had not lost 'scores' of people in the first six months of 1925, with hundreds more preparing to leave.

Yet the emigrants' experience in Canada was not without controversy either. The Canadian press, having expected the arrival of a 'race of giants' in 1923, was at first disappointed to find the new arrivals quite ordinary, and before long began to vilify them for taking up non-farming employment, defecting to the USA, and allegedly breaking a strike in a Toronto brewery. These charges were later corroborated by an internal Canadian Immigration Department memorandum and a comment in the *Stornoway Gazette* that, because of the 'good many disappointments' experienced by the Ontario government in respect of young unmarried Hebridean settlers who 'broke their agreements almost immediately on landing', William Noxon had decided by 1925 not to nominate any more young men from Stornoway but instead to target recruitment on family groups rather than unattached individuals.[69] Some *Metagama* emigrants subsequently recalled that they had left farming employment within a few weeks or months because of unpaid or low wages, poor living conditions and unremitting work. Others confirmed that they had gone over to the USA (often initially as illegal immigrants) because of better job opportunities and higher wages, ironically in the new motor industries of Detroit. At least one man, Angus MacDonald from Ness, deliberately used the Canadian assisted-passage scheme as a means of entry into the United States, from where two uncles had been sending home letters and remittances for more than a decade. Like several fellow-islanders, he preferred employment on the water to farm work, vindicating the criticism of a correspondent of the *Victoria Daily Colonist* who argued that the Lewismen should have been brought to the coast of British Columbia rather than to Ontario.[70] Donald MacLeod was another who soon left farming for two years' seasonal employment on the Great Lakes, subsequently going over to Detroit to work in the motor industry when large numbers of Lewis emigrants began to go directly to that city in the mid-1920s. And although John MacLeod remained in Canada, he left his farm placement near Ingersoll after only three weeks for construction work in Toronto, followed by sporadic farming jobs in Ontario and the west, a seven-year spell with the Goodyear tyre factory and, ultimately, civic employment in Woodstock, Ontario, secured through the good offices of South Uist-born Lachie Morrison, a policeman in Toronto.[71]

Casual employment and frequent changes of workplace were common, particularly as economic conditions worsened, and the Ontario authorities sometimes hounded emigrants' parents in Lewis in an attempt to track down defaulters. But some did pay back their $94 passage debt to the Canadian government, and most of those still alive in the 1980s – both permanent settlers and returnees – were generally positive about their experiences when interviewed. Summer fishing or freighting work on the Great Lakes might be interspersed with winter employment in American factories, and significant numbers of Lewismen also worked as labourers on construction projects at Niagara Falls and in New York State. Many made use of Hebridean connections in finding employment and accommodation, while secular and religious associations in places such as Toronto, Buffalo, Cleveland and New York ensured that most emigrants married fellow-islanders. John MacLeod recalled a strong community spirit and an excellent social life among the *Metagama* passengers for some years after their arrival, and he met his Barvas-born wife, Chrissie, a nurse, at a function in Toronto, she having emigrated in 1922 on the *Marloch* to join a brother who had come out immediately after the war.[72] Norman MacKenzie, who emigrated on the *Canada* in 1924 and went over to the USA after three months, estimated that there were more than 200 Lewis people in Buffalo in the 1920s, while in Harlem in the 1930s it was customary for around 400 members of the Lewis, Lewis and Skye, Celtic, and New York Gaelic societies to congregate every Saturday evening for a dance. Free Church ministers also preached in Harlem en route to Detroit, another centre of Hebridean settlement; the Gaelic Free Church in Toronto was always full of Lewis people – 'just like being in the island'; and in 1925 a Winnipeg correspondent of the *Stornoway Gazette* expressed the wish that a recent mission to Gaelic speakers in Winnipeg could be followed up by the permanent establishment of a highland church and minister in the city to which so many highlanders were then flocking.[73]

While most Canadian emigrants from Lewis were young, single men and women – at least until the Ontario government's change of policy in 1925 – the southern Hebrideans who left in equally large numbers in 1923 and 1924 were primarily families destined for more concentrated settlement in northern Alberta. They were nominated collectively, not through a federal or provincial agency but by Andrew MacDonell, an erstwhile Scottish Benedictine monk who had been dabbling in migration schemes since 1912 and who, in the 1920s, undertook both to find agricultural employment for his nominees and to secure full repayment of their passages within three years of their settlement in Alberta. After persuading the Canadian Immigration Department to send him on an expenses-paid recruitment visit to Scotland in 1921, during which he selected 150 ex-servicemen to go to Ontario under SSB auspices, MacDonell broadened his horizons to civilians, urging the Canadian authorities to capitalize on the prevailing spirit of restlessness in the highlands. The result was the embarkation of 291 emigrants on the *Marloch* at Lochboisdale on 15 April 1923 bound for Red Deer, Alberta, where MacDonell had been given a five-year lease on a disused farm school to receive and train his recruits before moving them on to waged work or farms of their own. In order to benefit from collective nomination under the ESA, MacDonell formed the Scottish Immigrant Aid Society as a charitable organization, incorporated in Canada but with directors and administrative staff on both sides of the Atlantic. While he was responsible for the nomination and resettlement of the migrants in Canada, recruitment in Scotland was delegated to the Castlebay priest, Donald MacIntyre, who in autumn 1922 had – on MacDonell's invitation – led a four-man delegation to the prairies to identify the best location for the colony before returning to the islands to promote the venture. The initial settlement was followed in 1924 by the arrival of two further large contingents from the southern Hebrides after MacDonell returned to Scotland to supervise the recruitment campaign and subsequently accompanied both parties across the Atlantic. His most ambitious venture followed in 1926, when, on a property at Vermilion, northern Alberta, which he named Clandonald, he attempted to create a colony of Hebridean Catholics. The 30,000-acre tract of land was purchased on mortgage from the CPR, funding being shared by the Scottish Immigrant Aid Society, the CPR and the British government under the terms of the ESA.

All MacDonell's colonization ventures were attended by controversy, opinion being divided as to whether he engineered a 'notable piece of work in Canadian land settlement'[74] or an ill-conceived and mismanaged fiasco. Awarded the MBE in recognition of his 'great work for emigrants',[75] he was undoubtedly a man of remarkable vision and determination. Undeterred by setbacks, he pursued single-mindedly his goal of importing to Canada large numbers of colonists from the Hebrides and other parts of the British

Isles in order to create close-knit communities that would be religiously, even more than ethnically, autonomous. Despite his assurances that the schemes were non-sectarian, MacDonell was clearly striving to establish Catholic colonies in Canada, and most of his recruits were of that faith. Parties of colonists were always supervised by at least one priest, the assistant managing director of the Scottish Immigrant Aid Society was the former Barra priest, Donald MacIntyre, and one of MacDonell's earliest priorities on establishing Clandonald in 1926 was to provide a church, followed in 1929 by a convent school staffed by Benedictine nuns.[76] His enthusiasm for promoting Catholic colonization also led him to try to organize the transfer of young boys, an area in which he had pre-war experience, as well as female domestic servants. But by acting as the paid agent of juvenile and female Catholic emigration societies, MacDonell not only compromised the alleged non-sectarian stance of the SIAS, he also became sucked into complex administrative duties, dissipating his energies and aggravating a problem (about which the Canadian authorities often complained) that he had 'too many irons in the fire' and left too much to chance – or to the Immigration Department.

> The trouble with Father MacDonell's business is that he carries his head office around with him and when he is in England [sic] the head office is there and similarly when he is in Canada the head office is here. I am afraid that a good deal of business is allowed to run itself or drift because of the utter impossibility of Father MacDonell looking after it personally.[77]

Such over-commitment and carelessness damaged both MacDonell's own credibility and the welfare of his colonists. In both 1923 and 1924 his work was impeded by the exaggerated assurances of over-zealous associates, whose activities he should have monitored more strictly, and by his emphasis on quantity, rather than quality, of recruits. First impressions were crucial to the future success of the work – particularly in 1923, when better-off Hebrideans who had been unable to gain release from their tenancy obligations were keeping a watchful eye on the fate of their countrymen who had sailed on the *Marloch* – and the Canadian authorities felt that more care should have been taken to avoid negative publicity by ensuring that the pioneers were established on a firm foundation.[78] Perhaps unreasonable ambition then lured MacDonell into the strategic error of neglecting the area and people whose needs he knew well – the Western Isles and their inhabitants – for wider, but less familiar, recruitment grounds, and it is striking that most deportees and failures came not from the Hebrides but from Ireland or Glasgow. In 1924 MacDonell admitted that lack of care in selection was partly to blame for the failure of several Irish recruits in particular, most of whom were 'on the move from the beginning', often to the United States, and very few of whom ever attained farms of their own.[79] Some years later, after his repeated failure to tackle his colonists' bad debts had rebounded on him in the refusal of the Immigration Department to recommence assisted passages in 1939, he conceded that he should have encouraged a greater sense of responsibility in the Clandonald settlers by drawing up formal short-term rental contracts instead of loose agreements of sale, with the tenants' suitability for long-term farming being assessed during that initial training period.[80]

But MacDonell was headstrong not just in his determination to expand his agency activity beyond manageable bounds. His single-minded commitment to large group settlement in specially created colonies ignored the lessons of history and ran counter to the general policy of empire settlement in the 1920s. The vulnerability of exclusive group settlements had been demonstrated in 1903 by the Barr colony at Lloydminster in Saskatchewan and, more pertinently for MacDonell, by the problems of indebtedness and adaptability experienced in the Hebridean colonies established at Killarney, Manitoba, and Saltcoats in the North-West Territories in 1888 and 1889, respectively. Whereas a few descendants of the island pioneers can still be found in two townships at Killarney, Saltcoats disappeared, almost without trace, within twenty years of its foundation, the victim of poor-quality land and the Imperial Colonization Board's interfering resident factor.[81] Against such a background it is not surprising that the *Stornoway Gazette*, in evaluating MacDonell's 1923 experiment, commented that 'emigrants cannot at once be settled in large colonies in any one area', while the Canadian Immigration Department opposed group settlement both on the theoretical argument that pioneers were more likely to succeed if they mingled with and learned from experienced settlers and on the practical grounds that large blocks of land were generally more expensive and inferior to dispersed purchases.[82]

The success of the ventures was prejudiced not only by MacDonell's own carelessness or poor judgement. He also had to contend with the equivocation of the Canadian Immigration Department and the outright opposition of anti-immigration elements in both Canada and Britain. Canadian resentment at the calibre of British immigrants was reflected at one level in the authorities' procrastination in dealing with applications, an attitude which MacDonell alleged was resulting in the loss of good material, not least to Australia.

> It cannot be questioned that many agents are in these days hostile to Canada because of the many difficulties put in the way of intending migrants. Many intending migrants are kept waiting as many as four or five months before they know whether they are likely to be accepted or not for Canada. Many resent the manner of their interrogation, and it is a commonplace that Canada seems to resent having people apply for migration, and it would almost appear to have bars up against British migrants.[83]

Evidence of deficiencies among MacDonell's recruits reinforced the Immigration Department's reservations, but when he offered to make an example of selected defaulters he came up against the Department's pre-occupation with maintaining a positive image of immigration in order 'not to give rise to the idea of persecution as that would be fatal to the work'.[84]

Official disquiet at the calibre of assisted migrants was paralleled and fuelled by caustic correspondence in the Canadian press. One letter in 1923 invoked precedent in warning the Immigration Department against assisting poor Hebrideans, claiming that the descendants of Cape Breton's nineteenth-century highland immigrants were 'absolutely unreliable citizens' who were crowding the asylums, 'living in poverty, and content to do so'.[85] Group settlement was opposed for fear that 'a group of Britishers would immediately set about forming a union and having a strike',[86] while MacDonell claimed that 'inimical interests' had tried to discredit the policy of empire settlement by fomenting discontent among the colonists. Singling out the Alberta Minister of Agriculture, the provincial press, and even his own erstwhile sub-agent, David Conroy, he alleged that all had at one time or another encouraged the colonists not to pay their debts or to demand immediate access to ready-made farms or other extravagant concessions.[87] Bad publicity from Canada also strengthened the argument of anti-emigrationists in Britain, both within and beyond the Hebrides. While at Westminster the Labour Party used it as a stick with which to beat the imperialists over the viability of the ESA, in the Western Isles the *Stornoway Gazette* on more than one occasion criticized MacDonell for his negative response to the 'Highland Problem', which, it claimed, simply depopulated the Hebrides and encouraged the government to neglect its economic responsibilities to the islanders.[88]

Perhaps MacDonell's main problem was that he became a victim of circumstances. He had to contend not only with over-expectant colonists and political opposition on both sides of the Atlantic. Having initiated his colonization schemes in the optimistic climate of the early 1920s, his recruits were still finding their feet when the depression put an end to any hope of debt repayment and plunged some families into absolute destitution. His 1924 scheme to guarantee employment and cottage accommodation to every colonist was thwarted by the growing inability of established farmers to offer a living wage or employ men all year round, and even the critical Immigration Department admitted in 1938 that the Clandonald venture had been bedevilled by depressed economic circum-stances over which the colonists had little control.[89]

In the final analysis, however, MacDonell did achieve his aim of estab-lishing a colony of Hebridean Catholics in western Canada. At the height of his activity, between 1923 and 1928, a total of 1,315 colonists crossed the Atlantic under his auspices,[90] and, although by no means all came from the Western Isles, surviving evidence suggests that Hebrideans formed the foundation and marrow of his enterprise. He was the best-known Scottish emigration agent of his day, and the Scottish Fishery Board seems to have taken it for granted in 1924 that he would escort crofter-colonists to British Columbia.[91] The Canadian Immigration Department, despite its reservations, not only renewed his temporary contract year after year, but also agreed to most of his wide-ranging financial demands, whether these were for the renovation of the Red Deer farm centre in Alberta, bills for medical emergencies, the salaries of sub-agents, or the travelling expenses of Scottish delegations brought to Canada to assess prospects for settlement. The criticism of detractors was matched by the commendation of supporters, both in official circles and among the colonists. Despite the hardships, settlers' complaints – at least in surviving correspondence – were remarkably few, and generally confined to urban recruits who were unable to adapt to pioneer farming.

Yet, although MacDonell and his helpers played a key part in bringing about a decrease of nearly 5,000 in the population of the Outer Hebrides between 1921 and 1931, his enterprise was not unique. As we have seen, he initiated his Alberta colonization scheme in the same week in 1923 as the *Metagama* embarked an equivalent number of emigrants from Lewis, Harris and North Uist for settlement in Ontario, and in the years that followed his recruitment campaigns were always matched by similar activity in the northern Hebrides. But whereas interest in the latter area was stimulated by government agents working on behalf of both Canada and Australia, MacDonell and his clerical colleagues operated to the exclusion of all other agents in recruiting Catholic Hebrideans; there is no record of either Stillman or Noxon visiting the southern Hebrides, and Anne MacDonald, the Canadian government agent in Inverness, complained on at least one occasion that MacDonell's controversial activities were damaging Canada's reputation amongst potential emigrants.

Why did controversy seem to court MacDonell to a much greater extent than agents operating in the northern Hebrides? How different were the attitudes and experiences of emigrants from the north and south of the Long Island, and can the apparently more negative results of MacDonell's enterprise be attributed simply to flaws in his motives, selection procedures and settlement patterns? Although the magnetic pull of the United States affected both groups, MacDonell always maintained that group settlement of entire families in a prepared location was more successful than the dispersal of single, footloose farm workers and domestic servants across Ontario – a point with which the Ontario government apparently concurred by 1925, when it tried to tackle the problem of broken contracts by concentrating recruitment on family groups. On the other hand, the northern Hebrideans' freedom from family commitments seems to have rendered them more adaptable to the demands of the Canadian and American labour markets, while MacDonell's colonists were not only inflexible but also incited each other to complacency and recalcitrance in respect of their financial obligations. Perhaps MacDonell's paranoia about communist infiltration of his settlements indicated that he was not unaware of some of the drawbacks of large group colonization.[92]

The islanders' different religious affiliations probably also shaped their attitudes. Whereas the confidence of Presbyterian emigrants from the northern Hebrides was perhaps reinforced by a subconscious sense of cultural superiority, to be a Catholic in Scotland in the 1920s was to be a second-class citizen, at least for those of Irish descent who lived in the central belt. Some of MacDonell's recruits may therefore have been driven to emigrate partly by a reluctance to expose themselves to xenophobic attack by moving to the urban lowlands, and partly by a determination to protect their traditional highland Catholicism from lower-class lowland associations by exporting it across the Atlantic. The spirit of emigration that infected the Hebrides in the 1920s may well have been more fervent in the Catholic south since it was promoted from within the community by the all-powerful priests, supported by the Catholic hierarchy, and turned into practice by priests-turned-agents. But the acute disillusionment and sense of betrayal subsequently felt by unsuccessful colonists and their relatives at home soon produced a backlash which led to vilification of MacDonell as a mercenary, self-promoting charlatan, whose notoriety outlasted his own considerable lifetime.

A further possible explanation of the bitterness which characterized the exodus from the southern isles compared with that from the north is the enduring memory of the brutal evictions and enforced emigration perpetrated by John Gordon of Cluny in the 1850s and reinforced by his daughter's anti-Catholicism, support for emigration and unsympathetic attitude to land redistribution after the Crofters' Act, compared with Sir James Matheson's reputation as a more humane landlord of Lewis. Controversy surrounding the will of Lady Emily Gordon Cathcart after her death in 1932 reflects the depth of public antagonism against emigration. Included in the will was a proposal to establish an emigration fund to assist empire colonization. It was to be administered by trustees nominated by Lady Gordon Cathcart, one of whom was her neighbour, Sir Reginald MacLeod of MacLeod. The laird of Dunvegan, however – while ultimately agreeing to accept the post – feared for his reputation, according to a letter from John Macdonald, the estate factor in Lochboisdale, to Lady Cathcart's solicitors in Aberdeen.

MacLeod was anxious to know how the people in the Islands are likely to view the provision in the Will applying to emigration, and I could plainly see that he was very much concerned as to how he should act. He seemed to think it strange that although he had been visiting Lady Cathcart frequently during the past two years she did not give him the faintest hint of her intentions in regard to the Long Island Estates, and did not ask for any advice on the matter. It was very plain to me that MacLeod had feelings of disappointment that the Island Estates should be used for the purposes of Emigration which, in these days, is such a hopeless proposition. His fear is that by acting as a Trustee he would run the risk of getting into bad grace with his crofting tenants, and at the same time he feared that Lady Cathcart would be held up to a good deal of ridicule by a certain section of the press throughout the country. I have a good deal of sympathy with MacLeod's point of view and I certainly told him so very candidly. At the present time the very word 'Emigration' meets with a hostile reception among the Islanders wherever the word is used and, after reading many of the letters received by relations in the Islands from some of those who emigrated to Canada in 1921 and 1923, I am not surprised at the hostility of the people to emigration. The emigrants who left the Islands in the years mentioned have had a hard struggle for existance [sic] and the outlook for them is everything but bright according to their letters. Some of those who emigrated in 1921 have returned to the Islands with very black accounts of conditions in Canada with the result that emigration among the Islanders is doomed for a good many years at any rate. MacLeod quite realised that for the present there is little likelihood of any of the Islanders taking advantage of the fund to be set apart for assisting emigration but he mentioned that if the outlook in the Colonies improved there might be some inducement in the Islanders to emigrate. Personally I have not much hope of anything of the kind but one never knows what may happen. It must not be forgotten that the people in the Islands are at present very comfortable. They do not, of course, make much beyond a living but they all make a comfortable living under better conditions than those existing in many other parts of the world. When it is considered that over £30,000 finds its way annually into the pockets of the people in Benbecula, Barra and South Uist for old age pensions, and pensions of several other kinds, which did not exist thirty years ago, it will at once be seen that the circumstances of the people are very much improved so that on that account it will take a long time for anything in the nature of emigration to take root among the people.[93]

John Macdonald himself was wary of encouraging emigration for fear that multiple renunciations would cost the estate a considerable sum in compensation. But although the depression prevented any such movement in 1932, he predicted that, once conditions improved, assisted emigration might appeal to younger crofters from large families provided that they had been adequately briefed – but not pressurized – by a 'responsible person' from the islands, who would also be able to advise the trustees on the suitability of each applicant. In his view, indiscriminate selection had been the 'ruination' of the 1920s scheme, since 'every person who came forward was taken whether good bad or indifferent. The good made good but the bad and indifferent have in most cases returned to the Islands and in order to justify their return have given the blackest accounts possible of conditions in Canada.'[94] MacDonell's request that the Long Island Estates Emigration Fund should be activated in 1939 was rejected by the trustees, who disbelieved his claim of having found several families willing to leave a region where 'the very word "emigration" is anathema'. In fact, the money was never used as Lady Cathcart had intended, partly because of continuing Canadian reluctance, but not least because the trustees themselves clearly regarded emigration as nothing more than a form of poor relief, which had become obsolete in the light of what one of them described in 1939 as 'the present facility for abuse of the dole, transitional benefit, and parish relief'.[95]

For many Hebridean and other highland emigrants in the 1920s, funding assistance provided under the ESA was indeed primarily a source of poor relief. Some participated with enthusiasm, others with reluctance, and no doubt their initial expectations helped to predispose them to success or failure. Equally important, however, was their perception of the agencies that arranged their transplantation and the quality of the soil into which they were transplanted. The 'excellent spirits' that characterized the *Metagama*'s unattached young passengers were reinforced both by the apparent professionalism of the Canadian emigration agents and the emigrants' relocation at Canada's urban hub, where all they had to do was 'go to the Employment Office and pay a dollar and they gave you a job'.[96] A minority of the *Marloch*'s southern Hebridean exiles who found work with the Gas Company in Toronto apparently shared this satisfaction, but, for most of the *Marloch*'s passengers, frustration generated by the limited opportunities of their isolated settlement in northern Alberta provoked sustained and bitter criticism of the agent who had masterminded their emigration. Their disillusionment became all the more acute as they began to suspect Andrew MacDonell not merely of incompetence but of treacherous collusion with Lady Gordon Cathcart and her factors in a plot to banish undesirable Catholic tenants to undeveloped and unsuitable prairie colonies. The contrasting experiences of Canadian colonists from the northern and southern Hebrides in the 1920s demonstrates both the complex psychology of highland emigration as it evolved over more than a century and the way in which specific local issues shaped crofters' reactions to ventures promoted under the ESA.

Notes

1 John P. Day, *Public Administration in the Highlands and Islands of Scotland* (London, University of London Press, 1918), pp. 393, 400.
2 Leah Leneman, *Fit for Heroes! Land Settlement in Scotland after World War I* (Aberdeen, Aberdeen University Press, 1989), p. 203.
3 Scottish Record Office (SRO), AF51/212, Emigration and Empire Settlement: Memoranda on Economic Conditions etc in the Highlands and Islands, 11 Aug. 1916.
4 *P&J*, 14 Nov. 1923.
5 *P&J*, 28 Sept., 14 Nov. 1923; Stornoway Town Council minutes, 24 Dec. 1823, vol. 12, p. 676.
6 *P&J*, 8 Oct. 1925.
7 *SG*, 26 Apr. 1923.
8 *SG*, 3 Apr., 22 May 1924.
9 *SG*, 5 June 1924. See also 10 July 1924, 21 Jan., 1 July, 9 Sept. 1927.
10 *SG*, 9 Aug. 1923; *P&J*, 7 Aug.1923.
11 *SG*, 25 Dec. 1924.
12 *SG*, 25 Jan. 1923, 10 Jan. 1924.
13 *SG*, 1 Mar. 1923, letter from Iain Macghora, Glasgow.
14 *SG*, 14 Jan. 1927. The defender of the motion pointed out that no islanders were ever able to go to Canada or the USA for a holiday. See also *P&J*, 19 May 1924.
15 SRO, AF51/212, BOAS, internal memorandum on emigration from the Outer Hebrides and Skye, 16 Dec. 1921.
16 SRO, AF62/1964/1, Emigration of Fishermen: Proposed settlement of Scottish crofter fishermen in British Columbia, 25 Nov. 1924.
17 *P&J*, 3 Oct. 1923.
18 *P&J*, 23 Apr. 1923.
19 Eoligarry, which had been raided by cottars in 1917 and purchased by the BOAS in 1918, suffered from absenteeism in the early 1920s. For details of this, and the attitudes of tenants who emigrated, see Leneman, *Fit for Heroes!*, p. 110.
20 SRO, AF51/167, 'Emigration from the Hebrides', BOAS memorandum, 3 Feb. 1922. My italics.
21 See chapter 1, p. 35.
22 Vancouver City Archives, ADD.MSS.181, Alexander Begg papers; Jill Wade, 'The "Gigantic Scheme"; crofter immigration and deep-sea fisheries development for British Columbia, 1887–1893', BC Studies, 53 (Spring 1982), pp. 28–44; Marjory Harper, *Emigration from North-East Scotland, vol. 2, Beyond the Broad Atlantic* (Aberdeen, Aberdeen University Press), pp. 153–7.
23 SRO, AF62/1964/1, T. D. Pattullo to F. C. Wade, Agent General for BC, London, 13 Mar. 1924.
24 SRO, AF51/173, Rev. M. McKerracher to the Rt Hon. Sir John Gilmour, 11 Mar. 1923.
25 *Oban Times*, 5 Apr. 1924.
26 *Oban Times*, 5 Apr. 1924; internal Scottish Office memoranda, including G. A. Steel to Mr Rose, 25 July 1924; Rose to Steel, 26 July 1924, 'JJ' to Rose, 28 July 1924; notes on the visit of the Under Secretary for Health to the Hebrides. The crofter-emigrant, who had been employed in the northern BC fishery for three years, had come home temporarily because of his father's terminal illness. The official did also admit, however, that some years earlier a 'large number of the young men' from North Uist had emigrated to British Columbia, but 'having found the conditions of labour unpalatable, some of them returned home'.
27 SRO, AF62/1961/1, George Hogarth, Fishery Board for Scotland, to OSC, 11 July 1924. (Information repeated in SRO AF51/172).
28 SRO, AF62/1961/1, Bankes Amery to Fishery Board Secretary, 22 Sept. 1924; Bankes Amery to Under Secretary for Scotland, 25 Sept. 1924; SRO AF62/1964/1; Bankes Amery to Jones, 24 Nov. 1924, dossier of confidential documents.
29 *Hansard*, vol. 153, 10 May 1922, Leo Amery to J. C. Wedgwood, quoted in SRO, AF51/172.
30 SRO, AF62/1964/1, internal OSC memorandum, 23 July 1924.

31 *Ibid.*, MacDonald to Jones, 21 Nov. 1924.
32 SRO, AF62/1964/2, David Jones' report on his visit to BC, 23 Feb. 1925.
33 *Ibid.* Jones suggested that if the Highlands and Islands Distress Committee placed $400–$500 in a British Columbian bank, needy colonists could draw on the fund subject to the approval of the provincial government's treasury.
34 *Ibid.*, Jones to Under Secretary for Scotland, 17 Mar. 1925. In view of the likely publication of Jones' report on both sides of the Atlantic, the Scottish Office revised his draft comments on the questionable calibre of Hebridean colonists.
35 SRO, AF51/173, Jones to Plant, 30 June 1925; AF 62/1964/3, Pattullo to F. A. Pauline, Agent General for British Columbia, London, 20 Oct. 1925. Although British Columbian tents were low wooden structures with canvas roofs, Jones believed they were suitable only for temporary summer accommodation (Michael E. Vance, 'British Columbia's twentieth-century crofter emigration schemes: a note on new sources', *Scottish Tradition*, 18 (1993), p. 6.)
36 SRO, AF62/1964/1, Deacy to Wade, 3 Mar. 1924.
37 SRO, AF 62/1963, MacDonald to Little, 1 June 1925.
38 SRO, AF62/1964/1, Wood to Fishery Board for Scotland, 25 Nov. 1924. He also mentioned that an attempt had been made to attract Lewis fishermen to British Columbia about eighteen years earlier, but 'owing to financial difficulties it did not come to anything'.
39 SRO, AF62/1961/1, Alexander Stephen, Fishery Office, Barra, to Secretary, Fishery Board for Scotland, 7 Apr. 1923.
40 SRO, AF62/1964/1, Motherwell to Professor Robert Wallace, Edinburgh, 15 Feb. 1924 (Wallace had been sent out by the Scottish Office, in conjunction with the Canadian government, to report on the Killarney and Saltcoats settlements).
41 *Ibid.*, Bankes Amery to Secretary, Fishery Board for Scotland, 4 June 1924.
42 SRO, AF 62/1964/2, Jones' report, 23 Feb. 1925; A. J. Rose, Scottish Office, to Jones, 12 Mar. 1925.
43 SRO, AF 62/1964/2, Jones' report.
44 *Ibid.*, MacDonald to Jones, 12 Mar. 1925.
45 Vance, 'British Columbia's twentieth-century crofter emigration schemes', p. 16; SRO AF62/1961/1.
46 SRO, AF51/186 and AF62/1964/4, Plant to T. D. Fairgrieve, Scottish Office, 23 Mar. 1937; *GH*, 22 May 1937.
47 *Ibid.*, memorandum by Payne to OSC, included in internal OSC memorandum by Plant, 14 Jan. 1937.
48 SRO, AF51/186, Plant to Canadian High Commission, 27 Sept. 1937, quoted in Vance, 'British Columbia's twentieth-century crofter emigration schemes', p. 19.
49 *GH*, 25 May 1937. The scheme was likely to be delayed by the provincial elections on 1 June 1937. SRO, AF51/186, F. Floud to Plant, 26 Oct. 1937.
50 'Some account of the Falkland Islands', *Colonial Magazine*, 7:28 (Apr. 1842), p. 438; letter to the editor, *Colonial Magazine*, n.s. 1:5 (Dec. 1842), p. 615.
51 PP 1849 1082 XXII. Ninth annual report of the Colonial Land and Emigration Commission.
52 Ian J. Strange, *The Falkland Islands*, 3rd edn (Newton Abbot, David & Charles, 1983), pp. 82, 94–5, 160.
53 Michael J. Mainwaring, *From the Falklands to Patagonia. The Story of a Pioneer Family* (London, Allison & Busby, 1983), pp. 21–2.
54 Greta MacKenzie, *Why Patagonia?* (Stornoway, Stornoway Gazette, 1995); Joni Buchanan, 'Lewis families who made the long trek to Patagonia', *West Highland Free Press* (*WHFP*), 22 Nov. 1996, p. 11. By the beginning of the twentieth century Menendez's company had expanded by merger and was renamed La Sociedad Importadora y Exportadora de la Patagonia.
55 Mainwaring, *From the Falklands to Patagonia*, pp. 242, 273; unattributed information from Aberdeen and North-East Scotland Family History Society files.
56 Interviews with Mrs J. A. Coupland, 26 July 1994, 16 Oct. 1996.
57 Highland Council Archives, CR6/1/6, Applecross Parish Council, Record of Applications, 1901–1930, 25 March 1914.
58 *SG*, 5 Apr., 26 July, 30 Aug. 1923; 11 Dec. 1924. *P&J*, 25 Aug. 1923.

59 *SG*, 5 Apr. 1923.
60 *SG*, 30 Aug. 1923.
61 *SG*, 28 Feb. 1924.
62 *HN*, 7 Mar. 1925; SG, 12 June 1924.
63 For detailed discussion of the two ventures, see Jim Wilkie, *Metagama. A Journey from Lewis to the New World* (Edinburgh, Mainstream, 1987) and Marjory Harper, 'Crofter colonists in Canada: an experiment in empire settlement in the 1920s', *Northern Scotland*, 14 (1994), pp. 69–108.
64 SRO, AF51/212, memorandum no. 13a, 18 Dec, 1921; Wilkie, *Metagama*, p. 60.
65 *SG*, 26 Apr. 1923; *P&J*, 20 Feb. 1923.
66 Donald MacLeod, Livonia, Michigan, to Christina Smith, Comunn Eachdraidh Nis, 5 Mar. 1980. See Macleod's obituary in *The Monthly Record*, Nov. 1997, p. 345.
67 Oral testimony of John MacLeod, Woodstock, Ontario, to Dr George Macaskill, Nov. 1996. MacLeod recalls paying £20 4s 1d for his passage, but once in Canada, he 'got away' without repaying the balance loaned to him.
68 *SG*, 24 Apr., 1 May 1924; *P&J*, 19 May 1924.
69 NAC, RG76, C-4661, vol. 6, file 41, part 2, unattributed memorandum to W. J. Egan, 7 Feb. 1925; *SG*, 19 June 1925. The Immigration Department memorandum referred to 'the decision reached by the Ontario Government representative in London not to nominate any further men from Stornoway owing to the failure of a percentage of those who have come to Canada in the past couple of years, to repay their loans'.
70 G. S. Macgregor, 14 Apr. 1923, quoted in *SG*, 17 May 1923; Wilkie, *Metagama*, pp. 114–25.
71 Wilkie, *Metagama*, pp. 105, 131, 138, 150; Donald MacLeod to Christina Smith, 5 Mar. 1980; *Daily Sentinel–Review* (Woodstock), 25 Jan. 1995.
72 MacLeod to Macaskill, Nov. 1996.
73 Wilkie, *Metagama*, pp. 151, 153–4, 133; *SG*, 21 Aug. 1925.
74 *Saturday Night* (Toronto), 21 July 1923.
75 *Inverness Courier*, 2 Dec. 1960.
76 Diana Sim, 'Clandonald: a rural Catholic colony' (unpublished undergraduate paper, University of Calgary, 1979), p. 27.
77 NAC, RG76, C-10446, vol. 633, file 968592, part 3, Blair to Little, 2 Apr. 1925; Blair to M. V. Burnham, Supervisor, Women's Branch, DIC, 26 May 1926.
78 NAC, RG76, C-10446, vol. 633, file 968592, part 1, Featherston to MacDonell, 6 June 1923; *SG*, 28 June 1923. See also *P&J*, 18 July 1923.
79 Andrew MacDonell, 'British immigration schemes in Alberta', *Alberta Historical Review* (spring 1968), p. 10.
80 Sim, 'Clandonald', appendix (n.p.), notes from MacDonell's undated typescript; NRAS 1883, Skene, Edwards & Garson papers, MacDonell's undated memorandum to Empire Migration Board.
81 Wayne Norton, *Help Us to a Better Land. Crofter Colonies in the Prairie West* (Regina, Canadian Plains Research Center, 1994). Further information on Killarney and Saltcoats was kindly provided by Dr Domhnall Uilleam Stiùbhart.
82 *SG*, 28 June 1923; *Saturday Night*, 21 July 1923; NAC, RG76, C-10446, vol. 633, file 968592, part 2, Blair to W. J. Black, 20 Aug. 1923.
83 NAC, RG76, C-10446, vol. 633, file 968592, part 3, MacDonell to Egan, 16 July 1925.
84 *Ibid.*, part 4, Blair to MacDonell, 16 Nov. 1925.
85 *Ibid.*, part 1, R. Law, Toronto, to the DIC, 22 Feb. 1923.
86 *Ibid.*, part 5, MacDonell to Forke, 4 Jan. 1928.
87 *Ibid.*, MacDonell to Blair, n.d. (late autumn 1925); MacDonell to Little, 7 Aug. 1927; *ibid.*, part 7, MacDonell to Blair, 17 July 1939.
88 *SG*, 7 Feb. 1924, 10 July 1925.
89 MacDonell, 'British immigration schemes', p. 9; NAC, RG76, C-10446, vol. 633, file 968592, part 6, Blair to Mrs Harry Reynolds, Los Angeles, 23 July 1938.
90 NAC, RG76, C-10446, vol. 633, file 968592, part 5, Forke to Blatchford, 28 Jan. 1928.
91 SRO, AF62/1961/1: internal memorandum by G. Fraser, Scottish Fishery Board Chairman, 7 July 1924. See also pp. 85 and 86.
92 St Francis Xavier University, Department of Special Collections, RG30-2/1/2533–2542

and 2544–2549, correspondence between MacDonell and Dr Moses Coady, Director, St Francis Xavier Extension Department, 1929–32.

93 NRAS 1883, Skene, Edwards & Garson papers, John MacDonald, Askernish, Lochboisdale, to Skene, Edwards & Garson, WS, Aberdeen, 26 Aug. 1932.

94 *Ibid.*, 5 Sept. 1932. According to Mrs Bella Mackay of Torlum, Benbecula, who was born in Clandonald in 1930 but returned to the Hebrides with her widowed father in 1939, many colonists had wished to come home but had been unable to afford the passage (oral testimony of Bella Mackay to author, June 1995).

95 NRAS 1883, Skene, Edwards & Garson papers, Commander Hood Linger, 1 Queen's Gate Place, Kensington, to Francis Chalmers, WS, Messrs Skene, Edwards & Garson, Edinburgh, 5 Apr. 1939; *ibid.*, Gordon A. Glennie, CPR, to Messrs Skene, Edwards & Garson, 19 Feb. 1953.

96 John MacLeod to George Macaskill, Nov. 1996.

1 (*left*) Transatlantic shipping advertisements (*Scottish Farmer*, 8 January 1927, p. 31)
2 (*right*) Canadian government advertisement for farmers and farm workers (*Scottish Farmer*, 29 January 1927, p. 133)

Farming in Canada

THE CANADIAN PACIFIC RAILWAY
MAKE IT EASY
for the farmer and farm worker
TO SETTLE IN CANADA

Farms can be selected in the best agricultural districts, close to markets, railways, schools and towns. Farm telephone system available.

Easy terms of payment spread over 34 years if desired.
Conducted Parties to view the Lands at frequent intervals.

Farm Workers—Married or Single – wanted in Canada. Employment guaranteed at Good Wages.

£2 to Canada for Approved Applicants.

SEND this COUPON TO-DAY
for booklet about

How to Own a Farm in Canada
and information about

How to Obtain Farm Work in Canada
and the

Free Passages and
Greatly Reduced Fares – No Repayments

DISTRICT REPRESENTATIVE, Colonization Dept.,
Canadian Pacific Railway,
25 Bothwell Street, Glasgow, C 2.

To DISTRICT REPRESENTATIVE, Colonization Dept.
8.2 Canadian Pacific Railway, 25 Bothwell Street, Glasgow. C.2, or Local Agents.

Please send me information without obligation as to

* How to Own a Farm in Canada
* How to Obtain Farm Work in Canada
* The Free Passages and Greatly Reduced Fares
* Strike out those not needed.

Name ....

Address ....

....

....

Married or Single.............................

---

100 Boys Wanted
for
CANADA
PASSAGES FREE

H.M. Government of Manitoba undertakes to place 100 British boys between the ages of 15 and 17 years with selected farmers in Manitoba to learn practical Canadian agriculture. Boys must be of good character and physique, and have parents' consent. Passages from Liverpool to destination in Canada will be free, and wages of 10/- a week will be paid with full board and lodging, washing and mending.

DOMESTIC SERVANTS WANTED

The Canadian Government undertakes to place experienced British girls in good Canadian homes as household workers where they will have most considerate treatment, good wages, and comfortable conditions.

FAMILIES with Agricultural Experience

Are wanted for placement on Canadian farms in New Brunswick, Ontario, and in the Western Provinces. Land selected; assistance given in settlement; reduced passage rates.

SINGLE MEN WITH FARMING EXPERIENCE

Will be placed by the Canadian Government with good farmers in Canada immediately on arrival. This employment is guaranteed by Government. Going wage will be paid and the Settler's oversight undertaken for at least a year after arrival.

For full information apply to Department 245A

Canadian Government Emigration Agent,
107, Hope Street, Glasgow, C.2.

3 (*above*) Canadian Pacific Railway advertisement for farmers and farm workers (*Scottish Farmer*, 15 January 1927, p. 60)
4 (*below*) Canadian government advertisement for boys, domestic servants, farming families and individuals (*Scottish Farmer*, 28 April 1928, p. 561)

SOUTH AFRICA

....

The Experienced Farmer's Attractive Prospects

....

South Africa offers wonderful scope for the energies of farmers or farmers' sons with capital from £600. Land is cheap, labour is plentiful, and the climate cannot be surpassed. Training in local conditions for long or short periods  according to individual needs is arranged. Reliable expert advice is given on the purchase or leasing of land, stock, and implements, &c. Settlers incur no expense for such service. In certain cases loans can be granted.

A WELL-KNOWN FARMER'S REPORT

Mr F. Herbert Padwick, C.B.E., Leader of the party of British Farmers who recently toured the country, reports:—"After our travels through South Africa, during which we saw something of every phase of her farming, it is the considered opinion of the party that South Africa offers attractive prospects to the young settler from Britain, but he must have enough character to stand on his own feet, plenty of enterprise and some capital, and he must not be afraid of hard work. . . . The 1820 Memorial Settlers' Association has won universal approval for the excellent and disinterested work it does in fathering the settler in South Africa through his first difficult years. No sounder advice can be given to the intending settler."

Particulars on request. Apply Secretary, 1820 Memorial Settlers' Association, 199 Piccadilly, London, W.1.

The 1820 Memorial Settlers' Association is unique because it is an absolutely disinterested body, existing solely to help and safeguard newcomers.

5 Memorial Settlers' Association appeal for farmers for South Africa (*Scottish Farmer*, 15 January 1927, p. 67)

MR. J BRUCE WALKER.

6 J. Bruce Walker, Canadian government emigration agent, Glasgow, and subsequently Director of Emigration for Canada in Britain and Europe (*Emigration and Settlement*, 21 November 1925, p. 22)

MR. WM. C. NOXON,
Agent-General in London for the Province of Ontario.

7 William Noxon, Ontario Agent-General (*Emigration and Settlement*, 21 November 1925, p. 18)

8 Canadian government emigration office, London (National Archives of Canada, PA124866)

9 Canadian government emigration office, Inverness, decorated for the visit of the Duke and Duchess of York, 1929 (National Archives of Canada, PA127068)

10 Fraserburgh family for Nova Scotia (*Press & Journal*, 24 April 1925)

11 William, Thomas and Frank Reid, Mains of Cowie, Stonehaven, recruited for farm work in Western Australia under the Empire Settlement Act (*Press & Journal*, 19 February 1923)

THINGS TO BE PROUD OF AT LLOYDMINSTER, SASKATCHEWAN.
A Farmer's Healthy, Sturdy Sons, and Oats Averaging 40 Bushels to the Acre.

12 Harvesting oats at Lloydminster, Saskatchewan (*Emigration and Settlement*, 21 November 1925, p. 14)

GRAPE PICKING IN THE AULDANA VINEYARDS. SOUTH AUSTRALIA.
This is work which your youngsters will enjoy if you take them or send them out to Australia.

13 Grape picking in the Auldana vineyards, South Australia (*Emigration and Settlement*, 21 November 1925, p. 8)

14 (*Facing page, above*) Group settlement in Western Australia (*Emigration and Settlement*, 13 November 1926, p. 145)

15 (*Facing page, below*) Portraits of early members of the Scottish Canadian community from the Isle of Lewis in Ripley, Ontario, 1952 (Ontario Archives, F1405 040-001 2445-4, Christina Picot Collection)

SIR T. HICKS BEACH AND PARTY MAKING A TOUR OF THE SETTLEMENTS.

CHAPTER FOUR

The lowland clearances

The undoubted importance of the highlands and islands in the long history of mass emigration from Scotland has tended to obscure the equally significant – if less dramatic – movement from other parts of the country. Recent scholarship has begun to highlight the neglected contribution made by lowland emigrants to the nineteenth-century exodus[1] and provides an essential foundation for any study of inter-war emigration – which was primarily a lowland phenomenon, most prominent in the towns and cities of the central belt. Insofar as it has been studied at all, it has been portrayed as a reluctant diaspora of Scotland's frustrated youth, most of whom were provoked by industrial unemployment, while others were driven into exile by a simultaneous contraction in the agricultural and fishing sectors of the economy. Although the vast majority of emigrants came from urban areas, discussion and promotion continued to focus persistently – as in the nineteenth century – on agricultural issues and opportunities, which the dominions were anxious to highlight in preference to the much more limited openings for urban-industrial employment. The following survey of the exodus from lowland Scotland's fishing, farming and urban-industrial communities seeks to evaluate the validity of negative claims about the emigrants' motives vis-à-vis the well-publicized inducements offered, particularly to farmers, through both official and informal channels. It scrutinizes the emigrants' expectations and experiences of continuity and change against the backdrop of over a century of large-scale emigration and, more specifically, of new initiatives spawned by the ESA.

The fishing emigrant

Emigration from fishing communities probably approximates most closely to the image of the reluctant emigrant. The difficulties suffered by the herring trade in the 1920s 'arguably were as great as in any British industry' and blighted fishing centres all round Scotland, not just those in the west highlands.[2] After a century of steady expansion up to 1914, which had seen the herring dominate western European fishing and the Scots dominate the herring trade,

> The main continental markets were reduced and disorganised, while competition from a number of other countries was increasing. To make matters worse, the home market was also in serious decline. As a result, production was curtailed, costs rose considerably faster than prices, and the share fishermen and hired hands on what was now an over-sized and ageing herring fleet struggled grimly to survive. A variety of measures were taken to alleviate the situation, but the maladjustment was so deep-seated that there could be no real solution to the industry's problems.[3]

An optimistic memorandum of 1918, in which Scottish Fishery Board Secretary (subsequently Chairman) David Jones anticipated that wartime dislocation in the fishing industry would be overcome by state aid and improved organization, proved unfounded as the herring trade became crippled not only by poor export markets but also by financial over-commitment and the withdrawal of government guarantees to purchase unsold stock in 1921. The coal dispute of 1921 aggravated the industry's problems, while the white fish trade, too, struggled with increased operating costs, inefficient transport and distribution systems and competition from Norway and Newfoundland.[4] Employment in all branches of the fishing industry fell from 90,710 in 1913 to 65,327 in 1921 and 58,780 in 1934, affecting curers, coopers, gutters and packers as well as the fishermen themselves. Fishermen who had strained their resources to buy heavily mortgaged steam drifters before the war became more and more indebted in the 1920s and 1930s, often to fish salesmen, and the number of curing firms and ancillary shore-based employees halved during the 1920s.[5] The reports of fishery officers in individual Scottish ports reflect a widespread crisis – with catches reduced in value (and often in volume), falling wages and fishermen unable to replace worn-out equipment due to shortages of nets and gear.

The poor state of the fishing industry is also reflected in applications for poor relief made to parish councils by unemployed fishermen and ancillary workers. In Fraserburgh, for instance, coopers William McNab and John Whyte became destitute after returning from the East Anglian fishing in autumn 1921, while Donald McPhee and John Clark were in the same predicament in December 1922.[6] Some applicants were the victims of unsuccessful emigration. Cooper John Simpson (aged 27) and fishworker William Mennie (25) both failed to make their way in the United States, where they had been employed at Ford's Detroit car factory in 1923–24, and returned home to Fraserburgh after less than a year, when they were placed on short-time working.[7] Also in 1924, Elizabeth Noble (21) applied for relief for herself and an infant child on the grounds that they were 'quite destitute and depending on her friends for food'. Her husband, cooper Robert Noble, had gone to join his sister in the United States five months earlier but had failed to find work and, by January 1924, was on his way home.[8] Four years later domestic servant Jane Mowat (42) applied for relief on the grounds of disability, having had her fare home from Toronto paid by the St Andrew's Society there, and in 1930 William Mitchell (34), having failed to find employment in Canada, worked his passage home to Fraserburgh on a cattle boat.[9] Several women also applied for parish relief when their husbands overseas failed to remit money home. In 1924 they included Margaret Birnie (45), whose husband had been 'very neglectful of his wife and family' since going to Detroit in 1923, and Catherine Ritchie (27), whose husband, a former engineer on a drifter, had failed to support his family since emigrating to Winnipeg twenty months earlier.[10]

Throughout the nineteenth century emigration had never featured prominently in the demographic history of Scottish coastal communities, as men whose capital and loyalty were heavily committed to family fishing enterprises exhibited little of the wanderlust that characterized many of their countrymen in agricultural or industrial occupations. Only with the severe downturn of the herring trade in the 1880s did significant numbers resort reluctantly to emigration, a short-lived expedient that was abandoned as soon as the crisis was over. Renewed difficulties just before the First World War, stemming from the introduction of expensive steam drifters, provoked a second, rather patchy, exodus, which some witnesses to the parliamentary investigation of the North Sea fishing industry in 1914 claimed was composed of disillusioned fishermen who felt they no longer had any prospect of independence through part ownership of a boat. Half a dozen Lossiemouth men had emigrated to Canada because of peer pressure, 'the difficulty in getting boats, and the difficulty in getting money to get into a steam drifter'. Emigration, again mainly to Canada, had also taken place from Montrose, Buckie, Peterhead and Fraserburgh, and thirteen emigrants had left St Combs 'because of the hard living', the St Combs witness adding 'I have never seen a fisherman emigrating from my locality in my life before'.[11]

The post-war crisis provoked a similar, though probably more widespread, response as unemployed fishermen who could not find alternative work in the depressed industrial sector emigrated as a last resort. By 1922 the emigration of crofter-fishermen to Canada had 'attained dimensions sufficient to attract popular attention, and Shetland also lost some of its fishing population through their departure overseas.'[12] A year later, after a glutted market had pushed prices down even further, the annual report of the Fishery Board for Scotland commented on the 'disquieting' amount of emigration that had taken place to Canada, the United States and Australia:

A number of fishermen have emigrated both from the East and West Coast, those from the former being mostly young herring fishermen who have found it impossible to provide or maintain the necessary equipment of drift nets, as well as a number of trawl fishermen, including skippers, whose income depends directly on their vessels' earnings, and those from the latter being crofter fishermen attracted by the better economic conditions of farming in Canada ... . Such a departure of capable and energetic men is a loss to the industry and the country, which it will require years of prosperity to rectify.'[13]

It is ironic that Hebridean crofter-fishermen, traditionally portrayed as reluctant exiles, were by 1923 regarded as more enthusiastic about emigration than their east coast counterparts. This view was confirmed both by the *Press & Journal*'s annual review of Fraserburgh's economy on 31 December 1923, which noted that as a result of 'widespread unemployment ... emigration is making a serious drain upon the population', and by Stornoway fishery officer James Wood the following year.[14] On the whole, however, emigration from fishing communities remained, as in previous generations, a response to economic hardship rather than overseas opportunities. It featured in only one further Fishery Board report, that of 1927, and by the late 1930s, despite continuing problems, the Department of Agriculture and Fisheries noted that 'The Emigration statistics published by the Board of Fisheries Journal from time to time have ... become Immigration statistics'.[15]

Attempts made to interest fishermen in schemes promoted under the ESA were generally unsuccessful. Duff Pattullo was not alone in failing to attract Scottish fishermen to Canada. In 1925–26 David Jones poured cold water on a proposal to send crofter-fishermen to Newfoundland, while James Wood, who had moved from Stornoway to become fishery agent at Fraserburgh, was equally dismissive of the merits of encouraging herring curers to invest there. Most curers did not have the capital required to set up in business in Newfoundland, and in any case were likely to be deterred by the financial failure of a previous venture undertaken by the Buckie firm Messrs A. Flett & Company. Robert Spink, fishery officer at Peterhead, corroborated Wood's opinion, thinking it improbable that many gutters and packers would go to Newfoundland without the assurance of good wages and steady, year-round work. Even the combination of a lengthy depression in Scotland and the offer of attractive inducements by the Newfoundland government was, he predicted, unlikely to produce a significant response.[16]

A subsequent proposal by the CNR to bring fifty Scottish fishermen from Banffshire to Nova Scotia also fell on stony ground. On 13 January 1927 CNR agent Alexander McOwan visited Buckie fish market to secure recruits for a six-month contract working out of Lunenburg, promising them a minimum wage of £100 and the prospect of settling down and developing inshore fishing ventures on their own account once their contract had expired. For their part, the fishermen had to pay their own passage (about £20) and subsistence – an unrealistic requirement according to Buckie fishery officer A. Munro, 'as those who would be prepared to take advantage of the scheme are unable to pay their passages out'.[17] In another demonstration of the link between fishing depression and emigration, approximately twenty interested parties applied unsuccessfully to Buckie Parish Council to pay their fare, but most fishermen apparently regarded the venture as an ill-founded 'goose chase'. W. Taylor of the Ministry of Labour deprecated the vagueness of Canadian businesses, which 'appear to be under the impression that we are all "on the dole" here and that they can in consequence come into the market with any kind of half-explained project'. In his opinion, the CNR might have been more successful if it had financed one or two Scottish fishermen to undertake a fact-finding mission and then used them as recruiting agents, since 'the fisherman is an extremely suspicious type who will generally believe only his own people' and was highly unlikely to commit himself to a speculative venture in which emigrants were recruited impersonally and indiscriminately.[18]

An attempt in 1927–28 to bring Scottish and English fishermen and ancillary workers to Australia under the £34 Million Agreement also foundered on the rocks of insufficient information and investment and, probably, lack of private recommendation.[19] The continuing significance of precedent and the personal touch compared to the more modest appeal of formal ventures is demonstrated in the recollections of those who participated in the exodus to North America. They included the late Annie Noble of Inverallochy, who claimed that some east coast fishing villages lost up to half their inhabitants overseas during the 1920s.

> After the First War … families were just lifting and going to America, and a lot of people left this village, and I'm sure same time they'd been leaving other villages and other towns, so you can see there was a massive evacuation to America at that time.[20]

Her claims were corroborated by the late Gilbert Buchan, from the same village, who recalled not only the steady leakage of emigrants 'every week' but also that these people, who constituted the cream of the fishing community, generally went out in 'little colonies' to join family members previously settled overseas. After the war Annie Noble herself went with her parents to join their extended family at Elgin, forty miles from Chicago, the town to which her grandfather had first gone in 1890. She soon became part of an extensive Scottish network and found work in a television and radio factory, where the employees included emigrants from Lossiemouth and Fraserburgh. Her Fraserburgh-born husband, whom she met through fellow-Scots in Illinois, was one of several brothers, all former fishermen, who had emigrated in response to the depression and encouragement from another brother already in the United States. Unlike her grandparents and uncle, Annie did not intend to return permanently to Aberdeenshire but was reluctantly obliged to do so when her mother took ill during a holiday at home nine years after the family had emigrated. She was later joined by her husband, who, having worked as a salesman in the United States, ultimately reverted to fishing in Scotland.

In the same period fishermen from Fife and (to a lesser extent) Aberdeenshire developed links with the Lake Erie fishing community in the Port Dover area of Ontario, again through word of mouth recommendations rather than formal schemes promoted under the ESA. The Port Dover connection seems to have been established as early as 1850, with the arrival of Captain James Lowe from Aberdeen.[21] It was reinforced in 1914 by the arrival of five Scots, mostly related, from Cellardyke in Fife. These men and their families were part of a bigger Cellardyke contingent which had emigrated to join relatives in Hamilton two years earlier after several years' poor fishing in the North Sea but moved to Port Dover when Steven Doig, a Cellardyke-born employee of fish processors W. F. Kolbe & Company, told his employer that there were experienced Scottish fishermen in Hamilton. Once established, the Cellardyke men purchased their own boats and were joined by at least eight other 'Dykers' between the wars, as well as families of Nobles and Downies from Rosehearty and Fraserburgh. Most of the Aberdeenshire families returned home, as did some of the 'Dykers', either in the 1930s when the Great Lakes fisheries were in the doldrums or after they retired. Others settled permanently, and some were rumoured to have been involved in smuggling 'the midnight herring' across Lake Erie during Prohibition.[22]

The farming emigrant

Throughout the inter-war period farmers and farm workers displayed a much keener and more consistent interest in emigration than did their counterparts from the fishing community. In view of their long experience and reputation as enthusiastic emigrants during the nineteenth century, the ongoing problems of socio-economic insecurity and the relentless canvassing to which they were subjected by agents, it was no surprise that they should respond to agricultural depression and attractive inducements by turning their attention overseas. The vast majority of ventures promoted under the Empire Settlement Act clearly aimed to attract recruits with agricultural experience, aptitude or ambition, and it was within such a constituency that officially sponsored and subsidized schemes made their greatest impact.

British agriculture was hit by two waves of depression between 1870 and 1940. The first crisis, from the 1880s to 1896, was largely the result of an influx of cheap cereals from the North American prairies and Russia, but its effect was mitigated by buoyant demand and, in Scotland, by the strength of mixed farming – particularly the relatively profitable livestock sector. The second crisis, from 1924 to 1940, was more serious, affecting both arable and livestock farming, with farmers exposed to the full blast of foreign competition when, in 1921, the government repealed the year-old Agriculture Act, which had guaranteed the price of grain. Subsequent legislative attempts to address the problem were of only limited relevance and success, and agriculture continued to suffer throughout the 1930s because of the depressed international economy.[23] Scottish farmers, many of whom had become owner-occupiers as large estates were broken up and sold, reacted to cheap food imports and inadequate government intervention by holding rallies throughout the country to press for reform and the more effective marketing of domestic produce. In January 1930, a protest meeting at Dingwall was attended by 3,000 farmers and farm servants, while a similar rally at Pittodrie stadium in Aberdeen a month later attracted 10,000, with gatherings at Perth and Laurencekirk attracting 6,000 and 2,000, respectively.[24] Branch meetings of the Scottish NFU regularly petitioned Parliament for import restrictions – the Banffshire branch, for example, complaining to local MP Sir Murdoch McKenzie Wood in March 1933 about the rock-bottom prices at which dumped oats and oat products were being sold and, in November, about 'the deplorable condition of the livestock industry in Scotland'.[25]

Government attempts to stem rural depopulation through the creation of smallholdings enjoyed mixed success. Although the Land Settlement (Scotland) Act of 1919 increased the financial and legal authority of the BOAS, reduced the complexity of compulsory purchase procedures and restored something of a ladder of opportunity for farm workers, delays in administering the scheme exasperated many applicants.[26] Living and working conditions for farm servants – a controversial issue since the early nineteenth century – continued to generate public debate, particularly after the establishment of the Scottish Farm Servants' Union in 1912. Much rural depopulation was, in the opinion of the SFSU, attributable to thwarted ambitions, job insecurity, inadequate social amenities and execrable housing, as well as an acceptance, by both farmers and employees, of the inevitability of 'flitting' and the mutual exclusiveness of their interests.

> Farm servants are mostly such by force of circumstances, not from choice, so naturally finding it at best a rather thankless business, as soon as opportunity offers a change they take it, for better or maybe worse, but they don't mind so long as they get clear of farm service. What has farm service to offer any lad of ambition? A grieve's job at best. He never gets past that

stage, as the farm managerships are picked up by the less skilled but 'diplomaed' farmers' sons. Why should that be so? In every other occupation one can, with merit, reach the top, but not on the farms. At best the farm billy has only a dreary life as a cottar to look forward to. Lack of incentive is one good reason [for leaving the land].

Discontented wives may be said to be another – and who can blame the wives? In many cases they are miles from anywhere or anyone, with nothing to divert them but making ends meet; houses neither weather proof nor having any pretence to sanitation, where even the common decencies of life can hardly be observed; and water to carry anything up to half a mile. The houses could often be made nicer, but the cottar has to do it at his own expense, and with the chance of a flit at the end of twelve months. Is it worth while, he asks? Lack of security is another reason. 'Why do the yard up, why bother with this, that, or the next thing; maybe we won't be here another year.' He has no part in the amenities of the district, and his children are backward at school from continuous shifting about.[27]

Rural rootlessness generated both migration and emigration, and, according to the *Scottish Journal of Agriculture*, a higher proportion of the agricultural labour force emigrated in 1924–26 than from any other occupation. Of a labour force which averaged 22,480 for the three years in question and which recruited only 2,370 per year, 8,300 emigrated – 4,050 to Canada, 1,650 to Australia, 1,120 to New Zealand, 550 to other parts of the empire, and 930 to foreign countries.[28] The farming community was kept abreast of the emigration debate and overseas opportunities partly through newspapers, but more directly through the *Scottish Farmer*, a weekly farmer's journal founded in 1893, and the *Scottish Farm Servant*, founded in 1913 as the monthly mouthpiece of the SFSU.

Not all the views expressed were favourable to emigration per se or painted a glowing picture of prospects overseas. The socialist *Scottish Farm Servant* regarded it purely as a negative reaction to hard times at home, and in 1920 warned emigrants – particularly to New Zealand – not to believe unreservedly the promises of 'posters, pamphlets, and other advertising means' which lured 'enterprising young men and women' to the colonies.[29] Two years later an Edmonton correspondent, after reminding readers that circulation of the journal was 'not confined to the land we couldn't find a living in', gave a detailed description of working conditions in Alberta, mainly to dispel the false impressions created by 'the posters with their visions of waving wheat'. It was, he claimed, 'a land where future crops are always looked forward to and never satisfy' and farmers took advantage of the ignorance of new recruits, working them into the ground and then illegally withholding their wages when they quit their jobs in disgust.[30] In 1924 SFSU founder and journal editor Joe Duncan warned that the conditions of hired workers in both Canada and the United States were inferior to those in Scotland, and, following a transatlantic trip six years later, he was even more convinced that young single men would be 'very foolish' to emigrate to Canada, although prospects were brighter for married men with ambitions to make themselves and their families independent on the land.[31] Yet in 1926 the *Scottish Farm Servant* bemoaned the relentless departure of large numbers of such ambitious emigrants – 'the most enterprising and venturesome of our workers' – who were enticed to Canada by the combination of assisted passages and settlement schemes:

> We do not blame those who leave. We know how pale is the gleam of hope, and how little encouragement there is for those who work for better conditions. We cannot blame any father who feels his responsibility to his children and decides that any risk is better than to condemn his children to the conditions of life on the average Scots farm. Yet we cannot bring ourselves to believe that emigration is any solution of the problem.
>
> We do not possess sufficient information to judge between those who contradict each other so flatly as to the conditions in the colonies. We are quite clear that the wages offered to farm workers in Canada are no better than can be earned in Scotland, and such reports as we have had from New Zealand and Australia, do not show that wages for farm workers, and regularity of employment are such as to justify anyone making the journey across the world. If the lure is the hope of being able to secure a holding, then we cannot understand why the towns in these countries should have such large bodies of unemployed workers. A very large number of those unemployed workers left farm work in this country to go to the colonies. Why should it be necessary to pay the passages for other farm workers from this country, if farm workers who left a few years ago are walking the streets idle in their own towns?
>
> If the opportunities in the colonies are so much better than at home, there ought not to be the room left for those emigrating now, unless many thousands of those who emigrated during the past twenty years have failed to make good. What guarantee is there that those going now will do any better? It is probably true there as here that a few struggle through by virtue of greater perseverance, or through fortunate circumstances. There may be more opportunities for the fortunate minority in the colonies but for the great bulk of the workers the struggle for a living seems to be as unremitting as at home, and perseverance and spirit put into the work of improving conditions here would soon make it less necessary for our people to go abroad.[32]

While deploring the need for emigration, the *Scottish Farm Servant* was equally hostile to farmers who opposed state-aided colonization schemes on the grounds that they aggravated labour shortages and forced up wages. In 1925 the Scottish NFU, particularly in Aberdeenshire, complained about the activities of emigration agents and army recruiting sergeants, and, as we have seen, some farmers even tried to forbid communication between agents and the farm labour force.[33] The response of the *Scottish Farm Servant* was to reiterate that the reason for rural depopulation lay not in the attractions of an emigrant or military life but in the hopelessness of farm service in Scotland – especially in the northeast, where four years earlier farmers had taken advantage of a plentiful labour supply to make big wage reductions.[34] The journal lampooned the inconsistent arguments of farmers such as Scottish NFU President Alex Batchelor in accepting assisted emigration for 'any other workers except farm workers',[35] although it remained opposed to emigration on principle and continued to warn of the pitfalls of the emigrant life – as in this imagined interchange between two doric-speaking farm servants in 1926.

> 'The farmers are no' very pleased aboot the lads gaun awa, are they?' said the Soutar.
> 'They're short o' men now, Hilly [the farmer] says, and it's no' fair o' the Government to tryst awa mair wi' cheap passages,' said Dyker.
> 'But gin it was cheap passages for Canadian stots comin' here, Hilly wadna object,' said Molie … .
> 'I canna say that I'm awfu' ta'en with the prospects in Canada,' said Postie. 'I saw in the papers that they were offerin' £5 a month, and £7 for specially good men.'
> 'That wad be wi' board an' lodging,' said the Soutar.
> 'Aye,' said Postie. 'It's no' so muckle mair nor they're gettin' here.'
> 'The board'll be better, though, I expect,' said the Soutar.
> 'But it's gey chancy,' said the Postie. 'A lad wad hae to be gey sure that he was to be keepit on in the winter, and that's sometimes no' the case.'
> 'Maist o' them'll be think' o' getting' a bit grun' o' their ain, after a year or twa,' said Dyker.
> 'You aye need a carrot in front o' the cuddy to keep him gaun,' said Molie.
> 'You're no sair ta'en on wi' Canada, are you, Molie?' said the Soutar.
> 'I dinna ken muckle aboot it,' said Molie, 'but there's been a gey curn o' lads left this countryside for Canada, an' I never heard that hauf o' them got farms.'
> 'They seem to do better nor here, though,' said the Soutar.
> 'They couldna weel do waur,' said Molie, 'but they dinna mak' fortunes there, ony mair nor here.'
> 'I some doo't there's no fortunes to be made oot o' wark in Canada ony mair nor here,' said the Soutar.
> 'There's no mony comes back,' said Postie.
> 'They're maybe no' able,' said Molie, 'though there's nothin' to come back for.'[36]

Warnings and hard-luck stories also appeared from time to time in the *Scottish Farmer* to deter gullible emigrants, particularly those who were in a position to take up land. New Zealand came in for unfavourable comment on three occasions in 1922: in April on account of an unfavourable harvest at Hawke's Bay, in July because of farming bankruptcies which had resulted from falsely inflated land values in the Taranaki region, also in North Island, and in September because of the deepening agricultural depression at Taranaki.[37] In 1923 the same regular correspondent from Hawke's Bay repeated his warnings to those with limited capital not to invest in land settlement in New Zealand if they wanted to remain solvent.[38] A year later Australia came under the critical microscope when a female correspondent from Lanarkshire – who had spent three years in Canada before settling on a 1,870-acre farm in the Hunter Valley in New South Wales in 1917 – compared her experiences in each country, to the latter's detriment. Australians, she claimed, did not welcome newcomers, housing and other amenities were poor, and farmers who were doing well in Scotland 'should stick to it'. Her warnings did not fall on stony ground, for by 1925 some of the Scots who had in 1924 made agreements with a visiting agent to take up farms on the 20,000-acre Martindale estate in the Hunter Valley were either asking for reassurance about specific issues raised by the Lanarkshire emigrant or, in one case, demanding the return of a deposit.[39] In 1926 Stirling correspondent P. Marshall, having just returned from a twelve-year sojourn in Victoria, Tasmania and New South Wales, alleged both that Victoria had no land available for immigrants and, more generally, that 'the aim of this immigration stunt is to lower the standard of living for the farm worker in Australia, as the native-born Australian won't put up with the low wages and rotten conditions on the farms'.[40] Nor did Canada, particularly the prairie west, escape criticism. In 1919 a correspondent reminded readers that drought or frost had caused the failure of the last three harvests in both Alberta and Saskatchewan and warned them to verify the glowing promises of federal agents before leaving Scotland. According to a British Columbian newspaper quoted in the *Scottish Farmer* four years later, there was a 90 per cent bankruptcy rate among the Dakotan farmers who had bought irrigated land from the CPR in Alberta during the previous few years, mainly because their crops were generally mortgaged either to the banks or to the railway company, and in 1924 Scottish farmers were warned against the sharp practice of land companies which duped unwary newcomers into buying farms at inflated prices.[41] Farm workers were apparently even more vulnerable to hardship and failure. In 1924 and 1927 they were warned of severe unemployment in Alberta, while in 1926 an anonymous correspondent, who had gone to the province expecting to earn $40 a month but had found himself working a 17-hour day for only $25, returned home in disgust, claiming that thousands more would do the same if they could only save the fare. Meanwhile another correspondent, quoting the experience of his own son, warned against the practice of some Canadian farmers who, by subjecting their employees to excessive work and unfair criticism, deliberately goaded them into leaving their situations without payment.[42]

But while the *Scottish Farm Servant* was unequivocally and consistently hostile to emigration, criticism in the *Scottish Farmer* was more sporadic, sometimes more constructive, and often robustly contested. Alongside warnings, its readers found positive encouragement to emigrate, as well as practical factual information and weekly advertisements for a variety of assisted passage and settlement schemes. Regular features such as 'Notes from Eastern Canada', 'Canadian Letter', 'Saskatchewan Letter', 'Notes from New Zealand' and 'Queensland Letter', which gave a running commentary on colonial life and agricultural issues, both reflected and stimulated readers' interest in overseas opportunities, as did periodic book reviews and editorials. Several correspondents presented a balanced view of the pros and cons of farming overseas, generally echoing the advice of generations of commentators that success was dependent on hard work and thrift – a point also made in editorials that tried to reconcile the conflicting statements of some letter writers.[43]

Information in specialist farming publications was reinforced by advertisements, features, correspondence and anecdotes in the provincial press. Although the *Press & Journal* reflected the hostility of its Aberdeenshire readership to the emigration of farm workers, particularly under state sponsorship, it still gave extensive coverage to dominion land settlement schemes. But both this daily newspaper and the weekly *Scottish Farmer* were selective in their recommendations. Almost no attention was paid to agricultural opportunities in the United States, although the achievements of individual Scots were sometimes mentioned. In 1919, for instance, Joe Muir from Ayrshire was profiled by the *Scottish Farmer* as one of Montana's leading sheep farmers with a holding of 12,000 acres, and in 1929 a Lewis correspondent pondered why several of his friends who were farming in the United States and Canada could come home periodically while he could not afford even a week's holiday on the mainland.[44] Three years earlier the *Press & Journal* had commented on the preponderance of Scottish herdsmen and exhibitors at large livestock exhibitions in the United States, and identified sixteen Aberdeenshire men who had attended the recent American Royal Livestock Exhibition in Kansas City.[45]

Opportunities in South Africa were open only to the monied emigrant and were usually canvassed in general terms rather than by identifiable Scottish agents or settlers. Enterprising young men were encouraged to go to Southern Rhodesia, provided they had a minimum of £2,000–£3,000 capital to establish and operate a mixed farm. Land could be purchased either privately, from the Crown, or through the Land Settlement Department of the British South Africa Company. In 1925 readers of the *Press & Journal* were assured of the 'great number' of Scots in Southern Rhodesia, where the 1920 parliament had been nicknamed 'the Caledonian Society' and where the Chief Agriculturist at the Department of Agriculture was Aberdeenshire man Major Mundy, formerly of Balcairn, Oldmeldrum.[46] In May 1924 A. H. Tatlow, publicity manager for South African Railways and Harbours, delivered an illustrated lecture at the Aberdeen YMCA under the auspices of the Royal Scottish Geographical Society, and the following month the Press & Journal announced the forthcoming visit of a representative of the African Irrigated Land Company Ltd to Mackay Brothers' Aberdeen office to discuss farming opportunities at Kendrew, Cape Colony, with small capitalists who preferred to avoid the rigours of pioneering in isolated locations.[47] In 1925 Caithness man Alister Miller came to Scotland to promote emigration to the Transvaal, where his own interests lay, at the same time as the Scottish Farmer reported the arrival of eight young Scots in Cape Town en route for farming careers in the Graaf Reinet district, where they had been attracted by the glowing recommendations of an earlier settler. Colonel Morris, general manager of the 1820 Settlers' Memorial Association, was anxious to attract Scottish settlers with £800–£1,000 capital to the Great Fish River Valley in Cape Province, and in February 1926 the Press & Journal reported a lecture given to past and present agricultural students at Marischal College, Aberdeen, by the Earl of Leven and Melville, similarly targeted on wealthy would-be farmers who could not find a niche in Scotland.[48] In the same month 100 British and Irish farmers, including Scottish NFU President Alex Batchelor, went on a fact-finding visit to South Africa, and some of the delegation subsequently publicized their favourable impressions in the press.[49]

Relatively little practical advice and encouragement was received from the Antipodes, although in December 1922 the Press & Journal predicted that Australia was about to replace Canada as the favourite destination of discontented farm workers, attracted by the promise of land work 'on a vast scale'.[50] The assisted colonization schemes were fully explained and specific openings regularly advertised.[51] Following his Scottish tour in 1924, W. C. Stillman was reported to be 'greatly satisfied' with the farm servants who had applied for assisted passages, and four years later one advertisement for eight shepherds for Australia apparently attracted more than 800 applications.[52] In 1923 the Scottish Farmer compared Queensland favourably with Scotland as a place where small-time purchasers of farms could work their way up to prosperity; in 1924 the Press & Journal featured the successful career of Midmar emigrant John Abernethy, a large dairy farmer and field supervisor of a group settlement scheme in Western Australia; and in 1928 a Scottish correspondent of the Scottish Farmer in Gippsland, Victoria, reported an encounter with three successful Scots who had been settled on fruit farms under the Big Brother Scheme.[53]

Predictably, the farming press accorded Canada more factual and promotional coverage than any other destination. Negative criticism often drew a sharp riposte from advocates of Canadian land settlement, with a particularly long-running debate in the *Scottish Farmer* over conditions of farm service. When in 1926 'JSW' of Vancouver warned farm labourers of the likelihood of excessive hours, winter unemployment and hardship, and claimed he had met 'thousands' who would return to Britain if they could afford it, his allegations were immediately refuted. He was attacked not only by W. T. Cranfield of the Canadian Press Bureau in London and F. B. Robins – a Toronto correspondent of the journal, who likened his attitude to that of the disgruntled Victorian remittance man – but also by Scottish settlers Thomas Boyle of Kingston, Ontario, and W. G. Lennox of Saskatchewan.[54] Lennox, who was on holiday in Glasgow when he wrote to the *Scottish Farmer*, complained that some press correspondence on Canadian emigration 'should never have been allowed to go into print, because if a person is discontented he immediately writes to a newspaper, which is not the case when everything is going smoothly'. His statement was echoed by Vancouver Island farmer A. D. MacDonald, who alleged that Canada was plagued by 'a plethora of misfits' who blamed everyone but themselves for their lack of success and were all too ready to write damning and damaging letters to British journals 'warning all and sundry not to be trapped by the florid inducements held out to intending emigrants'.[55] When the following year David Sands of Edmonton revived the unemployment theme by citing the case of an inexperienced farm labourer from Dundee who was in prison awaiting deportation after quitting his job and becoming destitute, Cranfield agreed that emigrant farm labourers should be robust, industrious and have no illusions about 'dollar bills flying loose around the country', but challenged his claim about the inevitability of winter layoffs.[56] And after prolonged debate in 1928 as to whether Canadian farm service was better paid, less stressful and more egalitarian than in Britain, editorial endorsement was given to the view that, if agricultural wage labourers could cope with hard work and adverse climatic conditions in the Dominion, they were more likely to attain ultimate independence on a farm of their own than their counterparts who stayed in Scotland.[57]

Editorials as well as letters in the press were more likely to inform and encourage than deter would-be farming emigrants. In a nine-part series of articles recounting his tour of the Dominion in autumn 1923, *Scottish Farmer* editor Archibald MacNeilage emphasized the high reputation of Scots throughout the country, and noted, perhaps surprisingly, that in British Columbia in particular 'one breathes the atmosphere of Glasgow and Scotland rather than the atmosphere even of London and England'.[58] *Press & Journal* manager E. W. Watt was one of a number of Scottish journalists who undertook a similar tour the following year, reporting his findings in a nine-part series in the newspaper, as well as in public lectures after his return. Having undertaken the trip at the invitation of the CNR, which was perturbed at British criticism of conditions of settlement, he expressed himself well satisfied with western and Maritime farming opportunities for Scottish settlers, several of whom he encountered. In Saskatchewan Duffus man W. G. Duncan, district agriculturist with the Dominion's Land Settlement Branch at Prince Albert, Saskatchewan, explained the training and aftercare given to new settlers, and in Prince Edward Island Watt visited the farm of Aberdonian Robert Rhymes, formerly an engine driver with the Great North Railway. Untypically wealthy, he had in 1910 spent $4,000 on a 140-acre farm on the island after an agent he met at the Kittybrewster Show in Aberdeen persuaded him to look east instead of west, and, although inexperienced at the outset, he had built up a successful mixed farming business.[59]

Several correspondents were anxious to encourage settlement in the neglected Maritime Provinces, one regular columnist in 1926 urging emigrants to consider settling in that 'garden of the Dominion ... before making up their minds that nothing can be done unless West of Winnipeg'.[60] Three years earlier a former teacher from Glasgow had sent to the *Scottish Farmer* the first of a series of letters from the neglected side of Canada in the hope that 'the experience ... of a couple of elderly immigrants would be interesting and encouraging to those who are debating whether or not to go'. While teaching in the Hebrides she had married a crofter when they were aged, respectively, forty and forty-seven, and then, inspired by a guidebook which they had read during their engagement, they emigrated to New Brunswick in 1921.

> Our Island friends wished us the best of luck, but many of them thought it was a most foolish and reckless undertaking. One man told us that we were going to certain ruin, that there was no good farming land in New Brunswick, it being a land of rock! Others thought that, as I was entirely ignorant of a farm-wife's duties, I would find it too hard and difficult, and would break down in health. I was pressed to stay and continue teaching, even although I was married, but I was getting pretty sick of the confining life of a teacher, and longed for some life and adventure, no matter what hard work it entailed.
>
> So we followed the advice of our book and chose a Province which would not be such a radical change for elderly folks as the West. The climate here does not go to such extremes as in the West, and crop failures are almost unknown. Fortunes may not be made, but, to balance that, fortunes are not lost by sudden climatic changes affecting the crops, as unfortunately does happen at times in the West. We also wished to be as near to the Old Country as possible, to give our friends there an opportunity of visiting us without incurring a heavy train fare as well as that of the steamer.[61]

Using the services of an agent in St John, they purchased a 200-acre farm for $750 and, after three years, despite the hard work and the loss of their house by fire in 1923, they had no regrets and were growing accustomed to the Canadian ways of farming. Their nearest neighbours were fellow-Scots who had done all they could to help them succeed, and she concluded her letter by recommending New Brunswick to others who were prepared to take advice and knuckle down to the hardships of pioneering.

Official colonization schemes in Canada were well covered in the agricultural press. The extension of Canadian soldier settlement to civilians was described by the *Press & Journal* in 1923 as a scheme which offered 'no get-rich-quick promise' but 'solid, if apparently slow, advantages' to those prepared to work hard under the auspices of disinterested, experienced officials, not untried theorists.[62] When a year later the 3,000 Families Scheme was approved under the ESA, it was stipulated that every family member had to be interviewed and approved. The attitude of the farmer's wife was regarded as the key to success or failure, particularly by Inverness agent Anne MacDonald, who believed that 50 per cent of the success of the scheme depended on settlers' wives.[63] New arrivals, while being settled immediately on farm holdings, were required to work for wages until they were competent to launch out on their own and, during their probationary period, they were to be visited approximately once a month by farm supervisors employed by the Land Settlement Branch of the SSB.[64]

> Families will not necessarily be established in homes of their own immediately on arrival in Canada, but each family will be provided with suitable accommodation. The adult male members will be expected to acquire local farm experience by accepting employment on farms in the vicinity. They cannot expect large wages while so employed, as they will be inexperienced.
>
> While the male members of the family are gaining experience, their wives and daughters may be expected to learn to look after cows and poultry, so that they may be able to do this work on their own farms.
>
> As soon as the family have had adequate training and experience, they will be allowed to start farming on their own account. The farm offered to them will in some cases be the farm on which they have been living, but if that farm is not available, they will be given the choice of one or two other farms, probably in the same neighbourhood.[65]

Commended by the *Press & Journal* to emigrants with 'grit and "smeddum"', the 3,000 Families Scheme was similarly endorsed by *The Scotsman* for ensuring 'that wider and better opportunities will be provided for thousands who are hampered under old-world conditions, and that the health, vigour, and unity of the Empire will be improved by the operation'. Equally supportive was the *Edinburgh Evening Dispatch*, which described it as a 'rational and co-ordinated plan of settlement' under which 'the Dominion

Government will provide houses and farms ready for cultivation, not in the back of beyond, but in settled and convenient regions, where the farmer can find a market for his produce'.[66] While the *Scottish Farmer* claimed that it was 'no part of our policy to recommend all and sundry to emigrate', it too welcomed the 3,000 Families Scheme, particularly for the promise that settlers would not be left to their own devices but would be trained, supervised, advised and, wherever possible, located together in groups of families.[67]

Opportunities for land settlement through provincial ventures, the railways and the Hudson's Bay Company were also well publicized. In 1924 John Martin, the Ontario Minister of Agriculture, in an interview with the *Press & Journal*, commended the calibre of agriculturists who had taken advantage of assisted passages.

> I have been greatly struck with the splendid quality of the selected farm labourers sent out from Scotland to Ontario during the past spring by the office of the Agent-General of Ontario in London and Glasgow. I never saw a better class of settlers. We will have as great a demand for suitable settlers next spring, and I hope that we will be able to make arrangements for granting the necessary assistance under the auspices of the Overseas Settlement Act, to enable many hundreds of suitable farm labourers to migrate to Ontario from this country. We are especially pleased with the new settlers who have been coming from the Hebrides and Scotland.[68]

When in 1925 the Land Settlement Branch (LSB) of the Canadian government's Soldier Settlement Board set aside 550 acres in British Columbia's Fraser Valley for subdivision into 15 Scottish-run dairy farms, readers of the *Scottish Farmer* were encouraged to take up 'one of the best opportunities which has ever been presented to Scottish dairymen who desire to become established on a farm of their own'.[69] And, in a Maritime imitation of the 3,000 Families Scheme, the imperial, dominion and provincial governments in 1927 made a joint agreement under the ESA to settle 500 British families in New Brunswick over a six-year period from March 1928, the scheme being fully explained and recommended in both the *Scottish Farmer* and the *Scottish Farm Servant*.

Like its larger predecessor, the New Brunswick venture provided assisted passages and settlement loans, spread over twenty-five years, to selected families with a minimum of £25 landing money to purchase and stock partially cultivated farms of 100–200 acres. Greeted by the *Scottish Farmer* as an enterprising imitation of the 'successful' 3,000 Families Scheme, the New Brunswick experiment immediately began to attract Scots, including seventy to one parish alone in 1927,[70] it was also endorsed by the more critical Joe Duncan, editor of the *Scottish Farm Servant*, after he had visited seventeen farms in the province and met several old – and satisfied – friends among the settlers. Although many of the farms were run down, they were capable of improvement and in a mixed farming environment that was not too dissimilar from Scotland.

> If any man were to ask me whether he should consider making application for a farm in New Brunswick, my reply would be something like this: 'If you are keen on farming and can handle stock as well as land, and your wife can milk and handle poultry, and you are both willing to work hard, and ready to adapt yourselves to different conditions, it is worth your while making enquiries about your chances under the scheme, but it is a choice you must make yourself, and you must take a chance because nobody can give you any guarantee. You will not make money, but you are not likely to fail in making a home and a living if you have ordinary luck and you have the capacity to run a place of your own. The prospects for your family are better than if you remain working on a farm in Scotland.'
> There are a good many 'ifs', as you will see there, and they have to be carefully considered. Much will depend upon the man himself, more upon the wife, and everything on both being able to make a good team job of it. I am satisfied that every reasonable assistance is given by those responsible for the working of the scheme to settlers who tackle the job in the right spirit. The officers I met were not only competent and keen on their work, but it was evident that they had the confidence of the settlers, and that they were genuinely interested not so much in securing settlers as in giving the settlers such help as they could to make a success of their venture. And although two or three of those I saw did not look too promising to me, I was satisfied they were getting a square deal, and that the defect was in themselves and not in the scheme or on the part of those who were responsible for the work in New Brunswick.[71]

While press reports and agents' records provide sporadic insights into the impact of government-sponsored colonization schemes on Scotland, it is from emigrant correspondence and memoirs that we learn most about the realities of farming overseas. The four Scottish cases uncovered in a sampling of Australian immigration records in the 1920s are not statistically significant, but they do indicate that farm labourers could meet with both adversity and success. Writing to a representative of the New Settlers' League, a voluntary organization created to befriend and place young immigrants, William McKinnon expressed complete satisfaction with his situation and prospects at Atherton, North Queensland:

> I am well established now and I like the job no end. I think I can say that I have struck the best billet on the tableland. I enjoy the work when [sic] I have a good boss. He is more like a pal than an employer [and] we get on very well. There is plenty of work just now, it being the corn pulling season. We are quite near town about ten minutes ride, but I am so well

treated that I never have any inclination to go in. I am studying the farming in real earnest and I mean to start for myself as soon as I am free ... . I was here about a month when Mr Armstrong took over another twenty [acres] for corn next season [and] seeing what a lot of extra work it was going to give me, he suggested that I have a share in the profits as compensation. I think that is all right for a new chum, don't you?[72]

Tom McKenzie (16), on the other hand, did not satisfy his employer, Clarence Roberts of Drillham, Queensland, when he went out at the end of 1923, and only six months later he was moved on 'through no fault of his own'.[73] An even less positive experience was that of twenty-three-year old J. C. McLaren, who arrived in Queensland from an unspecified part of Scotland on 1 January 1923, to discover that his nominator had no work for him. After finding a temporary milking job he had become unemployed by mid-May, with little prospect of fulfilling his ultimate ambition of joining the police force.[74] And Alexander Holburn, who emigrated from Edinburgh to South Australia as an inexperienced and penniless farm apprentice in 1924, was equally dissatisfied, but for different reasons, alleging that he was both overworked and unduly restricted in his social life by an employer who had been asked by Holburn's mother to act *in loco parentis*.[75]

Surviving evidence about farm settlement schemes relates primarily to Canada. According to the *Daily Record* of 2 May 1925, 'Family emigration from Scotland increases every week, and the British Settlement scheme, under which capital is advanced to farming settlers, has done much to encourage the movement.' Recruits came from all over Scotland, but particularly from the north – including the McLellans, a family of eleven from Lochmaddy, who joined around 1,000 emigrants on the maiden voyage of the Anchor Donaldson liner *Letitia* to Canada in April 1925.[76] In May 1926 the *Scottish Farmer* noted that the 3,000 Families Scheme had accounted for a 'large number' of recent emigrants on the SS *Montcalm* from Greenock,[77] and the *Stornoway Gazette* attributed a continuing enthusiasm for Canada in 1926 and 1927 to the combination of passage rebates and the 3,000 Families Scheme. It noted that eligibility had been extended to single men with no experience of farm work, and in June 1927 reiterated that the lure of assisted land settlement was the main reason for an upsurge of departures, particularly after the biannual term days, when farm servants either renewed or concluded their six-monthly employment contracts.[78] According to W. J. Egan, the Inverness agency was the second most successful in the UK in generating family settlement business between 1924 and 1926, with 379 agents' nominations and 387 nominations under the 3,000 Families Scheme, compared with figures of 118 and 245, respectively, from the Aberdeen office.[79] By 1928 the Glasgow agency

[131]

was confident that increasing publicity was leading to the recruitment of a superior type of emigrant because, as a result both of rural Scotland being 'very thoroughly combed' and vanguard settlers sending home successful reports, several 'real good farmers' were selling up when they heard of former agricultural labourers making better progress than their erstwhile employers in Scotland.[80] And a Dominion Office investigation in 1929 claimed that Scotland was probably the easiest recruiting ground for emigration in the UK, the two Scottish agencies having sent more families and domestics than any other British office between 1 January and 30 September, including 100 of the 291 families sent out under the 3,000 Families Scheme.[81]

Positive correspondence from recruits was incorporated into the propaganda of the Canadian government agents in Aberdeen, Glasgow and Inverness. When Aberdeen-based D. E. Lothian explained the details of the 3,000 Families Scheme to a meeting of the Drumlithie (Kincardineshire) Social Club in December 1925, he highlighted the experience of R. B. Morrice, who, having moved with his family from Lonmay in Aberdeenshire to a fifty-acre farm at Sebringville, Red River, Ontario, expressed unqualified satisfaction with his accommodation, treatment and prospects in an area where he had encountered several other Buchan families and in which there was 'ample room and good prospects for more Scottish families'.[82] On 30 January 1926 Thomas Boyle, who ten months earlier had emigrated to Ontario with his wife, three children and relatively little capital, wrote to the agent in Glasgow that the scheme was 'one of the best that has ever been put before the British farm servant, if he only takes advantage of it'.[83] And in 1928 Anne MacDonald received a glowing letter from a woman who three years earlier had emigrated to the 'splendid country' of Hardisty, Alberta, with her husband, and now, having broken forty-nine acres and begun to establish a farm, wanted to arrange for her sister-in-law in Newtonmore to join them.[84]

A more detailed account of the decision-making process, as well as of its outcome, was given in a letter by fifteen-year-old Cissie Stevenson from Lanarkshire, whose family decided to emigrate in the aftermath of the General Strike:

> It was before we had decided which country we would go to that we began to hear stories of Scottish families who had gone to Canada under the 3,000 Family Scheme, at practically no cost to themselves. These families wrote of the hearty welcome which they had received on arrival, of the pleasant farms they had been placed upon, and the exceptional kindness shown them by their neighbours, and seemed by the hopeful tone of their letters to be fully assured of future prosperity. In every case the families gave full credit to the Family Settlement Board, writing at length of the wonderful help received from this department in time, money and good advice.

My father wrote to the immigration authorities in Glasgow, asking for particulars of the Scheme. These were immediately forthcoming and we decided to apply for permission to participate. We were then interviewed by James L. Malcolm, chief of Canadian immigration in Scotland, and after passing a stiff medical examination were accepted as suitable settlers and sailed for Canada in the spring of 1928.[85]

Also in 1928 – and under the 3,000 Families Scheme but from the other end of Scotland – Daniel and Mary Campbell emigrated with their two children from Caithness to Alberta, sailing on the SS *Montclare* from Greenock. On arriving at Calgary they were met not only by a Land Settlement Board official but also by representatives from the Anglican Church and voluntary organizations. Their farm lay fifty miles further north, twelve miles from the town of Olds, where the first person they encountered was Aberdonian hotel clerk Jim Ritchie. Like their Scottish neighbours, the Elliotts, the Campbells had come to Canada 'because they felt the prospects for a better future for their children were here, rather than in the old land',[86] and they were soon impressed both by the widespread neighbourly kindness and by the paternalistic care shown to them by the LSB. Local representative Alec Findlater accompanied them to their somewhat dilapidated farmhouse and arranged their acquisition of stock, while his Calgary headquarters made sure that the family received Christmas gifts as well as pamphlets of practical information. After a year Mary was realistic, but cautiously optimistic, about the family's prospects on a farm where they were to remain for thirteen years.

> Was it worthwhile? This leaving behind of the old life and all that it meant to us, to venture into something entirely new and different? We did not realise, not in any shape or form, how entirely different this new life was going to be ... . However, we are not unhappy here, but it is too early to say that it was all worthwhile, but we will make it worthwhile if we live long enough. We are learning – we hope – the customs and the life-style of our good and kind neighbours, and we have achieved success with some of our efforts ... . We do feel that we have been accepted as members of this community, but we know that we have much more learning and living to do before we can truly say that yes, it has been worthwhile![87]

On the other side of Canada several recruits to the New Brunswick 500 Families Scheme spoke equally positively of the care shown by land settlement officials. William Forbes was grateful for the 'splendid chance ... of making a home for ourselves – a chance we would never get in the Old Country'; and the only regret expressed by another correspondent of the *Scottish Farmer* was that he had not emigrated forty years earlier to 'a great country for farmers with good experience and little capital' where those who did not succeed under the SSB had only themselves to blame.[88] John Jackson, a tenant farmer from Lesmahagow, wrote to the Canadian government agent in Glasgow five months after his arrival in New Brunswick in 1931:

> I have been very lucky regarding the farm that they have given me. It is in the best of condition … . We were met at Halifax by the Settlement official, and he arranged everything for us and got my things checked through the Customs right away. When we arrived at St John, Mr Scott met us, and got us out right away on the last part of our train journey, and we were met at our final station by Mr Gamblin, who arranged for us to stay at the hotel all night, as he thought that the river was rather rough and cold for late crossing. We crossed in the morning, and were in our new homes about 9 o'clock that morning, about 36 hours from landing at Halifax. The place had been standing empty for about one year, as the people who were in it both died suddenly. It is a lovely place, about 250 or 300 acres, with about 120 cleared, and the rest with good saw logs coming along.[89]

But endorsement of Canadian land settlement was not universal. Attention has already been drawn to the Canadian Immigration Department's questionable allegations about the extent of Scottish family settlement business and a general reluctance among Scottish emigrants to become embroiled in potentially debt-ridden and bureaucratic colonization schemes.[90] Perhaps a lack of concrete information deterred some agriculturists, for in 1924 Anne MacDonald appealed unsuccessfully for more detailed information with which to answer her clients' questions, particularly about the location of schools, churches, creameries and water supplies, as well as the size of houses, cultivated acreages and timbered lands on the farms.[91] In 1926 the Aberdeen agent noted that, in his area, 'The Family Placement Scheme, owing to its disadvantage of applicants having to wait a long period of time before they can be accepted, has not proven a favourite choice among the families intending to migrate.'[92] Others may have been discouraged by occasional items of negative correspondence, such as the attacks that were made in the *Scottish Farmer*'s letter columns on the efficacy of soldier settlement schemes. In 1925 and 1928 female correspondents wrote of hardship, loneliness and exploitation under a scheme that was 'too good to be true'. According to the later correspondent (an emigrant of seventeen years' standing) it was a mistake to give apprentice settlers start-up loans with easy terms of repayment since 'the emigrant can lose money much easier than he can make it in the early years' and would build a better foundation for his settlement if he started with nothing.[93]

Most of the negative publicity surrounding Canadian farming settlement arose not from family colonization schemes but from the badly organized recruitment of British harvesters in 1923 and, more particularly, in 1928.[94] This may well have been because the vast majority of those recruits who, before the winter, found themselves destitute and often subject to deportation were not trained agriculturists with marketable skills but redundant artisans, tradesmen and labourers who had jumped out of the frying pan of British depression into the fire of short-term Canadian employment. Although the *Scottish Journal of Agriculture* claimed that a higher proportion of emigrants came from farming than from any other occupation between 1924 and 1926, statistics presented to Parliament in 1923 showed that absolute numbers were greater in respect of skilled tradesmen, 13,537 of whom emigrated between 1 April 1922 and 31 March 1923, compared with 2,393 from agricultural occupations.[95] That so many of them became agriculturists overseas was probably a reflection of necessity rather than desire, in that the choice was made to benefit from the financial assistance which was confined largely to farming ventures, but it is not surprising that these often unsuitable, ill-prepared emigrants should have been disproportionately represented among the flotsam and jetsam of Canada's cities when hard times came. Despite the rural orientation of schemes promoted under the ESA and the preponderant publicity given to farming opportunities, most Scottish emigrants were town-bred, and their experiences demand closer attention than they have hitherto received.

The urban-industrial emigrant

It is hardly surprising that Scottish emigration between the wars was primarily an urban phenomenon. Well before 1918 Scotland had become one of the most highly urbanized countries in Europe, with four-fifths of the population resident in the industrial central belt, and that area of demographic concentration was also the area worst affected by the post-war depression. Labourers, tradesmen, skilled artisans, women workers and representatives of a variety of professions were all susceptible to the lure of better opportunities overseas, and either invested their own savings in emigration or took advantage of one of the colonization schemes mounted under the ESA, even if the latter sometimes meant that the recruits' skills were ill-matched to colonial needs.

Although frequently ignored and rarely advocated in contemporary emigration propaganda, the evidence for a non-agricultural exodus from Scotland is widespread and convincing. In addition to frequent press references, passenger statistics included in a sample of the Board of Trade's shipping returns reveal an overwhelming preponderance of both skilled tradesmen and central belt addresses among those who left Glasgow for Quebec, Montreal, St John and New York during the 1920s. Most of the 335 passengers who left Glasgow for New York on the SS *Assyria* on 5 April

1923 were young single adults, 113 of whom were travelling steerage, with 222 in the cabin. With the exception of one farmer, one farm worker and four fishermen, three of whom came from Golspie, they were all artisans, labourers or professional people, with engineers, joiners and miners predominating. The most common places of origin were Glasgow and its environs (150 emigrants), with Ayrshire, West Lothian and Edinburgh also prominent, and a smattering of emigrants from Dundee, Fife, Angus, Aberdeenshire, Inverness and Peebles. The contribution of the urban central belt was even more evident among the 1,102 passengers on the SS *Tuscania*, which left Glasgow for New York on 21 April, and a similar pattern emerged among the 1,436 passengers aboard the RMS (Royal Mail Steamer) *California*, New York-bound from Glasgow, on 25 August 1923. Slightly more variety of origins was evident among the 177 passengers who embarked on the SS *Marloch* at Glasgow on 14 April 1923, before it made its way to Lochboisdale, and a greater variety still among the 1,134 passengers who sailed from Glasgow to Stornoway with the *Metagama* a week later. Included among the *Marloch*'s passengers were emigrants from the rural and coastal northeast, upland Perthshire and Shetland, as well as the dominant Glasgow conurbation, and the *Metagama* transported a smattering of emigrants from almost every Scottish county, including a few from the eastern and western Borders, Kintyre, Orkney, Caithness and Sutherland. Twenty-three individuals or families on the *Marloch*, and 124 on the *Metagama*, intended to settle in the United States, all but one farm worker from Turriff in that group belonging to trades, professions or the unskilled labour force. Although 39 agriculturists were represented among the 1,311 Canada-bound Scottish passengers on the two liners, the fact that many of these individuals had urban addresses suggests that farming was their intended pursuit rather than their most recent occupation, and, as on the New York-bound liners, the vast majority of passengers represented urban occupations.[96]

A sample of Glasgow's transatlantic passenger lists six years later reveals a similar pattern. The Canadian Pacific liner *Duchess of York*, which left for Quebec and Montreal on 18 May 1929, carried a total of 461 passengers, and although the vast majority came from urban occupations and locations in the west-central belt, the list also included farming families from Insch in Aberdeenshire, Creetown in Kirkcudbright and Beattock in Dumfriesshire, as well as individual farmers from Montrose, Tillycoultry, Bathgate, Armadale, Stirling, Fraserburgh, Dumfries, Pitlochry, St Boswells, Edinburgh, Dundee and Glasgow, several of them with urban addresses. Archibald Campbell, who was described as a rancher from Portree in Skye, was one of the *Duchess of York*'s seven highland and island emigrants, who also included a Stronsay fisherman, a Cromarty accountant, a Dingwall engineer and a waiter from Inverness. There was only one highlander, however – a woman from Inverness – among the 522 passengers on the RMS *Cameronia*, which left Glasgow for New York on 25 May 1929, and none at all among the 82 passengers on the SS *Albertic*, which left for Boston and New York the following day, both vessels carrying mainly tradesmen, labourers and domestics from central Scotland.[97]

Emigrant departures from the port of Leith were negligible, but, as in the nineteenth century, a significant number of Scottish emigrants embarked at Liverpool. Twenty-seven of the 308 passengers on the White Star liner *Cedric*, which sailed from Liverpool to New York in January 1923, were Scots, as were 16 passengers on the *Montclare*, from the same port to St John, New Brunswick, the following month. And of the 280 passengers on board the SS *Montrose*, which sailed from Liverpool to Quebec and Montreal on 29 October 1927, 148 were Scots, only four of whom were agriculturists.[98] Artisan occupations and central belt origins were equally prominent among emigrants to the Antipodes, but they seem to have been slightly less significant among Scottish passengers to South Africa, which always attracted a significant proportion of affluent emigrants. The *Grandtully Castle*, for instance, which sailed from London to Beira via the Cape on 29 March 1923, numbered 24 Scots among its 169 passengers, while the *Walmer Castle*, which left Southampton for South Africa on 11 May 1923, included 12 Scots in a complement of 149. In both cases the passengers came from various locations, including Argyll, Aberdeen, Buckie and Inverness, as well as the Glasgow and Edinburgh areas, and represented a range of occupations including the law, the civil service, medicine, the priesthood, dressmaking and planting, as well as familiar trades such as mining, engineering and shipbuilding. Colliers, skilled tradesmen and labourers were much more prominent in Australian passenger lists. Several appeared among 75 Scots included in the 743 passengers who sailed on the *Jervis Bay* from London to Australia on 30 January 1923, and among 204 Scots included in the 846 passengers aboard the *Themistocles*, which left London for Australia the following day. Although most came from the environs of Glasgow and Edinburgh, north-east Scotland and the eastern highlands were also represented among the emigrants, and one family came from Selkirk. The SS *Athenic*, however, which sailed from Southampton to New Zealand on 31 May 1923, included 100 Scots representing a variety of locations and jobs among its 461 passengers – for, alongside the Glasgow shipyard workers, Fife miners and other central belt artisans, shopkeepers and domestics, we also find farmers from Stornoway, Inverness, northeast and southwest Scotland, a ploughman from Campbeltown and a tailor from Selkirk.[99]

Indirect evidence of artisan emigration is found in applications made to parish councils for relief, particularly by elderly indigents whose children were following a variety of occupations overseas, a significant number of them in the motor industry in Detroit. Some poor law registers also demonstrate the link between industrial hardship and emigration, particularly among female applicants whose husbands had gone overseas in search of work. Christina Strachan's husband, who had worked in Toronto for nine years before the war, returned there in 1924 after an unsuccessful attempt to work as a jobbing shoemaker in Fraserburgh. He left his wife and three children behind in the hope that he would find work as a french polisher and make enough money to bring them out, but in the meantime his wife was forced to apply for parish relief.[100] Two years later Agnes Penny came on to the Fraserburgh roll because her husband, who had gone to Detroit four years earlier 'and has sent her regular remittances all that time until 5 or 6 weeks ago ... has only been occasionally employed during the past 3 or 4 months'.[101] At the other end of the country, in Wigtonshire, Jane Wilson of Inch was given intermittent parish relief during the 1920s, when her estranged husband in Winnipeg failed to support her and their three children, while Isabella Neville of the same parish was added to the roll in 1927 because the erratic earnings and remittances of her husband in Montreal could not support the family.[102] Emigrants sometimes returned home as paupers after experiencing hardship or unemployment. Hawker Harriet Williamson claimed relief at Kingussie in 1921 after spending ten years in Canada;[103] baker James Noble, who 'has been in America since June 1923, but was not successful there', applied to Fraserburgh in November 1925, two weeks after returning from New York;[104] and Isabella Birnie, five of whose six children were scattered throughout Canada and the United States, applied to Rathen Parish Council in 1927 after returning from Winnipeg, where her husband had died nine years earlier.[105] By the late 1920s, as unemployment worsened, some parish councils became directly involved in assisting emigration. Records reveal both applications by would-be emigrants for help with fares, clothing and subsistence – often to allow them to participate in subsidized Canadian colonization schemes operated by the Salvation Army, the Hudson's Bay Company and the British labour exchanges – and deliberations in parish council meetings, at least in Edinburgh, about the viability of such schemes.[106]

Initially, emigrationists on both sides of the Atlantic were confident that artisans and labourers could be trained to be successful colonial farmers. In 1928 a correspondent of the *Scottish Farmer* in British Columbia notified readers of a written farm training course offered by the CNR, and he disparaged those who were 'content to live on their unemployment insurance benefits' just because they knew nothing about Canadian farming.[107] When the following year the Canadian Immigration Department published a pamphlet featuring prize essays written by successful settlers under the 3,000 Families Scheme, it claimed the publication's 'outstanding feature ... is that the writers were settlers from all manner of occupations in the mother country, and that many had had no previous experience on the land before they went out, but, by working for farmers at a wage for a year or two, they soon learned enough of farm work to be able to take on farms of their own'.[108] One of the Scottish essayists, already quoted, who belonged to a Lanarkshire mining family that had used up most of its savings during the General Strike, foresaw high unemployment and no alternative openings at home after the strike was over.[109] Another had previously been a railway carter at Portsoy in Banffshire, who, fluctuating between intermittent work and the dole, 'couldn't get enough money to feed and clothe my wife and seven of a family'. Having been located on a farm at Delburne, Alberta, under an assiduous supervisor, he recommended confidently: 'I have had experience of city life, but there's nothing to beat this life, so City dwellers, if you want to know what a real happy life is come to the prairie. Any working man with a family should be here, for you will all get employment.'[110]

Reassured by such glowing accounts, and conscious of the ever-growing pool of redundant industrial workers in Britain, the Ministry of Labour became less vigilant in the selection and training of emigrants. As a result the ESA was brought into considerable disrepute on both sides of the Atlantic, accelerating the premature demise of the 3,000 Families Scheme and other smaller land-settlement projects, and leaving a legacy of bitterness and recrimination that afflicted emigrants, sponsors and commentators alike. Even by 1928 Canada was perceived as a receptacle for Britain's dole queues, and there was strong Canadian opposition to the Ministry of Labour's proposal to negotiate cheap fares and loans to send 10,000 unemployed British miners to help bring in the prairie harvest in the hope that they might find permanent work. In the event, 8,500 of the 25,000 applicants were recruited, 6,876 of whom returned home – many of them at the expense of the British government when the Canadians refused to accept responsibility for unemployed 'harvesters'.[111] There was similar disillusionment the following year among town-bred migrants who were recruited by the Ministry of Labour and assisted to go to Canada after a brief preliminary farm training at government centres at Brandon in Suffolk or on the Lamfrits estate at Carstairs in Lanarkshire. While the Canadians justified their decision to deport large numbers on the grounds that recruits either refused farm work or were physically or temperamentally unsuited to it, the migrants complained of insecure employment at inadequate wages, farmers reneging on contracts and victimization of those who had taken the short four-week preparatory course rather than the longer, twelve-week training.

Neither migrant disgruntlement nor increasing Canadian antagonism deterred the British government from negotiating a reduced £10 fare for all British subjects in December 1928 and sending Employment Minister

J. H. Thomas to Ottawa eight months later in an attempt to reinvigorate assisted settlement schemes through an extension of the Ministry of Labour training scheme. Under the agreement arranged by Thomas, Canada was to guarantee farm employment in spring 1930 for 3,000 British recruits aged between 19 and 35 after their three months' training and passage had been funded by the British government, but, although £1,500 was spent on publicity, only just over 500 suitable men came forward, and the scheme foundered on the rocks of press criticism and international depression. Commentators on both sides of the Atlantic reminded readers of the harvesters' fiasco, the hardships of the 1929 drought and poor harvest, the lack of winter work, and the resulting stream of return migrants and deportees – with Canadian correspondents in particular attacking the 'utter failure' of an assisted immigration policy that threatened to bring civil unrest to the Dominion's cities.[112]

The consequence of such an unremitting barrage of negative publicity was to paint a picture of the late 1920s as one of the lowest and most ignominious points in the history of assisted colonization between the wars.[113] Unfortunately, it was an ignominy in which Scottish migrants seem to have played a particularly inglorious part. While several inadequately funded Glasgow Parish Council recruits became an immediate charge on the Canadian public purse, Scots who emigrated under the Ministry of Labour training schemes were branded as workshy troublemakers on both sides of the Atlantic. In October 1929 the manager of the Kirkintilloch employment exchange, having investigated the circumstances behind the recent deportation of four promising migrants, initially concluded that their failure was due to the poor harvest forcing down wages to an unacceptable level. But when his report was transmitted to the Ministry of Labour's London office, the interpretation was less charitable.

> The statement, of course, takes us down to the root of the whole trouble which is that our trainees, being drawn from industrial areas and being quite ignorant of the different kind of atmosphere in which farming is carried on, go out with all kinds of ideas about Trade Union rates of wages and hours of work. Rather than sacrifice their pre-conceived ideas they throw up perfectly good jobs which, with the exercise of a little patience, might well provide them with a secure and independent future.[114]

That view was corroborated in Canada by W. Duncan, LSB superintendent at Prince Albert, Saskatchewan, who in November 1929 dealt with nine Scots at North Battleford who wished to be deported unless they were paid $25 a month for winter farm work, for which they were totally unqualified. Duncan was 'sorry to see this kind brought out', youths whose training had not fitted them to command the high wages they had expected, who found fault 'very freely' with the farmers for whom they worked and 'who have clearly in their minds that they can go on the dole if work is not available in the Old Country'.[115] A month later Thomas Gelley's report on the season's Ministry of Labour trainees identified particular problems with Carstairs-trained recruits from Glasgow, Greenock and Dundee, 'many of whom appeared to hold "Socialistic" views, with little intention of working after arrival in Canada, in fact, gave the impression it was only a trip they wanted'.[116] Of the 576 applicants for Ministry of Labour training interviewed at the Canadian government emigration agency in Glasgow between 1 October 1928 and 28 February 1929, 225 were accepted and 351 rejected, a 61 per cent failure rate surpassed only by the Liverpool and York offices, which were also the only two agencies to receive more applications than Glasgow;[117] and although most of the unsatisfactory settlers deported by Canada during 1929 came from England, Scotland occupied second place with 516 deportees.[118]

But not all emigration from urban Scotland was a flight of alleged paupers, misfits or troublemakers who might have to be returned home. The skilled artisans, tradesmen and labourers who crowded on to the transatlantic liners at Greenock may have been anxious to escape the fact or fear of unemployment in Scotland, but that did not mean they were penniless, irresponsible or unadaptable. Trustee Savings Bank (Scotland) records for Nairn, Galashiels, Glasgow, Greenock and Paisley suggest that emigration was a recognized and accepted resort of the provident. While in Nairn and Galashiels emigration of depositors was mentioned in passing as a reason for withdrawals and the closure of accounts, when depression hit west-central Scotland the resulting exodus of careful depositors was highlighted – and commended – in at least three branch annual reports in 1923–24. The habit of thrift encouraged by the Greenock Provident Bank had permitted emigration of hard-pressed depositors 'when the emergency arose in their lives', while in Paisley 'a great many of their best young people found it possible to launch forth into new lands and new life just because they had acquired the habit of thrift, and had a certain deposit in the Savings Bank'. At the same time in Glasgow, reported the Lord Provost, 'numbers of the best class of their artisans had withdrawn their deposits in order to assist them to emigrate. They did not want to lose these artisans, but it was gratifying that the means accumulated in the Bank had enabled these people to seek their fortune in lands across the sea.'[119] Although some dominion emigrants might regard the availability of empire settlement funding as a welcome supplement to their own savings, others preferred to be completely independent, but for the significant contingent that went to the United States – particularly from central Scotland – such aid was irrelevant, and they had no choice but to finance their own emigration or have it funded by a sponsor in America who could guarantee that they would not become a burden on the state.

The oral history project undertaken by the US National Parks Service in respect of immigrants who passed through Ellis Island quarantine station on their way into the country reveals something of the motives and experiences of Scottish settlers. The archive currently contains twenty interviews with Scots who arrived before the Second World War, the earliest in 1902 and 1913, and eighteen during the 1920s. All but one of the eleven females and nine males in the survey came from the central belt – the vast majority from Glasgow – and all but four emigrated as children, either accompanying their parents or following them out to destinations which were mainly in the eastern seaboard states, where they took up urban or industrial employment. Eleven interviewees recalled that their fathers had initially gone to America alone, remitting money home until they had secured steady employment and could afford to sponsor the emigration of the rest of the family. But while most of the child migrants crossed the Atlantic under the supervision of one or both parents, two travelled alone. In 1920 seven-year-old orphan Margaret Cook from Chirnside in Berwick-shire left her younger brother, grandparents and aunts to join an uncle and aunt in Maine after her mother died in the 1919 influenza epidemic, while Thomas Allan (9) and his seven-year-old brother left the care of their grandmother and aunts in Tillycoultry in 1927 to join their father, who had emigrated to Nebraska some years earlier after the death of his wife.[120] Five emigrants settled in Scottish enclaves. Margaret Cook's first home in Maine was in an area where Scottish settlers – including some from her Berwickshire homeland – had built 'a tremendous number of paper mills', while the steel-making town of Gary, Indiana, had, according to Helen Hansen, a 'regular Scotch colony' on its eastern side. Maisie Pedersen, who worked for a Scottish sea captain and his wife in Brooklyn, recalled that the suburb contained a 'big Scottish population ... from different parts of Scotland', while both Anne Quinn and Isabella Rohan settled in textile communities in Carnie, New Jersey, and Ludlow, Massachusetts, respec-tively, which recruited large numbers of emigrants from parent firms in Paisley and Dundee.[121]

In most cases the stimulus to emigrate was provided by family or friends who were already in America or were planning to settle there, which itself was probably a consequence of the American requirement for contacts, sponsors and financial guarantees. Isabella Rohan from Dundee arrived in Springfield, Massachusetts, in 1913, at the age of nine, accompanied by her mother and sister. They joined her father, who had emigrated the previous year, and an aunt and uncle, who had arrived six months before that, the fares being paid either by her father or her aunt. The first of Patrick Peak's family to emigrate was his sister Mary, who left Glasgow in 1920 to join an uncle and aunt who had emigrated three years earlier. She was joined six months later by another sister and brother, and shortly afterwards by another brother and their father, before the mother and the remaining five brothers and sisters completed the family transfer to Connecticut. David Saltman, who emigrated with his mother and five siblings in 1922, was untypical. His parents were Jewish refugees from central Europe who had sojourned in Glasgow for almost twenty years before moving to New York. As Saltman recalled, 'My father always suffered from asthma, and it was very damp there, and he was thinking of between coming [sic] to the United States or going to South Africa. He preferred South Africa, but my mother had relatives in the United States, in the New York area, so we came to the United States ... . My father came with my oldest sister, as a visitor, to see how he would like it, and he stayed with relatives in Staten Island ... and my mother followed with the other five children later.'[122]

Also in 1922, nineteen-year-old miner Joseph Delaney left Glasgow for Pennsylvania in a family party of seven, the fares being paid by his two step-uncles, who had sponsored his stepfather's emigration eighteen months earlier and had arranged employment for Joseph in a rope factory. The following year eighteen-year-old Mary Dunn left Stirling alone, also to join relatives in Pennsylvania, while in 1924 Maisie Pedersen (18) from Greenock followed an ex-schoolfriend to New York, and was followed in turn by two of her sisters. In 1925 Allan Gunn emigrated with his mother and brother from Dennistoun, Glasgow, to New York to be reunited with his father, a boilermaker and crane operator, who had gone to America almost three years earlier as a result of encouragement from a former neighbour who 'used to write and tell how nice it was here [and] had a job lined up for my father if he was interested'. Lillian Hopkins also emigrated with her mother and sister in 1925, aged nine, two years after her father – a shipyard electrician who had moved from London to Clydebank in search of work – had been persuaded to accompany some friends to Pittsburgh, where he worked first on the railway and then in a bank. Mary Kendrick's father emigrated a year ahead of the rest of the family in response to encouragement from cousins already in the United States, and by the time he was joined by his wife and three children in 1927 he had found a job as a crane operator in Utica, New York. William McGuire's coalminer father was sponsored by a sister and brother-in-law to go from Blantyre to Columbus, Ohio, where he worked as a landscape gardener, being joined first by his wife, who came back to Scotland eighteen months later, in 1928, to collect their three children. Also in 1928, Anne Quinn (10) emigrated from Paisley to New Jersey with her parents and youngest brother, sponsored by her eldest brother, who had been in the country for six years with the rest of the family. Her mother's brother, a judge in Kansas City, had used his influence to gain entry for them since Anne's father had been partially disabled by a stroke in 1922, and the American authorities on both sides of the Atlantic were initially unwilling to allow him in.[123]

Virtually every interviewee claimed that they, or their parents, had come to the United States in pursuit of better opportunities. Agnes Schilling from Motherwell, who persuaded her parents to let her go to New Jersey alone in 1922 at the age of fifteen, was caught up in the post-war mania for America:

> My whole idea was to get to the United States, and that I could work when I got here and help to bring my family eventually, each one would come over, because there were many people migrating, so I was very insistent, and of course, much to my parents' dislike, they were afraid to let me go at that young age. I had no relatives in America, no relatives whatsoever, but we did have neighbours who had young girls working in a factory making good money and I thought I could get work – get a job and work and send money home to my parents. So after lots of red tape, it wasn't easy for me to convince my parents, my family, everybody, that I was capable of going over and taking care of myself, but I was determined, and no matter what obstacle came up I always found a way out of it. So I finally got my way.[124]

As she had anticipated, Agnes was soon joined by her brother, followed by a sister, three other members of her family within a year and, eventually, by her parents. After working in service initially, Agnes went into business, managing a successful boutique and dress shop.

Equally adventurous was Glaswegian Margaret Kirk, who waited two years for a visa and had to recruit a sponsor before going to New York in 1923 at the age of twenty-two. Thwarted by lack of finance in her ambition to be a doctor, she too was caught up in the post-war enthusiasm for America.

> There was loads of work while the war was on. Shipyards were booming. As soon as the war was finished, everybody was getting laid off. There was depression in the country, and everybody wanted to come to America. Everybody was putting in to get to America, to go to Canada, anywhere, so that that was when everybody came to America, 1918. The men came over to America first, and then they brought their families over, you see, so that it was – that's why so many people came from Scotland, because of the depression. There was nothing, there was no work, so they were gasping for a job. And America sent out signals that everything was wonderful here, so they came to America, and that's why they all came.[125]

Caught up in the same enthusiasm in 1923 was Mary Dunn, who emigrated 'to better myself' after working as a milliner's message girl in Scotland,[126] while John Will, who went from Cupar in Fife to Los Angeles at the age of seven, explained how the family's emigration was precipitated by the decline of his father's coachbuilding business in the uncertain post-war economic climate, and emphasized that by no means all who were detained at Ellis Island were impecunious refugees. The business had been purchased before the war with money his father had earned during a five-year sojourn in South Africa in the 1890s, so it was not entirely surprising when he decided to invest in America in 1924, sponsored by his wife's second cousin:

> he tried to bring his business back but the economic conditions as a result of World War I in Scotland were very very poor. The farmers were not making any money, and if they had a broken down wagon they didn't have any money to fix it, or they'd bring it in and he'd fix it and put it on the books. They were not buying hardly anything new. So, he kept trying to bring his business back but was not successful in that, and he was going broke. And also he had a secondary condition, thought in mind, and that was the education of his five kids. Scots people traditionally are very educational minded. They shove and push for better schools and better education. So, remembering his time in South Africa, – and he was a prolific reader, he had read a lot about California, the orange groves, the climate, land of opportunity, and all the things you hear about ... he decided that we should emigrate to Southern California. In this transition he auctioned off his shop and all the equipment. He auctioned off our home and then we were ready to go but there was a problem with the quota system. As I get the story from my folks, they had thought that they had the seven quota numbers necessary for the family to travel together, but when they came through only four came through, so this caused a big debate between my father and mother. My mother wanted my father to take the three oldest children and go, and she would wait for the additional quotas some time in the future. He didn't want to do that, so we ended up by being parked in a little town called Gourock, on the beach front, waiting for additional quota numbers, and that took several months before we got them. And we finally got them and the seven of us left from Liverpool on the ship *Baltic* for New York. The primary reason for emigrating was lousy economic conditions and it didn't look like very much opportunity for his kids, and he brought us all here. I might add, without trying to be too egotistical, that all my brothers and sisters did very well in our new country.[127]

For Anne Quinn's mother, coming to America in 1928 was the fulfilment of a long-held ambition to settle in the 'land of opportunity', while Joseph Daly recalled the image of the United States as a 'panacea country', where his father – a miner and IRA terrorist who had fled to Dumbarton in the early 1920s when being hunted by the Black and Tans – could find work.[128] The Dalys arrived in New York not long before the Wall Street crash, but some of those who arrived in earlier years were also disappointed in their expectations. Margaret Cook's unhappiness stemmed from parting with her younger brother and going to an aunt and uncle who neglected her physical and mental wellbeing, using her as an unpaid maidservant, while Mary Dunn's experience of hostile officials at Ellis Island brought into question the image of America as a welcoming land of opportunity.[129] Not surprisingly, though, most interviewees expressed satisfaction with their lot, and their stories serve as a further reminder both that urban Scotland's inter-war emigrants could be enterprising and ambitious and that they were not completely confined to ESA-funded opportunities in the dominions.

The female emigrant

Three of the Ellis Island interviewees had gone to the United States as young, single women in search of better opportunities. The foundations of systematic single female emigration had been laid in the half-century before 1914, when a variety of national and provincial societies emerged to orchestrate the redistribution of selected women within the empire in the hope of reducing the chronic female surplus in Britain while at the same time implanting a 'hallowing influence' in the male-dominated colonies.[130] Domestic servants in particular were bombarded with propaganda assuring them of 'high wages, good homes [and a] healthy climate',[131] although the influence of the eugenics movement and an upsurge of imperialistic sentiment in the early 1900s led to increasingly strenuous efforts to recruit 'distressed gentlewomen' as well as working-class girls. Over 22,000 women emigrated under the auspices of charitable societies in the thirty years from 1884 to 1914, while many more who did not belong to any society simply booked their passages through ticket agents, taking advantage of the assisted passages offered by Canada, Australia, New Zealand and South Africa.

After the war, the establishment of the Society for the Overseas Settlement of British Women (SOSBW) in 1919 marked the British government's commitment to female emigration as an integral part of its new empire settlement strategy. Created as the women's branch of the Overseas Settlement Office, the SOSBW incorporated the three leading pre-war female emigration societies and was awarded an annual grant of £5,000 to promote and direct women's emigration in conjunction with the dominions. In the event, just under 100,000 single women were assisted through empire settlement funding,[132] a figure that fell far short of the OSC's expectations and underlined the long-standing incompatibility between British supply and dominion demand. While from the British perspective pre-war arguments were reinforced by the desire to redeploy town-bred women who had gained experience and confidence through war work, the dominions were interested only in a continuing supply of cheap but capable domestics – not displaced urban-industrial workers who threatened to dislocate their vulnerable, agriculturally-based economies. Their reluctance to share the funding of training homes in Britain severely curtailed the OSC's ambitions, which were further eroded by the increasing distaste for domestic service among female emigrants. A jointly funded domestics' training home at

Market Harborough, opened in 1927, produced only 564 recruits for Australia, while four 8-week training courses run by the Ministry of Labour with a 25 per cent funding input from the Canadian government produced only 507 former factory and shopworkers from their centres in London, Newcastle, Cardiff and Glasgow in the two years from autumn 1928 until all the dominions withdrew assisted passages for domestics by the end of 1930.

Yet opportunities for household workers were relatively well advertised and patronized in Scotland throughout the 1920s. Urban booking agents who found it difficult to recruit agricultural workers capitalized on the insatiable colonial demand for domestic servants – who, both before and after the war, also carried a bonus payment – and itinerant recruiters regularly visited Scotland. New Zealand and Australia in particular often sent special female representatives to booking agencies to interview and select applicants for free and assisted passages, including Miss M. E. Hanlon, who in 1923 visited Scotland in the course of a nationwide campaign to add to the 1,500 domestic servants she had recruited for New Zealand since the war. In an interview with the *Press & Journal* she claimed that the calibre of Aberdeen girls was superior to their counterparts in Dundee, and she outlined the conditions under which they could obtain free, super-vised passages from Southampton and assistance in obtaining 'suitable posts in good households'. Four months later another New Zealand official spent two days interviewing girls at R. & J. Davidson's agency in Aberdeen, and Mackay Brothers regularly played host to female recruitment agents from Australia.[133]

At times female agents were licensed directly by the steamship com-panies to promote transatlantic emigration. Included in that category were Mrs Sanford, matron of the Winnipeg Girls' Home of Welcome, Mrs Radford and Mrs Francis from similar institutions in Montreal, and Miss Duff from Ontario, all of whom visited Scotland periodically to recruit parties of domestics on prepaid tickets. Both the Canadian government and the railway companies also expanded their agency organization to take account of the vibrant post-war market for female emigrants. The dominion immigration authorities were particularly concerned that recruits should be monitored, reminding booking agents in 1919 of the requirement to book unaccompanied females on ships that carried Canadian government conductresses. Women officers at the Canadian end oversaw the girls' medical and civil inspection, reunited them with their baggage and made arrangements for their onward journey. Beginning in 1920 with Liverpool, Glasgow and London, women officers were ultimately appointed to eight regional offices to supervise the selection of domestic servants and arrange-ments on board ship. The Glasgow representative, Miss Taylor, was kept particularly busy – notably after the £3 passage led to an intensified drive to obtain domestics – and in 1928 the chief Glasgow agent observed that Scottish women emigrants were more ambitious than their male counterparts.[134] According to the Dominion Office in 1929, Scots accounted for 1,355 of the 1,763 domestic servants recruited for Canada between 1 January and 30 September, a statistic which perhaps explains Miss Taylor's retention of her post in 1932 after the decline in emigration had resulted in six other female officers being retired.[135]

The emigration of domestic servants from urban areas was also facilitated by the Scottish Council for Women's Trades. In addition to finding home-based farm and domestic placements for those on unemployment benefit or parish relief, it operated an emigration scheme under the ESA, which it regarded as 'specially helpful to unemployed factory girls'. After undergoing six months' training on farms or in country manses, trainees were encouraged to apply to emigrate to Australia or, more commonly, Canada. In June 1929, reviewing a year that had seen fifty-two successful emigrants, the Council's secretary, Miss M. H. Irwin, commended the training scheme because it 'enables them to take good posts when they go overseas, and the general improvement in their health effected by the wholesome food and fresh country air enables them to pass the medical examination required by the emigration authorities, which many of them might otherwise be unable to do'.[136]

Systematic quantitative evidence of single female emigration from urban Scotland is found in Board of Trade shipping records – particularly for Canada-bound vessels, whose women passengers included not only domestics but also nurses, cooks, bookbinders, typists, weavers and hotelkeepers.[137] A significant amount of female emigration was also orchestrated by the Canadian railway companies so that unaccompanied females could travel in protected parties. In 1924 the CPR established a women's branch in London with a travelling female inspector, Mrs Waite, who in 1925, 1926 and 1927 used the offices of Mackay Brothers in Aberdeen and Murdo Maclean in Stornoway to recruit domestics for Canada, while Esther Mackie, supervisor of the Women's Branch of the Canadian Pacific Land Settlement and Colonization Service, appeared in Inverness in June 1925 offering to interview not only prospective settlers but also their anxious mothers.[138] The CNR also sent its agent, Miss Durham, to Scotland, and reported in April 1926 that 100 women – 62 English, 22 Scots and 16 Irish – had just left Liverpool, Glasgow and Belfast for Canada under its auspices in the largest such party sent out by the company since the war.[139] CPR records of specific sailing parties, available for 1924–25, indicate that most of the Scottish domestics were recruited from urban areas, particularly in the central belt, although Aberdeen and Inverness were also well represented and a smattering of girls came from Lewis, Easter Ross, Caithness and the Borders. One inmate of the Bonar Bridge poorhouse was assisted to emigrate to Chesley, Ontario, where her former mistress had connections, while others, such as sixty-one-year-old Elizabeth Sweet from Hamilton, whose age rendered her ineligible for assistance, joined a selected party after paying the full fare and showing proof of future employment.[140]

But female emigration was no less controversial in the 1920s than it had been before the war, incurring criticism from parents, the dominion authorities, employers, and the emigrants themselves. As early as 1916, William Ledingham of Glasgow complained to the Colonial Office about the manner in which his daughter and four other impecunious and inexperienced Glasgow girls had been persuaded to go to Canada by Marion Lindsay, an emigrant domestic who, on a visit home, recruited them for established agent Mrs McArthur of the Toronto Domestic Guild. Although Lindsay claimed that Ledingham was more concerned about losing his daughter's weekly board money than her company, the Canadian Emigration Office in London conceded that untrained domestics were unlikely to find work and instructed both its Glasgow agent and the Allan line to warn inexperienced recruits that they would not be allowed to land in Canada.[141] Concern about the dangers of indiscriminate emigration resurfaced after the war. In 1920 Cumnock booking agent James Ballantine complained that inadequate provision for advancing fares to impecunious domestics was preventing him from sending out large numbers of 'splendid girls',[142] and when in 1923 George McFarlane of Glasgow resumed his pre-war practice of assisting houseworker recruits with fares that were subsequently repaid by employers from the emigrants' wages, the Canadian authorities alleged that irresponsible application of that practice would lower the standard of recruitment:

> We get any amount of enquiries from females of every sort, but to none of whom do we guarantee their full passage realising that unless they have some stake in the matter, you are going to get a nondescript crowd no matter how careful the investigation. Does it not appeal to you in this way to a certain extent? Girls should at least have a few pounds interest in their fare besides an equal amount landing money, and if they are well trained and at domestic work, there is no reason why they should not have some small funds.[143]

Although the Canadian Immigration Department was generally willing to leave the selection of domestics to female representatives of the CPR and CNR, friction sometimes arose either when the railway company agents felt their decisions had been overruled or Dominion officials complained that they had been sidelined by the transportation companies dealing directly with receiving homes or giving inadequate notice of the forthcoming arrival of large parties of girls. Following a complaint in 1925 by Miss M. V. Burnham, the Dominion government's superintendent of female immigration, W. R. Little, Director of European Emigration for Canada, berated his colleague J. B. Walker, Canada's Director of British Emigration, for poor business practice. It was inappropriate, he reminded Walker, 'for representatives of transportation companies to be writing to hostels regarding Empire Settlement cases which should be handled direct through your office and through the Department', and when in 1929 Elsie Waite, the CPR's chief female selecting agent, asked for an assurance that her decisions would be rubber-stamped by Dominion officials in Canada, the request was rejected on the grounds that transportation officials were unaccountable.[144] By 1931 the CPR had developed its own arrangements for placing domestics through a woman representative in Montreal, irritating the Dominion authorities not so much because of the recruits' alleged inexperience but because the CPR's policy defied federal advice to transportation companies to discontinue advertising in the face of deteriorating economic conditions. Even though the recruits could pay their fares and possessed landing money, insufficient employment meant they soon ran out of funds, and in June 1931 Dominion Immigration Minister W. Gordon complained to the CPR's Chief Colonization Commissioner that the advice of his department's overseas agents was being undermined 'by persons apparently more interested in the selling of a steamship ticket than in the welfare of intending immigrants or Canada generally'.[145] Six months earlier overseas training at the Ministry of Labour's hostels at Lenzie, Newcastle, Cardiff and London had been suspended, the Canadian authorities complaining that the centres were more interested in tackling unemployment in distressed areas of Britain than in meeting Canada's demand for well-trained, high-class domestic servants.[146]

The sharpest criticism usually came from emigrants and employers who felt they had been misled or defrauded. In 1920 a correspondent of the *Scottish Farmer* complained about the practice of enticing inexperienced girls to New Zealand farms which were nothing more than uncomfortable wood shacks served by virtually non-existent transport facilities.[147] In 1928 Jane Hughes (20), formerly of Windygates, Fife – who six months earlier had gone to a pre-arranged situation at Freeling, South Australia – gave her notice and asked the state immigration authorities for a transfer to a less lonely location 'where there are other maids kept' and where she could work as a housemaid or take care of children.[148] Three years earlier, on 11 September 1925, Elizabeth Wray had left Ibrox, Glasgow, on the *Marburn*, having been recruited by Esther Mackie of the CPR to take up employment as a cook with Justine Calderwood of Barrie, Ontario. On 28 September Mrs Calderwood wrote to the matron of the Canadian Women's Hostel in Toronto complaining both that the girl had been left by a Traveller's Aid representative to spend the whole day in Toronto's Union Station, unaware of the hostel's existence, and, even worse, that she was a liability rather than an asset as an employee:

> On Monday at noon when she came down stairs, much refreshed, I asked whether she would care to wait until the next day to take over the cooking as my old cook is still here and it would be a good chance for her to learn the difference in our ways. 'Cook' she said 'I can't cook anything but the very plain things.' She has now been here a week and the only two things we have found that she knew were tea and porridge – I asked her how she came to engage for this position, her reply was 'When your letter was read I said "but I can't cook" and the lady said "Oh! if you can do anything at all you will do for Canada."'
>
> If she had ever seen the things before we might have done something with her, but at her age 35 it is hopeless. We have tried to show her how to dress and cook a chicken – she said she had once before seen one roasted – but it is impossible. We had a beefsteak and kidney pie, she had never seen such a thing, did not know what the kidney was and had never made pastry. I could go on ad. infinitum but these few samples are sufficient. She is absolutely unacquainted with what seem to us in Canada the ordinary articles of food.
>
> In 25 years of housekeeping many old country women have passed through my household some to marry and settle in homes of their own, others leaving for various reasons. Many I have trained as they had not previously been in housework in Great Britain but never have I encountered a woman as uncouth or hopelessly ignorant as Elizabeth Wray. She is I am sure thoroughly decent and respectable and feels as I do that we have not had a 'square deal'.
>
> I hope you may be able to find her work in an institution or hotel as dish washer or kitchen maid, in a private house she is impossible.[149]

The emigrant training schemes run by the Ministry of Labour and the Scottish Council for Women's Trades recognized that the emigration of working-class females was often provoked by unemployment rather than ambition and aimed to give recruits a better start to their new life than that experienced by Elizabeth Wray. Similar sentiments inspired many of the philanthropists who throughout the 1920s trained and assisted adolescent and young adult males – and some females – to emigrate under the auspices of a variety of charitable organizations that capitalized on the shared funding opportunities made available by the ESA. Voluntary society activity, which is examined in the next chapter, demonstrates continuities and changes in both the theory and practice of aided emigration in the inter-war years and, in particular, allows us to evaluate the effect of state involvement in a sphere of well-established, but hitherto private, assistance. Since the beneficiaries were almost invariably town-bred, it also offers another perspective on the vital but neglected phenomenon of emigration from the urban lowlands.

Notes

1 T. M. Devine (ed.), *Scottish Emigration and Scottish Society* (Edinburgh, Donald, 1992), pp. 3, 9–10, 104. See also Marjory Harper, *Emigration from North-East Scotland, vol. 1, Willing Exiles, vol. 2, Beyond the Broad Atlantic* (Aberdeen, Aberdeen University Press, 1988).

2 James R. Coull, 'The Scottish herring fishery in the inter-war years, 1919–1939: ordeal and retrenchment', *International Journal of Maritime History*, II:1 (June 1990), pp. 55–81.

3 *Ibid.*

4 PP 1919 Cmd 231 XXII 311, Thirty-Seventh Annual Report of the Fishery Board for Scotland, 1918, Appendix I, Post-war Problems. Memorandum by D. T. Jones, RNR, on the re-establishment of the Scottish fishing industry after the war.

5 Coull, 'The Scottish herring fishery', pp. 66, 70.

6 AA, AC6/27/26, Fraserburgh Parish Council, Record of Applications for Poor Relief, 24 Nov. 1921, nos 2 and 4; 4 Dec. 1922, no. 261 (McPhee); 2 Apr. 1923, no. 332 (John Clark).

7 *Ibid.*, 29 Aug. 1924, no. 729; 12 Sept. 1924, no. 751.

8 *Ibid.*, 11 Jan. 1924, no. 546.

9 *Ibid.*, 5 May 1928, no. 654. AC6/27/29, Fraserburgh Parish Council, Record of Applications for Poor Relief, 28 Oct. 1930, no. 673.

10 AC6/27/26, 22 Jan. 1924, no. 556; 31 Mar. 1924, no. 615.

11 PP 1914 Cd 7462 XXXI 733, Report of the Scottish Departmental Committee on the North Sea Fishing Industry, Part II, Minutes of Evidence, question 931, p. 22. See also pp. 37, 50, 90, 109, 171, 128, 429.

12 PP 1923 Cmd 1884 XI 445, Forty-First Annual Report of the Fishery Board for Scotland, 1922.

13 PP 1924 Cmd 2232 IX 615, pp. 10, 64, Forty-Second Annual Report, 1923.

14 See chapter 3, p. 80.

15 SRO, AF51/186, 'Employment of British Fishermen in British Columbia, 1937', note by unnamed civil servant.

16 *Ibid.*, AF62/1965, Emigration of Fishermen and Fishworkers to Newfoundland, James Wood to George Hogarth, 1 Feb. 1926; Robert Spink to Hogarth, 29 Jan. 1926.

17 *Ibid.*, AF61/1961/2, Emigration of Fishermen and Fishworkers, A. Munro to Fishery Board for Scotland, 26 Jan. 1927.

18 *Ibid.*, AF62/1964/4, appendix 3, Employment of British Fishermen in British Columbia, undated memorandum by W. Taylor.

19 *Ibid.*, AF62/1966, Emigration of Fishermen, Settlement of British Fishing Families in Australia.

20 Author's interview with the late Annie Noble and the late Gilbert Buchan at Inverallochy, 16 September 1985.

21 'Scottish immigrants came to Port Dover to fish', *Port Dover Maple Leaf*, 13 July 1988, pp. 6–7.

22 Harry D. Watson, *Kilrenny and Cellardyke: 800 Years of History* (Edinburgh, Donald, 1986), p. 192. I am grateful to Dr Watson for providing me with private correspondence and other information about emigrants from Fife to Port Dover.

23 Richard Perren, *Agriculture in Depression, 1870–1940* (Cambridge, Cambridge University Press, 1995), particularly pp. 37–51.

24 Bill Howatson, review of Angus MacDonald, *The Scottish Farmer, One Hundred Years* (Glasgow, Outram Magazines, 1993), in *P&J*, 21 Dec. 1993.

25 National Register of Archives (Scotland) (NRAS) 1202, SNFU, Banffshire Area, 27 Mar., 13 Nov. 1933. The SNFU had been formed in 1913, five years after its English counterpart, and saw a large increase in membership between the wars. By 1938, when it amalgamated with the Scottish Chamber of Agriculture, membership stood at 12,500.

26 Leneman, *Fit for Heroes?*, particularly pp. 20–52.

27 *Scottish Farm Servant (SFS)*, Oct. 1925, p. 101. See also *SFS*, June 1927, p. 264; Dec. 1927, p. 383.

28 Quoted in *SFS*, Aug. 1927, p. 305.

29 *SFS*, Aug. 1920, p. 96.

30 *SFS*, June 1922, p. 523.

31 *SFS*, June 1924, p. 48; Oct. 1930, pp. 128–9.

32 *SFS*, Apr. 1926, p. 193.

33 See chapter 2, p. 66 and note 9.

34 *SFS*, Feb. 1925, p. 170; Aug. 1925, p. 70. See also NRAS 1177, SNFU, Turriff District minutes, 2 June 1925.

35 *SFS*, Feb. 1926, p. 161.

36 'The Soutar's Shop' in *SFS*, Mar. 1926, p. 178.

37 *SFS*, 1 Apr., p. 383; 8 July, pp. 827–8; 30 Sept. 1922, p. 1192.

38 *SFS*, 20 Jan., p. 64; 3 Feb. 1923, p. 129.

39 *SFS*, 15 Nov. 1924, p. 1432; 28 Mar. 1925, p. 399.

40 *SF*, 6, 27 Mar. 1926, pp. 299, 413.

41 *SFS*, 11 Oct. 1919, p. 997; extract from the *Chilliwack Progress* in *SFS*, 21 Apr. 1923, p. 502; *SFS*, 24 May 1924, p. 669.

42 *SFS*, 16 Aug. 1924, p. 960; 23 Apr. 1927, p. 557; 1 May 1926, p. 592; 4 Sept. 1926, p. 1108.

43 *SFS*, 27 Mar. 1926, p. 430; 12 Nov. 1927, p. 1540; 17 Mar. 1928, p. 352.

44 *SFS*, 20 Sept. 1919, p. 911; 23 Feb. 1929, p. 224.

45 *P&J*, 22 Dec. 1926. See also *P&J*, 2 Nov. 1926, for details of Aberdeenshire emigrants James and Frank Napier. James was the manager of a pure-bred shorthorn herd in Missouri, and Frank was on the editorial staff of the Chicago-based *Breeders' Gazette*.

46 *SF*, 23 Dec. 1922, p. 1584; *P&J*, 8 July 1925.

47 *P&J*, 31 May, 25 June 1924.

48 *SF*, 10 Jan. 1925, p. 31; 24 Jan. 1925, p. 103; *P&J*, 13 Feb. 1926.

49 *P&J*, 15 Oct. 1925; *SF*, 17 Oct. 1925, p. 1347.

50 *P&J*, 26 Dec. 1922.

51 See, for instance, *P&J*, 1 Apr., 6 June 1924; 7, 15 Apr., 21 June 1925.

52 *SF*, 29 Mar. 1924, p. 406; advertisement for shepherds reported retrospectively on 18 Jan. 1930, p. 71. See also *P&J*, 28 Jan. 1924.

53 *SF*, 3 Nov. 1923, p. 1405; 28 Nov. 1928, p. 1567; *P&J*, 3 Jan. 1924.

54 *SF*, 6 Mar. 1926, p. 300; 20 Mar. 1926, p. 374; 24 Apr. 1926, p. 556; 1 May 1926, p. 606.

55 *SF*, 3 Apr. 1926, p. 453.

56 *SF*, 23 Apr. 1927, p. 557; 7 May 1927, p. 633.

57 *SF*, 19 May 1928, p. 656; 2 June 1928, p. 728; 9 June 1928, p. 755; 16 June 1928, p. 787; 23 June 1928, pp. 820–1; 30 June 1928, p. 852; 7 July 1928, pp. 887, 891; 14 July 1928, pp. 923–4.

58 *SF*, 6 Oct. 1923, p. 1273.

59 *P&J*, 6, 20 Sept. 1924. See also *P&J*, 27 Aug., 3, 10, 13, 17, 24 Sept., 1, 10 Oct. 1924.

60 *SF*, 20 Feb. 1926, p. 234, 'Notes from Eastern Canada', by WRJ. See also *SF*, 17 Jan. 1925, p. 74.

61 *SF*, 10 May 1924, pp. 590–1.

62 *P&J*, 26 Mar. 1923.

63 NAC, RG76, C-7396-7, vol. 248, file 179046, part 1, Scheme between British and Canadian governments, settlement of British families on land, 1924–5, undated memorandum (Oct/Nov. 1924).

64 *Ibid.*, confidential circular (ED Circ. 78/47, EDO 443/1924 – EID 14) to Ministry of Labour, Employment and Insurance Department. See also 'Assisted Settlement of Approved British Families on Canadian Government Farms' (Ottawa, NAC pamphlet, 2-5235, 1924).

65 NAC, RG76, C-7396-7, vol. 248, file 179046, part 1, White Star Line and White Star–Dominion Line advertisement for 3,000 Families Scheme.

66 *P&J*, 22 Aug. 1924; *The Scotsman*, 21 Aug. 1924; *Edinburgh Evening Dispatch*, 21 Aug. 1924.

67 *SF*, 14 Feb. 1925, p. 189.

68 *P&J*, 14 June 1924. See also *SF*, 23 Aug. 1924, p. 1062, *P&J*, 25 Feb. 1924, 26 Feb. 1926; *Edinburgh Evening Dispatch*, 23 Aug. 1924.

69 *SF*, 11 Apr. 1925, p. 507.
70 *SF*, 27 Aug. 1927, p. 1174; 7 Mar. 1931, p. 307.
71 *SFS*, 'Family Settlement in New Brunswick', Nov. 1930, p. 145.
72 Queensland State Archives, IMM/300, General Correspondence of the New Settlers' League, William McKinnon to Captain Mapleton, 5 Aug. 1923 (punctuation as in original). See also *ibid.*, Mapleton to McKinnon, 20 Aug. 1923, New Settlers' League memorandum, 29 May 1924.
73 *Ibid.*, General Secretary, New Settlers' League, to T. L. McKenzie, 19 Mar. 1924, and to Mrs W. H. Campbell, South Brisbane, 27 May 1924.
74 *Ibid.*, J. C. McLaren to Mapleton, 4, 30 June 1923; Mapleton to McLaren, 8 June 1923.
75 South Australia State Records, South Australia Immigration Department, GRG7/6/1159, Applications by youths for assisted passage as farm apprentices, together with applications for such persons by landowners in South Australia, 1922–4, nos 1–1476. Alexander Holburn to 'Mr Ryan', 22 July 1924. All correspondence pertaining to Holburn is dated 1924, although the file records his arrival in South Australia as 17 December 1926.
76 *The Bulletin*, 24 Apr. 1925, in Glasgow University Archives and Business Records Centre, UGD 255/1/8/6, Anchor Line, newspaper cuttings, 1924–25. See also *Daily Record*, 29 May 1925.
77 *SF*, 1 May 1926, p. 592.
78 *SG*, 4 Mar., 1 July 1926, 28 Jan., 10 June 1927. Term days were set at Whitsuntide (May) and Martinmas (November), with most emigration taking place in the spring.
79 NAC, RG76, C-4661, vol. 5, file 41, part 3, Egan to Walker, 28 Aug. 1926. See also chapter 1, p. 35. Egan conceded that the Aberdeen agency made more Canadian bookings overall.
80 *Annual Report of the DIC, 1928*, report of Glasgow agency, contained in the report of J. B. Walker.
81 Public Record Office (PRO), DO57/118/0164/2, Report of a tour in the North of England and Scotland, Oct.–Nov. 1929, by Kenneth Lindsay, Director of Voluntary Organisations, Oversea Settlement Department.
82 *P&J*, 12 Dec. 1925.
83 *SF*, 1 May 1926, p. 606.
84 *Annual Report of the DIC, 1928*, report of Inverness agency, contained in Walker's report.
85 PRO, DO57/119/0352/6. 3,000 Families Scheme, experiences of settlers, letter of Cissie Stevenson in *Winning Through: Stories of Life on Canadian Farms, told by New British Settlers* (Ottawa, DIC, 1929).
86 Mary E. Campbell, *In Yesterday's Footsteps* (n.p., 1986), pp. 109–10. I am grateful to Mrs M. E. Blackhall of Tarland, Aberdeenshire, for drawing this book to my attention.
87 *Ibid.*, pp. 147–8.
88 *SF*, 26 Sept. 1925, p. 1244; 9 Jan. 1926, p. 33.
89 *SF*, 24 Oct. 1931, p. 1453.
90 See chapter 1, p. 35.
91 NAC, RG76, C-7396-7, vol. 248, file 179046, part 1, Little to W. J. Egan, 5 Nov. 1924.
92 *Ibid.*, C-4661, vol. 5, file 41, part 3.
93 *SF*, 25 July 1925, p. 983; 17 Mar. 1928, p. 346.
94 See also chapter 6, pp. 204–5 and 207–8.
95 *SF*, 12 May 1923, p. 593.
96 PRO, BT27/1000, 27/1002, passenger lists for ships departing from Glasgow, April and August 1923.
97 *Ibid.*, BT27/1228. There were thirty-three cabin passengers and twenty tourists on the SS *Albertic*.
98 *Ibid.*, BT27/1004 (departures from Liverpool in 1923); BT27/1151 (departures from Liverpool in 1927). Three of the Scottish passengers on the *Montrose* were tourists.
99 *Ibid.*, BT27/1018 (departures from London), BT27/1029 (departures from Southampton).
100 AA, AC6/27/26, Fraserburgh Parish Council, Record of Applications for Poor Relief, 25 Apr. 1924, no. 648.
101 AA, AC6/27/27, 16 July 1926, no. 652.

102 SRO, CO4/32/7, Inch Parochial Board, Wigtonshire, General Register of Poor, 1845–1930, pp. 253, 308.
103 Highland Council Archives, CI7/15/9, Kingussie and Insh Parish Council, Record of Applications for Poor Relief, 1911–1926; 20 Mar. 1921, p. 74.
104 AA, AC6/27/27, Fraserburgh Parish Council, Record of Applications for Poor Relief, 2 Nov. 1925, no. 338.
105 AA, AC6/67/9, Rathen Parish Council, Record of Applications for Poor Relief, 30 Nov. 1927, no. 77.
106 See, for instance, AA, AC6/27/28, Fraserburgh Parish Council, Record of Applications for Poor Relief (4 Nov. 1926 to 7 Dec. 1928), Noah Birnie (no. 357), Robert Sim (no. 551), James Simpson (no. 552); AC6/27/29 (7 Dec. 1928 to 23 May 1931), George Hadden (no. 126), William Malley (no. 127), Henry Crighton (no. 132), Francis Chalmers (no. 136), Robert Sim (no. 143), William Clark (no. 166), John McKenzie (no. 200), Alexander Simpson (no. 201), Walter Thompson (no. 225). For discussion of parish council subsidies to pauper emigrants, see Edinburgh City Archives, SL14/1/29, Edinburgh Parish Council minutes, 18 June 1923, p. 347, 9 Oct. 1923, p. 513; SL4/1/30, 19 May 1924, pp. 251–2; SL14/1/31, 27 Apr. 1925; SL14/1/32, 26 Apr. 1926, pp. 257–8. For further discussion of Salvation Army colonization schemes, see chapter 5, p. 158.
107 SF, 1 Dec. 1928, p. 1582.
108 PRO, DO57/119, 0352/6, 3,000 Families Scheme, experiences of settlers, internal memorandum. (See also ibid., Australian Joint Copying Project, reel 6714–5). When in winter 1928–29 several leading western Canadian newspapers ran a prize essay competition for British families who had settled under the 3,000 Families Scheme, 86 letters were sent to the Calgary Herald, 50 to the Saskatoon Star Phoenix, 14 to the Regina Leader and 32 to the Vancouver Province. The prize-winning essays were subsequently published as the pamphlet Winning Through (see note 85).
109 Winning Through, Cissie Stevenson (see note 85).
110 Ibid., William Wilson, Delburne, Alberta, to LSB, Ottawa, 25 Mar. 1929.
111 John A. Schultz, 'Leaven for the lump' in Stephen Constantine (ed.), Emigrants and Empire. British Settlement in the Dominions Between the Wars (Manchester, Manchester University Press, 1990), pp. 164–5. See also SFS, Oct. 1928, p. 139, and PRO, LAB 2/1237/9 (Pres. No. A73/1926), Ministry of Labour, Employment and Insurance Department, EDO 985/1929, Report on returned trainees, Canada per Scotland, 4679/10/1929, 'Confidential note on Canadian deportations, 2 Mar. 1931'.
112 NAC, RG76, C-7385, file 135755, part 13, 'British Reduced Rate Settlers, 1928', A. J. Morris to Robert Forke, 27 Nov. 1929; British Welcome and Welfare League to Forke (undated).
113 PRO, DO57/14, Ministry of Labour, 3,000 Trainees for Canada, 1930 (24 Dec. 1929), memorandum on publicity expenditure.
114 PRO, LAB 2/1237/9 (Pres. No. A73/1926). Ministry of Labour, Employment and Insurance Department, EDO 985/1929. W. Taylor to J. M. Cairncross, Divisional Office, Edinburgh, 25 Oct. 1929. For further discussion of complaints made against the Glasgow Parish Council trainees, see chapter 5, pp. 170–2.
115 NAC, RG76, C-7385, file 135755, part 13, Duncan to Colonel Rattray, 16 Nov. 1929.
116 Ibid., Gelley to Jolliffe, 14 Dec. 1929.
117 Ibid. Sixty-three per cent of Liverpool's 1,264 applicants and 68 per cent of York's 992 applicants were rejected.
118 PRO, LAB 2/123/9 (Pres. No. A73/1926). Ministry of Labour, Employment and Insurance Department, EDO 985/1929. Cutting from an unnamed Canadian newspaper submitted to the Ministry of Labour by Mr McDougall of the Church of England Council of Empire Settlement, 24 Mar. 1930. Of the 41 countries represented among the deportees, England accounted for 1,313, Ireland for 300 and Wales for 207.
119 Glasgow University Archives and Business Records Centre, TSB14/1/1/3 (Nairn minutes, 24 Jan. 1922), TSB29/1/1/3 (Galashiels minutes, 30 June 1924)), TSB64/1/3/6 (Greenock annual report, 1923), TSB71/1/2/4 (Paisley annual report, 1924), TSB63/1/4/4 (Glasgow annual report, 1923, p. 4).
120 Ellis Island Oral History Project, interviews EI-435 (Cook) and NPS-149 (Allan).

Immigrants did not have to pass through Ellis Island unless there were queries over their sponsors or health which the authorities wished to investigate. The Allan brothers were detained, for example, because Thomas's brother caught chickenpox during the voyage, while Margaret Cook had an eye infection. The Oral History Project therefore covers only a tiny minority of Scots who went to the United States.

121 *Ibid.*, interviews EI-435 (Cook), DP-46 (Hansen), EI-442 (Pedersen), NPS-146 (Quinn), EI-823 (Rohan).
122 *Ibid.*, interviews EI-823 (Rohan), AKRF-84 (Peak), EI-97 (Saltman).
123 *Ibid.*, interviews AKRF-23 (Delaney), AKRF-127 (Dunn), EI-442 (Pedersen), EI-179 (Gunn), EI-70 (Hopkins), EI-492 (Kendrick), KM-77 (McGuire), NPS-146 (Quinn).
124 *Ibid.*, interview EI-172.
125 *Ibid.*, interview EI-440. Kirk was sponsored by an English family which had provided lodgings for an emigrant acquaintance who had left his job at John Brown's shipyard to work on the railways in America but kept in touch with his former boss, Margaret's father. Margaret later married the son of the family.
126 *Ibid.*, interview AKRF-127.
127 *Ibid.*, interview EI-547.
128 *Ibid.*, interviews NPS-146 (Quinn) and EI-558 (Daly).
129 *Ibid.*, interviews EI-435 (Cook) and AKRF-127 (Dunn).
130 Marjory Harper, *Emigration from North-East Scotland*, vol. 2, pp. 231–87.
131 Canada Wants Domestic Servants (Ottawa, Ministry of the Interior, 1909).
132 Janice Gothard, '"The healthy, wholesome British domestic girl": single female migration and the Empire Settlement Act, 1922–1930' in Constantine (ed.), *Emigrants and Empire*, pp. 72–95. For female emigration to Australia, see Margrette Kleinig, 'Independent women – South Australia's assisted immigrants, 1872–1939' in Eric Richards (ed.), *Visible Women: Female Immigrants in Colonial Australia* (Canberra, Division of Historical Studies and Centre for Immigration and Multicultural Studies, Research School of Social Sciences, the Australian National University, 1995), pp. 112–44.
133 *P&J*, 8 Feb., 14 June 1923. See also, for example, *P&J*, 3 Oct. 1924, 7 Jan. 1926.
134 *Annual Report of the DIC*, 1928, Glasgow agent's report.
135 *Ibid.*, 1930–32; DO 57/118 0164/2, Report of Kenneth Lindsay's tour in the North of England and Scotland, Oct.–Nov. 1929.
136 *SF*, 1 June 1929, p. 729.
137 PRO, BT 27/1000. See, for instance, the passenger list for the *Metagama* from Glasgow to Quebec and Montreal, 20 Apr. 1923.
138 *P&J*, 21 Feb. 1924, 20 Feb. 1925, 13 May 1926; *SG*, 28 Jan. 1927; *HN*, 23 May 1925.
139 *P&J*, 13 Oct. 1923, 12, 17 Apr. 1926.
140 NAC, RG76, C-7380, file 127825, parts 1 and 2, 'Colonel J. S. Dennis, CPR, Selection of domestics under the ESA, 1924–5', list of girls on the *Montnairn*, 17–18 July 1925. Mrs Sweet was accompanied by her twenty-eight-year-old daughter, who also prepaid the full fare, both having secured employment in the same household.
141 *Ibid.*, RG25, A2, vol. 152, file C10/36, Ledingham to Colonial Secretary, 27 Jan. 1916; J. K. Miller, Canadian government emigration agent, Glasgow, to J. O. Smith, 29 Jan. 1916; Smith to Miller, 31 Jan. 1916.
142 *Ibid.*, RG76, C-10260, vol. 356, file 402561, Little to Cory, 11 Dec. 1920.
143 *Ibid.*, RG76, C-10315, vol. 435, file 652806, part 3, D. J. Murphy to M. V. Burnham, 24 May 1923.
144 *Ibid.*, RG76, C-7380, vol. 230, file 127825, part 1, Little to Walker, 21 Nov. 1925, Burnham to Little, 30 Oct. 1929, Blair to Burnham, 6 Nov. 1929.
145 *Ibid.*, Gordon to J. N. K. Macalister, 14 June 1931; see also Deputy Minister to Gordon, 1 May 1931, Little to Blair, 4 May 1931, Macalister to Gordon, 29 June 1931.
146 Gothard, '"The healthy, wholesome British domestic girl"', pp. 86–8.
147 *SF*, 2 Oct. 1920, p. 1115.
148 South Australia State Records, South Australia Immigration Department, GRG 7/8/793, file 793.D.
149 NAC, RG76, vol. 230, file 127825, part 1, Calderwood to matron of Canadian Women's Hostel, Toronto, 28 Sept. 1925.

CHAPTER FIVE

Creating Christian colonists

Many formal emigration schemes between the wars addressed the specific needs of a generation of disillusioned or adventurous urban youths. By harnessing post-war legislation to Victorian and Edwardian concepts and practices, private and public enterprises together tried to tackle unemployment and poor prospects, creating one of the most significant, but also one of the most controversial, manifestations of assisted emigration in the entire history of the movement.

Inter-war philanthropists could build on a recognized foundation, for by 1914 assisted emigration had been incorporated into a variety of charitable ventures which attempted, from both a national and a regional perspective, to alleviate problems of overpopulation, unemployment and destitution. In the virtual absence of state welfare provision, churches and charities shouldered the burden of rescuing and rehabilitating needy men, women and children – particularly from the overcrowded and anonymous cities, where statutory relief barely scratched the surface of an endemic poverty that was sometimes aggravated to epidemic proportions by specific economic crises. Undergirding the relief programmes of most of these charities was an evangelical Christian commitment to offer both practical and spiritual help to needy individuals – a commitment that was increasingly reinforced by a eugenic confidence that the future of Britain and the empire could best be secured by the judicious transfer of suitable recruits from the debilitating environment of the mother country's city slums before their constitutions had been irreparably damaged. None of those sentiments was eroded either by the First World War or by the embryonic beginnings of state-funded welfare before and after the conflict, although eugenic arguments steadily, if sometimes imperceptibly, superseded Christian concerns. Organizations that had been established as part of the late Victorian enthusiasm for evangelical philanthropy continued to combine domestic rescue work with assisted emigration throughout the 1920s, in conjunction with a range of new ventures in youthful colonization, some of which concentrated on the plight of disadvantaged juveniles, while others courted more affluent clients.

Nationwide initiatives

By 1914 the Salvation Army was described as 'the world's largest emigration agency'.[1] It not only advertised extensively in provincial newspapers, but it also sent officers on recruitment visits to regional citadels, as in January 1924, when Colonel H. G. Miller selected at least twenty-four boys in Aberdeen, or in September 1927, when Colonel David Lamb, the Friockheim (Angus)-born head of the London-based Migration and Settlement Department, visited Inverness.[2] Carefully regulated migration had been a pivotal part of William Booth's social strategy, and such was the Salvation Army's reputation as a migration agency that within a month of the Armistice it had received nearly 6,000 applications from would-be emigrants. The Empire Settlement Act subsequently gave a new impetus to its work, which was singled out for particular tribute when the Bill was introduced into Parliament.[3] Encouraged by government grants and loans, in 1923 the Army undertook a new Boys' Scheme, whereby unemployed youths and those in blind-alley jobs could apply for assisted emigration as farm labourers. Successful candidates, aged between fourteen and seventeen, were either sent to the Army's farm at Hadleigh in Essex for three months' basic agricultural training before being shipped out to pre-arranged positions on colonial farms or, in the case of Queensland and New Zealand, trained on arrival at Salvation Army farms near Brisbane and at Putaruru in Auckland. Once placed, the boys were visited regularly, and periodic progress reports were sent to the Army's London headquarters on more than 5,000 boys who had been dispatched by 1930, mainly to Australia. David Lamb retained his charge of emigration work until the Department was wound up in 1932, by which time he had been round the world four times and had visited Canada almost annually in the course of his work.

The Salvation Army continued to operate largely autonomously, jealous of its reputation and fearful of the loss of goodwill and independence that might be entailed in collaborating too closely with the OSC. It continued to hold a licence as a passage broker's agent and was not prepared to forego the commissions it received from steamship lines on the booking of passengers, believing that the success of its emigration work was reflected in widespread and long-standing public confidence in its methods.[4] Other inter-war enterprises – new and old – were more clearly a response to financial inducements, since under the ESA juvenile emigration societies were given a grant of £14 10s per head to cover transport expenses as well as assistance with placement and aftercare.[5] But many antipodean and

South African ventures in particular courted privileged middle-class, rather than disadvantaged working-class, recruits.

Between 1909 and 1914 the Dreadnought Trust used half of a public subscription initially set aside to finance a battleship to bring 1,787 boys to a training farm in New South Wales prior to their distribution to farmers in the state. Between 1921 and 1929 it sponsored the settlement of a further 5,000 15- to 18-year-olds, who were selected by Commonwealth government representatives in Britain, granted assisted passages and given elementary or specialized farm training for six months or a year, respectively, at one of five training farms before being sent to work with carefully vetted employers. Aftercare was the responsibility of travelling inspectors and the 300 local branches of the New Settlers' League, and the ever-optimistic A. G. Scholes described the scheme as 'one of the best examples of voluntary effort in conjunction with Government aid ensuring that no detail of the Settlement process is neglected'.[6] Although it attracted more English than Scottish recruits, the Dreadnought Scheme was commended in December 1923 by the Aberdeen Advisory Committee for Juvenile Employment, which resolved to bring its advantages to the notice of local voluntary organizations.[7]

Victoria's particular contribution to juvenile migration was the Big Brother Movement, founded by Melbourne man Richard Linton in London in 1925 with the aim of offering personal attention to recruits in a way that would reassure parents anxious about sending their sons so far away. Boys were recruited for farm work between the ages of fourteen and nineteen and came mainly from public and secondary schools, although they were also recruited by organizations such as the Victoria League, the Navy League, the YMCA and various churches. If their character references and medicals were accepted by the officials at Australia House, their particulars were forwarded to the Big Brother Committee of the New Settlers' League in Victoria and, later, in the other states that adopted the scheme. Each recruit was assigned a Big Brother – a leading member of Australian society who might be a clergyman, a banker, a municipal dignitary or a government official – of the same nationality and religion as himself. This person's initial duties were to meet the Little Brother on arrival, arrange temporary city accommodation and, having ascertained that he was going to suitable employment, see him off on the train. His longer-term duties were to act *in loco parentis* until the recruit was twenty-one, writing to him at least once a month, visiting him at intervals and interceding with employers on his behalf. The Little Brother, for his part, was to follow and actively seek his mentor's advice, not leave his employer without the Big Brother's permission, and maintain correspondence, as well as fulfilling the more general requirements of abstaining from liquor and gambling, opening a bank account and giving good service in his work. The scheme was commended on the grounds that 'There are in Great Britain thousands of boys without any opportunities; there are in Australia thousands of opportunities without any boys to fit them. The Big Brother's task is to bring together British boys and Australian opportunities. It is a form of practical patriotism, and if it succeeds, Australia and the Empire will be the better for it.'[8]

The imperialist rhetoric and practical prospects struck a chord in Britain, and by 30 September 1928 868 Little Brothers had been sent to Victoria, 522 to New South Wales and 125 to Western Australia, of whom 914 were from secondary schools, 121 from public schools and 475 from elementary schools.[9] Like the Dreadnought Scheme, it was more important in England than Scotland, although in August 1925 Richard Linton visited Aberdeen and Inverness on a promotional tour, eliciting an editorial recommendation from the *Press & Journal* that since his scheme offered a viable means not only of tackling domestic depression and unemployment but also of ensuring that Australia was populated with suitable settlers, 'this policy of fraternity, at once statesmanlike and human, deserves every encouragement'.[10] Five months later the *Stornoway Gazette* indicated that Linton's visit had borne fruit – at least in the highlands, from where 250 Little Brothers had emigrated the previous autumn, including boys from Dingwall and Inverness. Arrangements had been made for parties of forty to sail in January, February and March, with a 'fair proportion' of Scots included in the February contingent.[11]

Neither the Dreadnought nor the Big Brother scheme catered for the destitute or disadvantaged, and many of Australia's juvenile migrants were sent out by solicitous parents rather than rescue homes. Perhaps the relative success of the Big Brother movement was because it was hedged about with comparatively few regulations, while attempts by South Australia to obtain several thousand boys of a similar calibre for land settlement under state government guardianship foundered on the rock of over-onerous apprenticeship conditions. Queensland also favoured parental involvement, operating a farm apprenticeship scheme for sixteen- to nineteen-year-olds, who, after being selected by the Commonwealth authorities in London and obtaining parental approval, put themselves under the guardianship of the state's immigration agent for three years. During that time they were apprenticed yearly to farmers, who could dismiss them only with the written consent of the Immigration Minister. By 31 October 1929, 2,536 boys had settled in Queensland under these arrangements and had accumulated over £28,000 in trust accounts.[12]

Less fortunate boys who wished to go to Australia could have recourse to the Salvation Army, Barnardo's Homes or the Fairbridge Society. In 1921 Barnardo's began to send children to New South Wales, operating a receiving centre and training home, which by 1928 had catered for 891 recruits.[13]

But most disadvantaged juvenile migrants went to Western Australia under the auspices of Kingsley Fairbridge's Child Emigration Society, founded before the war to bring out destitute children between the ages of six and eleven and train them with a view to their ultimate settlement on Crown lands. Fairbridge himself died in 1924, but by that time he had established a 3,200-acre training farm at Pinjarra, which purportedly offered not only agricultural instruction but also formal elementary education and a home life which the children had not enjoyed in Britain.

Between 1923 and 1928 New Zealand received 1,765 juvenile migrants from Britain.[14] Interest had been aroused in 1910, when 50 recruits from London boys' clubs were apprenticed to New Zealand farmers after Londoner T. E. Sedgwick had persuaded the Dominion government to act as guardian. Sedgwick's hope of extending his operations to all the dominions was curtailed by the war, but legislation in 1920 provided for apprenticeship agreements to be made, as in Queensland, between boys and the New Zealand Minister of Immigration, who selected employers and arranged for the compulsory saving of wages and repayment of loans. Recruitment was targeted on public schoolboys, 644 of whom had gone to New Zealand by March 1928, with the expectation that after suitable training they would invest their capital in farming on their own account. New Zealand's best-known juvenile migration scheme, however, was the Sheepowners' Fund, by which after the war 2,700 sheep-farmers assigned to trustees their share of profits on wool sales in order to benefit disabled sailors of the Royal Navy and Mercantile Marine, their dependents, and the dependents of those killed in action. By 1923 it had been decided that the money should be spent primarily on bringing orphaned children to New Zealand, establishing them on farms and subsequently helping them to obtain farms of their own. To this end a 9,000-acre training farm was purchased near Palmerston North, and the first party of boys arrived in June 1924, under the supervision of the YMCA, for eight months' training and an apprenticeship of up to three years. In 1925 a girls' training centre was opened in the same area, and by December 1928 429 males and 94 females had been recruited through the Fund.

The New Zealand Sheepowners' Fund was represented in Scotland by the Marquis of Graham, Brodick Castle, Arran, who made regular use of the press to promote and explain the scheme. In January 1925, six months after it was inaugurated, Graham reported receiving many 'happy letters' from Scottish recruits and expressed surprise that relatively few fishermen's sons from the islands had applied, 'for they are undoubtedly the boys who are wanted in New Zealand'.[15] Later that year Frank Ivey, the Fund's London-based secretary, gave an illustrated lecture at the Aberdeen YMCA, chaired by the Lord Provost and attended by, among others, 100 lads from the local employment exchange. Ivey's visit was prompted by concern at the lack of Scottish participation – which he blamed on poor publicity, although he highlighted the case of an experienced recruit from Fraserburgh who was earning up to 27s 6d a week in the first year of his apprenticeship. Ivey's claim that Aberdeen and Fraserburgh could supply many such recruits was supported by another member of the platform party, Bishop Deane, who 'thought they had got in Aberdeen as fine lads as any in the British Isles – and the one thing he was more sorry of than anything else was that they had got so many of these lads – who had the making of splendid men, and at the moment had not a job.'[16]

If a significant number of juvenile migrants to Australia and New Zealand were from middle-class homes, the minority who went to South Africa were even more well-endowed, since possession of a minimum of £1,000 capital was a prerequisite of acceptance by the 1820 Memorial Settlers' Association.[17] These countries were relatively new participants in juvenile migration programmes, but even Canada, the established destination for destitute juvenile emigrants, began to recruit a different type of young settler after the First World War. As the supply of orphans and illegitimate or destitute children dried up some encouragement was offered to middle-class recruits, as in the Antipodes; in 1924 both Macdonald College at McGill University, Montreal, and the Provincial Agricultural School at Vermilion, Alberta, launched sandwich courses designed for selected boys from British public and secondary schools. The fees of £72 and £50, respectively, were to be borne by the boys or their parents, and a similar two-year course was subsequently offered at the Ontario Agricultural College at £50 per year. The main Canadian emphasis, however, was on the good prospects for unemployed or temporarily employed adolescents, as established and new agencies alike began to test, train and transport urban recruits.

Barnardo's was the first organization to resume migration work after the war, when in 1920 it sent a party of 155 to Canada, the same year as Canadian government supervision was extended from poor-law children to all unaccompanied juvenile migrants. Scholes claims, somewhat questionably, that this move ended discrimination by merging the migration of state children into the mainstream of juveniles entering Canada and reassured anxious parents that placements would be monitored by government inspectors as well as the voluntary societies.[18] In 1921 ten agencies dispatched a total of 1,426 migrants, and pre-embarkation medical inspections were tightened up four years later. The Canadians also began to operate their own voluntary societies. The most notable were the Quebec-based British Immigration and Colonisation Association, founded in 1924, and the Ontario-based agency of the United Church of Canada, founded in 1927 and using the YMCA to select boys in Britain for dispatch to its receiving home at Norval, Ontario. Continuing friction between federal and provincial authorities over the quality of recruits and placements led to greater provincial involvement in 1927, when boys' training and settlement schemes were initiated under the ESA. Reception farms were established at Vimy Ridge, Ontario, and in Winnipeg and Saskatoon for the training of fifteen- to nineteen-year-old British boys as a preliminary to their placement with local farmers, the provincial governments continuing to act as guardians for three years. A simultaneous agreement allocated $5 million for loans to selected young British men to buy and equip farms of their own, preference being given to those who had passed through the provincial reception farms and saved $500 during their apprenticeships.

Scottish youths were often reminded about the range of Canadian opportunities by federal or provincial agents. In July 1925, for instance, Aberdeen agent D. E. Lothian intimated the extension of Alberta's farm training sandwich course from Vermilion to two extra centres, at Olds and Clareshome, and reminded applicants that they could obtain an interest-free transport loan from the port of embarkation to their destination. The Boys' Training Scheme at Vimy Ridge Farm, Guelph, was commended by the Inverness agent on the grounds that 'many poor neglected lads from the industrial centres of Scotland have gone out under this scheme, [and] have become healthy workers in a few months after their arrival'.[19] Lewis boys in particular had their attention drawn to farm training facili-ties by Alexander McOwan, CNR agent in Glasgow, and Murdo Maclean, the Stornoway booking agent, in a jointly placed advertisement in the *Stornoway Gazette* in September 1927:

> Under the Canadian Government Juvenile Settlement Scheme, boys under seventeen travel to Canada free from Glasgow. They have nothing to repay. They are placed in situations, receive wages from the start, and their wel-fare is strictly safeguarded. They are trained to be farmers, and encouraged to launch out for themselves. Three or four years' residence in Canada will qualify an industrious, ambitious boy to arrange nomination for his parents and other members of the family, so that they may join him.[20]

The YMCA and the Church Nomination Scheme

While small numbers of Scots participated in several UK-wide juvenile migration schemes, they had a much higher profile in a sponsored overseas settlement programme launched by the YMCA largely in response to the ESA. In the 1920s the YMCA took the initiative throughout the dominions in promoting the collective nomination of migrants, depersonalizing and extending the established procedure of personal nomination whereby individuals overseas proposed friends or relatives in Britain for assisted passages and assumed responsibility for the aftercare of their nominees.

Since its foundation in 1844 YMCA halls had frequently been the venue for promotional meetings addressed by both professional and amateur emigration agents, and YMCA members were well represented in the ranks of Victorian and Edwardian emigrants. It also quickly developed a sophisticated international network, which included a heavy involvement with the reception and welfare of newly-arrived migrants through its network of hostels. Its recognition that the emigrant was 'an international person without recognised international rights'[21] led to the establishment in 1909 of an Emigration Department within the YMCA World's Committee, a body that was revived with greater authority after the war. YMCA workers were placed in ports of embarkation and debarkation, and the Emigration Department liaised with the International Labour Bureau to create better transport facilities and employment opportunities for emigrants. YMCA welfare officers who sailed with the emigrants organized shipboard recreation and instruction, as well as religious meetings, and at the end of the voyage made sure that the new settlers were put in touch with local YMCA officials or churches at their destinations.

The YMCA clearly felt that emigration gave its organization both the opportunity and the duty to exercise Christian care and witness.

> Have we, then, any interest in the welfare of those colonists who go out from us to do the work of the Empire? Ought we to be concerned about the future? If men resolve to migrate, ought we to consider them as coming within our purview of work? Have we any responsibility towards our dispersed people? Surely the answer is in the affirmative. Where is the Association secretary who does not see in all this migration movement a great opportunity of service? ... Who does not want to help men at a time when the roots of their life are being pulled up; when ties are being severed; when dangers confront and when they feel as never before that their future is in the lap of the gods? Most men are conservative at heart, and it is usually a great wrench for one who loves his country to leave the old, and to enter upon a new life amid new surroundings and in strange places ... .
> At this juncture, men require counsel and guidance. The Young Men's Christian Association is in a position to help them, and assist them from the moment they give expression of their desire to migrate, right through the period of their voyage until they settle in their new homes on the other side.[22]

Post-war legislation made it possible for the YMCA to move from passive supervisory and aftercare work to a more active involvement. A London-based Migration Department was created in 1920 to marry colonial demand with British supply, and after the Department's general secretary, Major Cyril Bavin, visited Canada, Australia and New Zealand in 1922 at the invitation of churches in those dominions, a co-operative scheme of Christian nomination was devised. Colonial churches and charities were

encouraged to appoint local committees which, after liaising with employers and residents and obtaining guarantees of employment and accommodation, nominated eligible categories of settlers to their government's
immigration department. The initial recruitment of individuals was then
undertaken by the counterparts or agents of these organizations in Britain,
although the final selection was, as always, subject to the approval of the
dominion authorities. The local committees in the dominions assumed
responsibility for the reception and aftercare of recruits and also undertook
to find fresh openings for anyone who had been unsatisfactorily placed in
the first instance.

Such collaboration between the home and colonial churches was
welcomed by the OSC, which was confident that 'if we could enlist their
full support the whole question of migration might be raised to a higher
plane'.[23] Furthermore, as Thomas Pollock, one of the YMCA's Migration
Department secretaries, pointed out, collective nomination not only
inspired greater confidence among migrants because it was less risky than
individual nomination, it also strengthened the bond between the home
and colonial churches and 'enables the Church to make her contribution
towards the solution of some of the pressing problems of the day. It also
ensures that spiritual contacts made at home will not be severed by reason
of the change of locality, although this may be several thousand miles
distant.'[24] Such issues seem to have been of particular concern to the
Presbyterian Church of Australia, for when J. C. Milliken, the convener of
its Immigration Committee, came to Scotland in spring 1926 to promote
collective nomination, his visit was prompted partly by the alarming
number of presbyterian migrants who, once in Australia, failed to establish
contact with their Church, and the YMCA's programme, at least in its
initial stages, related more to Australia than Canada.

From its outset the YMCA scheme attracted a significant number of
Scots. On 23 October 1924 the *Press & Journal* intimated the forthcoming
visit of the YMCA's migration representative to Aberdeen, along with an
Australian delegate, to select twenty applicants for farm trainee positions
in the Colac district of Victoria, as well as a few employees for the Camper-
down, Gippsland and Hamilton districts. In June 1925 the Presbyterian
Church in Australia asked the YMCA and the Scottish churches to secure
forty-six domestics and thirty-six boys for Victoria. Three months later
it offered to place ten families per month in New South Wales, and in
February 1926 J. C. Milliken explained the scheme's rationale to a meeting
of the Aberdeen United Free Church Presbytery. The objective, he claimed,
was to maintain the Britishness of Australia against 'low class' Italian
infiltration by recruiting and nurturing presbyterian settlers – mainly for
farming, but also for domestic service and artisanal employment.[25]
Meanwhile, in Victoria, the Caledonian Society of Colac was particularly

active in forging links with the Scottish YMCA, which for its part was happy to send boys to presbyterian farmers in an area that was 'the centre of a large Scottish community'.[26] Youths were advised by the YMCA that Australia offered good farming opportunities to adaptable and hard-working recruits provided they were of 'good character, good health, good eyesight, and a reasonable standard of education' and were willing to accept the long hours and loneliness of country life.[27] Untrained recruits could earn a minimum of ten shillings a week, with board and lodging, and the prospect of doubling their earnings after training on government farms or through state-supervised farm apprenticeships. YMCA welfare officers accompanied the emigrant parties, and their recommendations, reports of the voyage and descriptions of Australian openings appeared regularly in the Association's monthly journal, *Scottish Manhood*.

Letters from satisfied settlers, also published in the journal, were particularly important in giving the scheme credibility – all the more when they also asked for friends and family to be brought out under its auspices. For example, one emigrant from Fife wrote to the YMCA in 1926 after only a few months in Australia announcing his intention of bringing out his parents and two brothers once he had acquired some land and asking the Association to assist the emigration of one of his former neighbours.[28] In the same month that his letter was published 100 emigrants left Scotland for Australia by the SS *Baradine* under the auspices of the Church Nomination Scheme, with subsequent sailings on 19 August and 14 October and enthusiastic continuation of the scheme the following year. In July 1927 *Scottish Manhood* reported that since 95 per cent of the 120 families sent to New South Wales under the scheme during its first year had made good, the Presbyterian Church there was keen to extend recruitment to 240 families per year, and by 1930 a total of 1,500 people had been settled in the Antipodes, mainly in farm work and domestic service.[29]

Even more recruits were sent across the Atlantic. In 1926 and 1927 the Migration Department liaised with the Canadian National Council of YMCAs in the recruitment of single men for farm service in the Dominion, but from January 1928 activity increased when the United Church of Canada took over sole responsibility for nominations. In 1928 and 1929 a particular effort was made to encourage the emigration of youths from the depressed mining communities of central Scotland, beginning with two parties, mainly from Cowdenbeath, sent 'from shadow to sunshine' in July and August 1928.[30] From the United Church's receiving hostel at Norval, Ontario, a total of 132 boys were distributed to farms in the locality in 1928, apparently with such success that by 1929 the United Church was expressing its willingness to absorb a further 600 suitable Protestant youths. The boys – who were required to supply only their clothing and £1 landing money – were to be shipped out in fortnightly parties under the

charge of a YMCA welfare officer, and were to remain under the guardianship of the United Church of Canada until they had reached the age of
nineteen, earning a minimum wage of ten shillings a week, with full board
and lodging, on carefully vetted farms.

According to *Scottish Manhood*, good reports from the 1928 contingent
led to the recruitment of a further seventeen boys from Cowdenbeath,
with other recruits drawn from Lanarkshire, Edinburgh, Glasgow, Dundee,
Orkney and Lewis.[31] A refreshingly honest account of the experiences of
the first party of forty-six boys was later given by the accompanying welfare
officer, George Simpson.

> Our party included the unemployed lads from Lanarkshire, colliers from
> Cowdenbeath and Lochgelly, quondam Morningside message-boys, and the
> public schoolboy apparelled in plus-fours – a conglomeration with the
> smouldering fires of local patriotism, class-consciousness, and snobbery
> ready to burst into flame at any moment. Fortunately or otherwise, the
> Great Leveller, sea-sickness, laid practically everyone low on the first day
> out on the 'Montroyal,' and probably this did more to produce an *esprit de
> corps* than all the exhortations which I periodically delivered during the
> voyage ... . On the whole it cannot be said that the ocean voyage is a very
> healthy experience for the boys, either physically or morally. The third
> class section of the 'Montroyal' was overcrowded. Most people were too
> sick at the beginning of the week to take much interest in anything.
> Towards the end of the voyage the weather was so rough that everybody
> had to stay below, with the result that all the available accommodation was
> crowded out ... . Ventilation below was poor, and usually had the effect of
> sending one to sleep in the more crowded parts. Food was abundant, but
> towards the end of the week tastes and smells began to pall on us, and we
> longed for really fresh food.[32]

The subsequent train journey offered some temporary relief before the boys
were subjected to the spartan regime and discipline of the Norval hostel,
where they stayed for three days until farm placements were arranged.
Here, too, Simpson was realistic about the problems encountered by city
boys trying to adapt to farm life, but, despite his reservations, he ended his
report with a ringing endorsement of the nomination scheme.

> Many boys will consider themselves fortunate to be placed in homes such
> as I saw, if they can conquer the initial home-sickness. The work will be
> fairly hard, and the hours long, but they must be prepared to get used to
> that. If they are in difficulty at any time they are free to write or go to the
> Hostel. The farmer hands over the boy's wages every quarter to the Hostel
> to be banked in his name after his pocket money has been deducted. In this
> way it is possible for a boy to have saved $100 at the end of his first year
> on the farm. The boy is not in the position of the farm servant in this
> country. He is treated as a member of the farmer's family, takes his meals

with them, has his own room, and enjoys all the social life they have. Some would perhaps envy them this chance to begin all over again. For the boy with grit and determination, this is really the wonderful opportunity it is made out to be.[33]

During 1928 and 1929 a total of 647 British boys were placed in Canada under the Church Nomination Scheme. At least 90 per cent appeared to be doing well, and 3 employers were so impressed that they arranged for the boys' families to join them. Only 6 had been deported, including 2 for medical reasons, and almost 60 per cent of recruits were still with their original employer. Success rates were slightly lower among the 715 single men who had also gone to Canada under YMCA auspices since April 1926, but in October 1929 54 per cent were still contentedly employed in farm work.[34]

The YMCA was so convinced of the efficacy and increasing urgency of its emigration work that in February 1930 it devoted a whole issue of *Scottish Manhood* to publicizing its various initiatives. These initiatives, it stressed, were completely disinterested, for the YMCA aimed not to make a profit as a booking agency but to offer free advice and assistance to those with a 'spirit of adventure', or, more particularly, a desire to escape from the threat or reality of unemployment. But such activities cost money, and included with the descriptions and commendations of the work in the dominions was a public appeal by the chairman of the Scottish branch of the Migration Department for £5,000 with which to send 400 boys and 100 families to Canada during 1930.[35]

Also included in the special issue was a firm endorsement of the YMCA's work by the moderator of the General Assembly of the Church of Scotland, for by 1930 the YMCA was administering the Church Nomination Scheme not only on behalf of itself and its colonial contacts, but as the agent and clearing house for a number of home churches that had been persuaded to participate. In 1925 the Overseas Committee of the Church of Scotland sent a circular to all parish ministers pointing out, like Thomas Pollock, the spiritual as well as the practical benefits of an enterprise that provided the migrant both with work and with the immediate opportunity to worship in his new country 'in the manner to which he has been accustomed'.[36] Ministers were invited to alert their congregations to the scheme and were required to supply character references to accompany the application forms which intending migrants submitted to Thomas Henderson, secretary of the Church's Overseas Committee. An initial selection was made by the YMCA Migration Department, assisted by participating churches and other organizations, which within two years included the Free and United Free Churches as well as the Church of Scotland and various English churches and societies. The names of selected applicants were then submitted to the appropriate dominion government office for approval.

The Scottish Presbyterian churches promoted collective nomination through a joint committee, which liaised with the YMCA as well as organizing preliminary training for recruits. The United Free Church of Scotland, which had for some time collaborated with the YMCA in home mission work, was enthusiastic about the arrangement from the outset, but the ultra-reformed Free Church of Scotland had a profound suspicion of worldly entanglements, not least through involvement with the YMCA, and only began to participate in 1927. It was persuaded to do so partly because it saw in the Church Nomination Scheme a means of influencing the emigrants' future environment, and partly because by 1927 this seemed to be almost the only way of persuading the increasingly reluctant dominions to accept colonists who faced a bleak economic future if they stayed in Scotland. As the Free Church mouthpiece, *The Monthly Record*, observed:

> There are inducements to the courageous in far off lands; but these countries have become critical of whom they will receive. Openings, with settlement on the land (for which most of Free Church people are suited), are not to be had by the penniless in any colony, unless the incomers be nominated to the Colonial Government by a trustworthy colonist who will give them work to do. Colonial Governments go further, and accept collective nominations by Colonial Churches. These Churches, on the other hand, are ready to nominate for admission young people recommended to them by the Churches in this country … . Our readers will see how good a thing it is for outgoing young people to be welcomed in the colony by kindly churchmen and women, ready to find them employment and to give them the guidance and supervision of Christian friendliness.[37]

Specifically Scottish enterprises: Cornton Vale, Craigielinn and Quarrier's

As well as participating in UK-wide juvenile migration schemes spawned by the Empire Settlement Act, Scots also took advantage of home-grown enterprises. Encouraged by government funding, the Church of Scotland became actively involved in migration schemes in the 1920s, both on its own account and in co-operation with other presbyterian churches and voluntary societies at home and abroad, making a determined effort to improve the quality of the exodus and influence its direction. Classified as a private organization under the ESA, its involvement took the form of offering colonial training courses and securing supervised passages and assured employment for emigrants whom it had helped to hand-pick. Training and selection procedures took due account of the dominions' unwavering emphasis on land settlement as the main vehicle for economic development, but also their preference that specific training of would-be farmers should be deferred until the emigrants had reached their destinations. Preparatory courses therefore consisted mostly of general instruction and testing in farming practices to eliminate unsuitable candidates before final selection took place, and the Church of Scotland was involved with two such institutions, Cornton Vale Farm Colony and the Craigielinn Farm Training School.

In 1907 the Church of Scotland had purchased the thirty-acre Cornton Vale farm at Bridge of Allan near Stirling as a rehabilitation and training centre for destitute men. After being requisitioned by the Army during the war, it was returned to the Church and resumed its original function under the auspices of the Social Work Department. But the lack of suitable adult recruits, combined with the difficulty of placing boys' home trainees in employment in Scotland in the 1920s, soon led to a change of policy, and in 1924 the Social Work Department resolved to use Cornton Vale primarily to train young men between the ages of eighteen and thirty with a view to their subsequent emigration. In 1926 the Department concluded an agreement with the Dominions' Secretary under the terms of the Empire Settlement legislation to share the cost of testing approximately 100 would-be emigrants per year at the farm, and to assist jointly the passages of eligible candidates who could not afford to finance their own migration and were not financed by parish relief or private charity. The convener of the Social Work Committee was instructed to admit to Cornton Vale 'only such men as are reasonably likely to prove suitable for settlement overseas',[38] and those selected for assisted emigration were to be single men proceeding to guaranteed agricultural work and who intended to settle permanently overseas.

In initiating the Cornton Vale enterprise, the Social Work Committee 'confidently expected that there will be a useful and fruitful sphere for the Colony in work of this kind'.[39] Its confidence was demonstrated in 1927 when, from a donation of £30,000 towards emigration made to the committee by retired Ceylon tea-planter Sir Leybourne Davidson of Huntly, Aberdeenshire, £2,000 was assigned to Cornton Vale to extend and improve the buildings and a further £1,000 was made available to purchase more land. In the same year the Parish Council of Glasgow negotiated an agreement whereby unemployed youths aged between fourteen and twenty-five were offered three months' training at Cornton Vale followed by a free passage to Canada and placement with farmers for a minimum three-month period, 'after which they will undergo a test for physical fitness to satisfy the authorities here that they [are] fit subjects to become worthy Canadian citizens'.[40] The first 7 recruits arrived in September 1927, followed by a further 45 the following March, and Govan Parish Council estimated that it could supply a total of 250 trainees during 1928 for distribution to Toronto, Winnipeg, Edmonton, Calgary, Saskatoon, Regina and Prince Albert.[41] The outfit, ocean passage and landing money of Cornton Vale recruits were paid for by the Social Work Committee, which also guaranteed their employment for a year, and in 1928–29 a record 67 of the centre's 191 trainees emigrated. They included several men from depressed mining districts, and the regular receipt of 'very cheering letters' from colonists in Canada and Australia continued to convince the Social Work Committee that it was performing a useful service.

Such optimism evaporated when the impecunious state of the Glasgow Parish recruits attracted sharp criticism from Canadian immigration officials who had to make unbudgeted cash advances for food and transport to the migrants' final destinations. Shortly after the arrival of the second contingent the Edmonton district superintendent of the LSB wrote in some irritation to his superior in Ottawa:

> Last Friday five Glasgow Parish Trainees reported at this office. Between the five they had 30 cents and we have been obliged to make advances ranging from $4.00 to $10.00 apiece in order to provide subsistence and transportation. In each case we have written to the prospective employers advising them of this advance and asking them to recoup us out of the first wages earned. Our experience in these cases is, however, that this money is often lost owing to the trainees failing to hold the position found for them.
>
> These Glasgow Parish Trainees advise me that by way of training they were put out to work with Scottish farmers for a period of about four months, during which time they received their board and about one shilling a week pocket money. Prior to sailing they were given £3.10 in cash, wherewith to meet their subsistence expense between the port of debarkation and their destination. These boys have been about eight days en route to Edmonton, and during this time this advance has been completely spent.
>
> By arranging the migration of these boys the British Authorities are relieving themselves of substantial further obligation for relief. I am sure that you will agree with me that it is only right that these boys should not be migrated under conditions which makes them a charge on the Dominion Government immediately on their arrival. I feel that the Glasgow Parish should be prepared, in addition to financing these boys, with the means of subsistence to the District Office point, to forward through you to us from $5.00 to $10.00 per migrant, which would enable us to meet the expenses incident on putting them in touch with their employer. The fact that we have to make them advances from our own funds is, I feel, a very dangerous precedent, as despite anything that we might tell them to the contrary it creates an impression in their minds that if they are dissatisfied with the job found for them all they have to do is to return to town and appeal to us again.[42]

When similar complaints were made by LSB officers in Winnipeg and Calgary, the Dominion government agent in Glasgow was instructed to ensure that he obtained from the parish council a deposit of $10 per recruit to cover the expenses of sending migrants from distributing centres to their places of employment, but ambiguities in the instructions meant that another Glaswegian contingent arrived penniless in May 1928.[43]

The recruits' penury was compounded by their alleged physical and moral failings, raising question marks over the parish council's selection procedure and the superficiality of the Glasgow agent's examination. Most deportations were made on medical grounds after the migrants claimed public welfare. They included John McLean, returned from Calgary after being diagnosed as suffering from 'heart trouble ... neuritis of the lumbar muscles following tonsilitis, and a septic cold in the head, possibly slight pleurisy and ... TB'; John Watson, sent back from Winnipeg after the recurrence of a hernia; John Currie, who had a tubercular knee; and George Watt, who the Canadian authorities claimed was a malingerer.[44] Among those deported for behavioural problems were Robert Sommerville, David Cartledge, Robert Church and Thomas O'Neill. After Sommerville was convicted for a violation of the Alberta Liquor Act in 1928, it emerged that five years earlier he had spent thirty days in Barlinnie prison, Glasgow, having been convicted of house-breaking and theft, while Cartledge, who had served two terms of imprisonment for vagrancy after coming to Canada in 1928, was considered by one of the LSB field supervisors in Manitoba to have 'red' tendencies.[45] Church, who was described by Canada's London-based superintendent of emigration as 'apparently a common Glasgow type, saucy, lazy, indolent and impertinent', was sent back from Nova Scotia in August 1928, and O'Neill was deported at the same time after being convicted of theft. But although J. B. Walker, the London-based director of emigration, admitted that neither recruit should ever have been selected and declared himself 'not favourably impressed with Glasgow as a scene for favourable operations in the selection of a desirable type of boy', he attributed his agents' mistakes to unrealistic deadlines rather than a flagrant disregard of selection criteria:

> In the pressure ... of a limited time to get the number of lads required it was not possible to give each one of them the once over as it should have been done, and I am afraid that several boys were accepted who would not have been accepted had we had more time to go into the boy's past character and even to get references with respect to the referees, many of whom have no idea of the responsibility they assume in giving a certificate which may have very little foundation in fact.
>
> It is not possible in the course of our ordinary work in the Spring of the year to fill a quota of 50 or 100 boys and give them the same time and attention as if we received the order a few months earlier. We are obliged

to conduct an intensive campaign, generally in the large cities from which most of the bad boys come. If, in the future, arrangements could be made with the Provincial Governments to have the orders for the number of boys sent here in October or November I am satisfied [that] with the additional time allowed at our disposal and with the results of our ordinary depart-mental advertising, we should not only get a better class of boy but as many as we could safely absorb.[46]

In fact, Walker's recommendations were never put into effect, for although in 1929 the parish trainee scheme was extended to include applicants from other parts of Scotland, it was abandoned at the end of that year in the face of a total loss of confidence which saw recruitment drop to only nineteen.[47] As for Cornton Vale, in its report to the General Assembly of the Church of Scotland in 1930 the Social Work Committee observed that although good reports had been received from that year's emigrants – thirty in Canada and five in Australia – many other applicants had not been selected because they fell short of the physical and intellectual standards set by Canada in particular. 'The gates to Canada are not so wide and easy of access as they used to be',[48] the report remarked ruefully, and at the end of 1930 Cornton Vale ceased to operate as an emigrant training and testing facility, reverting to its former status as a rehabilitation centre.[49]

The Cornton Vale scheme was run directly by the Church of Scotland through its Social Work Department, but the Kirk was also peripherally associated with another, more sophisticated, farm training venture operated by the Glasgow philanthropist Dr George Cossar, CBE, MC. While Cornton Vale catered for men and youths over eighteen, his farm at Craigielinn near Paisley in some ways provided a model for the Cornton Vale operation, training juveniles between the ages of fourteen and eighteen, including several who were selected for overseas settlement under the YMCA's Church Nomination Scheme. Cossar's charitable conscience had been aroused when, in his student days, he saw the plight of homeless men sleeping on the Thames Embankment, and in 1909, as a delegate of the Church of Scotland's Social Work Committee at the Winnipeg meeting of the British Association for the Advancement of Science, he petitioned the Canadian Minister of Agriculture for financial assistance to relocate suitable trainees from Cornton Vale on Canadian farms.[50] On being given short shrift by the Canadian immigration authorities, which took the view that the recruits would be 'social derelicts who have been taken under the sheltering care of the Church',[51] Cossar turned his attention to juvenile migration. This was an extension of his existing rescue work among Glasgow youths, which had already seen him open missions, soup kitchens and clubs in the city centre, establish a wood-kindling business to provide employment and purchase a training farm, Todhill at Kilwinning in Ayr-shire, to instruct and then place boys in farm service at home or abroad.[52]

His priority was to assist 'the poorer lads of our city', particularly the 75 per cent of poor Irish Catholic boys, whose plight he felt was largely ignored – not least by evangelical philanthropists like himself.[53] To facilitate Canadian placements, in 1910 he purchased a 700-acre farm at Lower Gagetown, New Brunswick, to which recruits were sent for training, either directly or via Todhill, before being placed with individual farmers in the province. In 1911 Cossar escorted his first recruits to New Brunswick, along with a man and wife from Stirlingshire to superintend the venture, and he subsequently purchased three adjacent farms to increase his holding to 1,000 acres. By 1913, when G. B. Smart, Canada's Chief Inspector of Juvenile Immigration, submitted a report on the farm, 250 boys had passed through its doors, and by 1922 this had risen to 800. Although Smart suggested that Cossar was naive in expecting his recruits to repay their fares, he reported that each boy, when interviewed individually, had expressed enthusiasm for his work, and concluded that 'Mr Cossar's plan of supplying a good class of young Scotch immigrants is not only commendable but advantageous to Canada and deserving of encouragement'.[54]

Until August 1922 Cossar assisted emigration entirely at his own expense. Then, encouraged by the funding made available under the ESA, he purchased for £2,000, with the aid of private donations, the thirty-six-acre Craigielinn estate at Gleniffer Braes, Paisley, for use as a basic training farm.[55] As before the war, trainees were to be mainly 'city boys of the poorer classes' who would be referred by schools, labour exchanges and presbyterian churches, as well as by individuals, and Craigielinn was given a grant in return for testing 100 boys per annum with a view to their permanent settlement as farm workers in Canada or Australia. The thirteen-week testing was to include, *inter alia*, 'elementary agriculture, milking, horse harnessing, the care of stock and personal laundry and if possible cooking, shoe-mending and rough carpentry.'[56] Like Cornton Vale later, the school's directors were to admit only those applicants who showed potential to be successful colonists, and from such trainees they were subsequently to make an initial selection of candidates for presentation to the colonial selecting authority. Boys were to be encouraged to contribute as far as possible to their maintenance, training and examination costs of twenty-two shillings a week, although inability to do so was not to prejudice their selection.

Eighteen months after its establishment on this subsidized basis, Cossar was in no doubt that his enterprise was proving a successful assault on poverty and unemployment and was therefore worthy of supplementary public support. In making an appeal for £2,000, he pointed out that of more than 250 lads from all parts of Scotland tested at Craigielinn, 160 had gone overseas, while others had been passed as fit and were waiting their turn to go.

Many of them, after several years of idleness, without the faintest prospect of work, are now amongst the real producers of the world and are earning good wages. Some are being joined by other members of their families. To read their letters from overseas, full of hope, with their accounts of steady work and good wages, is as good as a tonic in these depressing days.

They all have a good word for Craigielinn and their experience there, and, if a lad is willing to work, he is bound to learn something with us that will be useful later. The Farm not only provides a training for the boys, but supplies them with an outfit, so that parents in really poor circumstances need pay nothing towards the equipment of their boys ... .

We invite any Christian worker who is interested in the welfare of the young to submit the names of likely lads, and will be glad to show them some of the many letters received from boys and their employers in Australia and Canada that prove to us conclusively that the prospects we can offer to a willing lad are excellent.[57]

Cossar's interest was not limited to the impoverished, for he acted as a Scottish agent for the British Immigration and Colonisation Association from its inception in 1924, welcoming the opportunity both to orchestrate the migration of self-financing boys from affluent families and to extend his influence by arranging placements in Canadian provinces other than New Brunswick. In July 1924 he accompanied his first such party to the Association's receiving hostel in Montreal, where twenty-four Craigielinn trainees were joined by twelve self-funded boys for farm placements. At the same time his Gagetown farm was used by the Association as its reception centre in New Brunswick.[58] Cossar's conducted parties were regularly advertised – and sometimes pictured – in the Scottish press, and in June 1925 the CPR offered farm labouring openings to selected Higher Grade schoolboys who would emigrate under Cossar's auspices the following month.[59] Two months earlier, in a lecture to the Aberdeen Rotary Club, Cossar reported that over 500 Craigielinn boys had now been sent overseas and urged local businessmen to give particular support to his Canadian work.[60]

Cossar's canvassing and publicity did not fall on deaf ears, for Craigielinn was well supported by public subscriptions, and in 1927 it too received, like Cornton Vale, a substantial donation from the retired tea-planter Sir Leybourne Davidson to stimulate its colonial training scheme. In that year its accommodation was extended to admit 300 boys per year, and by 31 October 1928 a total of 1,076 boys had received training at Craigielinn, of whom 734 had been sent overseas – 535 to Canada and 199 to Australia. Only 90 had been placed on farms in Scotland, generally because they had failed the dominions' medical.[61] The directors remained well satisfied with their work, which had grown despite competition from more glamorous emigration agencies that offered boys immediate transfer to the colonies without the apparent drudgery of preliminary testing. Although the directors were mostly Glasgow-based, Craigielinn's recruitment field was Scotland-wide:

> We have taken boys from every part of Scotland, ranging from the Shetland Isles to Berwickshire, and, while most of the boys were from the cities, we were glad to have a leavening from the country, who helped to make the others more contented by their outlook on life away from the crowd. From the advantage that has been taken of our extended accommodation, it is evident that there is an increasing desire among many boys to get overseas, and that the thoughtful parent values the opportunity of a preliminary testing. A satisfactory feature is the number of younger brothers coming, whose brothers were at Craigielinn before emigrating.[62]

Like most of his contemporaries and predecessors, Cossar attempted to generate public support by peppering his annual reports with letters of gratitude and recommendation from successful emigrants. Perhaps because Australia was a less familiar and established destination than Canada, or perhaps because more recruits went there in the first year of the scheme, the 1923 report included eight letters from boys in the Antipodes but only one from Canada.[63] One recruit in Victoria had proved the validity of 'rubber udder' training and had already paved the way for another placement:

> My training at Craigielinn has come in more than useful, for the first thing I got to do was to milk a cow. The farmer asked me where I had learned and when I told him on a rubber cow at Craigielinn, he burst into a fit of laughter. I explained what it meant, and he said it was a capital idea. The farmer next door to us requires a boy, so my boss told him to get one of our boys when they land. Tell all the Craigielinn boys it is a fine country and if they do what they are told and trust in God, they will get on. No matter where you go in Australia the 'Scotch' are liked everywhere.

Several Australian correspondents thanked Cossar for giving them 'the chance of a lifetime' and, mindful of their benefactor's priorities, stressed their spiritual as well as their economic wellbeing – if sometimes as an afterthought. 'J.M.' wrote from New South Wales:

> We are very well satisfied with everything. We have learned to milk and turn our hand to all sorts of useful things. We are both getting 10/– per week and keep, and have started to pay back our passage money. On Sunday morning we go riding on horseback, so we manage to see a good deal of the country round, but we always try to attend the church as regular as we can. We have never regretted taking the chance you gave us. We hope to see more Craigielinn boys out here, and we are sure that they will quite surprise themselves by the way they get on.

Two others, in Victoria and Tasmania, welcomed the way in which their employers made them part of the family circle, and the report also included four letters of assurance from Australian and Canadian employers to the emigrants' mothers. One Australian correspondent praised a recruit taken on by his son-in-law for demonstrating 'those qualities of courage, persever-ance and adaptability that make the Scotchman a good asset in whatever country he settles'. Another, who seems to have been more solicitous of her charge than the boy's own mother, hinted at the prospect of secondary migration, thanks to her employee's good progress and reputation.

> Because I am a mother I write to ease your mind, if possible, and tell you that we will do all we can to give Robert a good home in every sense of the word, and that when you come out to him you will find he will still be conducting himself as you would wish. He seems very happy and not at all homesick, but says at times, 'I'll be real pleased when I get a letter from my mother.' Robert is [sic] such a happy disposition that I think he will make good friends anywhere, and he has made a good impression of the stamp of boys Scotland has, and one or two other people are going to see if there are more like him that they can get.

Appended to the 1927 annual report were ten illustrated letters from Cossar boys in New Zealand, Australia and Canada. One former city boy wrote from Taranaki, New Zealand, in praise of a country which offered modern conveniences in a familiar social environment. It was, he claimed, 'an ideal country for outdoor work … . There is infinite variety, and even in the routine work the more experience one gets the more interesting it becomes.' Three others wrote from Australia in slightly less enthusiastic vein, including one from a Queensland sheep station where the work was hard and the hours long, and one from Irriwarra, Victoria, who advised settlers to persevere even in unpalatable jobs and warned that 'You've got to look after yourself if you want to be of any use to the country.' The six letters from various parts of Canada were unanimous in their praise of the country and its opportunities. One correspondent, in his third year in Ontario, wrote:

> I found Canada was as civilized as Britain. I will never regret coming here. We have all kinds of fun all the year round. After work is over we go swimming or fishing, or go riding round the countryside horseback. No more running around the streets of Glasgow for me again. I get my good meals day in and day out. Yes sir, I am enjoying life now. The country seems to grip a fellow, the longer you stay in it the more you like it. So I've become attached to Canada. I mean to have a farm soon, and bring the rest of the family.[64]

Not surprisingly, selected success stories and reassuring accounts of chain migration, whereby boys congregated in particular areas, present only a partial picture of Cossar's activities. Even the propagandist annual reports contain some hints of bad conduct, the 'abandoning' of colonial life, and the damaging opposition raised against Cossar through negative press statements made by those who, he claimed, 'were failures in the Colonies and, in many cases, misfits at home'.[65] Canadian Immigration Department files contain more explicit complaints about the deficiencies of Cossar boys – and their sponsor. As early as 1913 sixty citizens of Gagetown petitioned the immigration authorities in Ottawa 'with a view to stopping the frequent crimes which have been committed in our community, by the boys brought out here from the Old Country by Mr. Cossar and others', asking that checks should be made to ensure that no recruits had a criminal record or had been inmates of a reformatory. Cossar dismissed the complaint as sectarianism on the part of the hostile Anglican majority in Gagetown and pointed out that only two of his 200 recruits had turned out badly.[66] Boys were periodically deported for vagrancy, criminal convictions, illness, laziness, unadaptability or, in one case, because the recruit was 'thoroughly unsatisfactory, and a bad influence on other boys'. Others were criticized for absconding from the Gagetown farm, whose reputation suffered further when in 1925 the British Immigration and Colonisation Association decided to send all its delinquent boys there instead of returning them to Scotland.[67] Employers sometimes complained that boys were undersized or spendthrift. One such derogatory – though not entirely damning – comment was made about recruit John Wemyss by a farmer at Andover, New Brunswick:

> John has but recently arrived. He is all legs and arms, and with the ever present cigarette, he looks like a centipede. Like all or more of Cossars Glasgow boys, he is an inverterate [sic] smoker. In fact Farquhar [the employer] tells me he has drawn the entire $6.00 for clothes and pocket money and spent it on cigarettes – leaving nothing to go towards clothes. He may pull through but it will take time. He is also very apt to tell lies. He is of good manners and attractive personality.[68]

In November 1924 a scathing attack on the management at Gagetown was made in a report by Margaret Waugh, a former matron, to G. G. Melvin, the chief medical officer in Fredericton.

> Dr. Cossar, a medical doctor in active practice in Glasgow, and who goes about preaching at times as well, collects boys in Scotland for emigration to his farm in the county of Queens at Lower Gagetown.
> These boys are supposed to be fed and clad and to get $10 a month and supposed to remain one year on the farm, at the end of which time they are supposed to be free of debt and to be trained to hire out to farmers ... . These boys seem never to be out of debt. After hiring out so many months there is always something to be paid out to the Meiklejohns ... . Mr. and

Mrs. Meiklejohn have been in charge of the farm for 14 or 15 years ... . There is nothing to work with nor to cook with and the boys do their own cooking and washing. There is no sanitary arrangement; one lavatory which is used only by Mr. and Mrs. Meiklejohn to which they hold the key. No patent water-closet. The only water laid on is in the kitchen, by tap. There is no bathroom; no means of bodily washing; no tanks, no boilers, no hot water system ... . The boys are neither well-fed nor properly clad ... . They get neither butter nor milk and no meat except once in a long while. Meal and water and bread, stewed apple cooked without sugar, constitute their food. A boy of about 16 [is] at present doing the cooking. They are obliged to carry water from the Meiklejohn kitchen and if it does not suit Mrs. Meiklejohn when they come for water or food to give it, they do not get either until she is ready to do so. Last week end, there was no bread and the boy doing the cooking was ordered to make scones. He did so and Mrs. Meiklejohn wishing the oven took the half baked scones out of the oven and put them on the boys' table to be eaten by them. Mrs. Meiklejohn is apparently suffering from asthma or consumption and is not careful respecting sanitary aspect of the matter. The boys appear to be much afraid of both Mr. and Mrs. Meiklejohn. No one will remain as matron in the home. The boys rise at 5 A.M., and have no light in the morning. At night a stable lamp is placed on the table. The house is cold. Mr. Meiklejohn made the statement to Mrs. Waugh that the boys were liars and thieves and had been taken out of reformatories and gutters.[69]

Although Margaret Waugh's claims contradicted Dr Melvin's earlier impression that the boys were well nourished, and were challenged by Cossar on the grounds of the matron's unsuitability for the post of assistant to the sickly Mrs Meiklejohn, Smart (the Chief Inspector of Juvenile Immigration) found some of her complaints substantiated and advised Cossar to renovate the buildings and improve procedure.[70]

Official opinion was divided about the calibre of the Meiklejohns' successor, John Jackson, a noted shorthorn breeder who arrived with his wife in 1927. M. J. Scobie, manager of the British Immigration and Colonisation Association, spoke highly of the new superintendent – perhaps not surprisingly given Cossar's close relationship with the Association.[71] Jackson came in for criticism from the Canadian immigration authorities, however, for his lax attention to the selection of employers and aftercare, being more concerned with farm management and agricultural experimentation than with the welfare of the boys. He admitted that pressure of time sometimes prevented him from checking employers' references, homes were not always visited in advance, and almost never thereafter – unless trouble arose – and there was no clear procedure regarding indenture, ensuring regular payment of wages, answering the boys' enquiries or even keeping track of them.[72] Although deficient inspection was addressed by the appointment of one Captain Clingo in 1930, his task was complicated by the fact that Cossar's recruits were mostly older boys who, having 'knocked about Glasgow for two or three years after leaving school', resented regulations about compulsory saving of wages and tended to find their own situations.[73] The scathing denunciation by D. J. Murphy, the Canadian Immigration Department's representative in St John, suggests that matters had deteriorated rather than improved by 1930. Writing to Smart, he claimed that his hard-hitting report simply reflected the opinions of many complainants.

> There is no doubt but the boys in many cases are being exploited by employers, and in others, Cossar throws them in without a semblance of investigation. I find boys all over the country working on roads for their employers who give the lads none of the earnings although these same boys do the chores at night and morning in addition to milking etc ... . In far the majority of cases I find Cossar's lads are farmed out without agreements, and seldom or ever do they get any real notice (outside of prayer circulars) and the loose check is not doing any good. Jackson lives in luxury and yet he can't keep boys about the place to give them some sort of idea of Canadian ways. I saw last year when there, grass growing out of his potato planter, that is not what boys should see on landing at the farm. Boys leave one job and find another on their own and it is all the same to Mr. J. As long as he is not worried, all is well. He is a farmer on the stock side, and has no real time for the most important of all work – the welfare of the boys. I also notice so often that I fear there is truth in my conviction, that after he gets the amount owing to Cossar for out fit [sic: clothing, etc., for boys' transfer to Canada], he is no longer vitally interested. It is only too self evident.
>   Then this awful heavy outfit. The hobnailed boots are a constant irritant to the woman of the house and of no real use on Canadian farms where there are no paved roads or stone floors to barns. In they bring heaps of manure stuck to the soles and the woman starts to whine, the boy starts to talk back, she calls him saucy, he asks for his pay and the man of the house comes in and throws him out. All due to Cossar's boots ... . Now this is not imagination, and if the Dr. on his visits would talk to the family instead of the boy behind the barn, and tell the family he wanted their view point he would get some of the truths I am writing.[74]

Complaints were also made by a few dissatisfied boys and their parents. Glaswegian Hugh Paterson, aged fourteen, who went to the Cossar farm with his seventeen-year-old brother William in July 1924, felt resentment at being pressurized to sign a contract which would prevent the brothers moving to Toronto, where two sisters and another brother were already settled and where his widowed mother was about to emigrate with two younger children. He also hinted that W. J. O'Brien of the British Immigration and Colonisation Association was the real power behind the Cossar enterprise:

Dear Mother,
I don't like starting this wrong but I've got to. The people from some Association here are trying to get us to sign a contract for a year, or rather to consent to the farmer signing it, to keep us for 1 year, the best pay being $10 a month with some given to us for pocket money and some put in a bank somewhere nobody around here has heard of. Willie and I refused to consent until we had heard from Alec or you. He led us to believe it was his scheme but its the Orangemen here with a guy called O'Brien at the head of it, that's bringing us Protestant boys out. Cossar's only an agent, darn him. He never told us about contract or anything else and he said he would come round and see us all, but he came and just visited one fellow as far as I've heard, and he was a chap that came from 28 Monteith Row [Cossar's Glasgow address] do you see through it? They're just twisting the contract business round so as the farmer could have us for a year and work us like – like – the dickens for $10 a month. I believe I could stick it for a year but I don't know about the boss sticking me. I'll sign the contract if you and Alec want me and so will Willie but if they come funny will show them how far a Scotsmans neck can shoot out. The man also mentioned that we might be deported if we didn't sign. I asked him what for and he couldn't say.[75]

Cossar and his staff not only defended themselves against allegations of neglect, lax policy and deception; they also attacked restrictive dominion regulations which, in both Canada and Australia, led to the rejection of many applicants on the grounds of underdeveloped physique. Australian selecting agents were accused by Cossar of inconsistency, bureaucratic short-sightedness and a reluctance to co-operate with private organizations such as his own. In January 1926 75 per cent of the boys who applied through the Glasgow labour exchange for assisted emigration to Australia were rejected or had their applications deferred, and the following month not a single Glasgow applicant was accepted. Stung by the rejection of three 'intelligent and physically fit' Craigielinn boys, Cossar complained:

So far as one can judge, the standard seems to vary with the representative and it would be of great assistance to those who are interested in the problem of the unemployed youth if a standard was set that it would be possible to expect a city boy to attain to. At present it seems a farce to invite boys, as is done through the Labour Exchanges, to come up to be interviewed by the Australian representative when this percentage is turned down and it is only fair, in my opinion, that the extreme unlikelihood, under present conditions, of boys under 18 years of age being accepted should be put clearly before the boys and their parents beforehand to prevent so many coming up just for the disappointment of being rejected in this wholesale manner.

It seems to me it would be only reasonable if Australia was to give boys who come from the poorer parts of our cities the same opportunity of going out as those who come from homes where conditions are better ... . I trust there is enough well-informed public opinion in this country to waken up our friends in Australia to see that they have a real duty to this portion of the Empire to take not only the cream (in the way of physique) of our population, but also to assist that class of boy who, through previous environment, is not yet up to the standard of a boy who has had the advantages of an English Public School and this work, (well worthy of Australia) of assisting in the development of these lads and girls who are healthy, but have not had the same opportunity of development, would not, I submit, prove unprofitable.[76]

Disputes with the Canadian immigration authorities increased after 1928, when – at Cossar's own suggestion – New Brunswick handed over to Gagetown farm responsibility for processing all the province's assisted juvenile immigrants, making it the provincial training centre for the reception, distribution and placement in New Brunswick of all boys recruited in the UK for that purpose under assisted-passage agreements. Cossar was henceforth required to bring out 100 boys per year under his own auspices as well as receive those recruited by other organizations, but his heightened role was a mixed blessing. On the one hand he seemed to have secured the future of his colonial training farm in an era of increasingly restricted operations, with the provincial and dominion governments now shouldering responsibility for placement and aftercare.[77] On the other hand he felt the new arrangements had seriously reduced his independence and control over the venture that bore his name. Because the farm at Gagetown had been turned into a provincial reception centre, Cossar was unable to require all recruits – particularly those from rural areas – to undergo preliminary training at Craigielinn as both he and John Jackson wished, and he suspected that his preference for 'city boys of the poorer classes' was being eroded by the federal and provincial governments' tendency to select rural recruits or boys who had received a secondary education. Craigielinn trainees were then put at a further disadvantage, he claimed, by stringent new federal medical regulations, and after 1928 he complained frequently that the enforcement of a minimum height requirement of five feet was resulting in two out of every three such trainees being rejected. Although he admitted that city-bred boys were often of below-average height before emigrating, he claimed that this did not impair their farming skills or their popularity with New Brunswick's farmers. But his threat to close down the Craigielinn centre and his proposal to take responsibility for the repatriation of any undersized boy who failed to find employment cut no ice with the Dominion immigration authorities, which argued that since the farm at Gagetown was now a provincial training centre, it should set an example by securing only 'strong, robust boys'.[78]

Far from lowering standards, the federal immigration authorities responded to the deepening depression by encouraging juvenile emigration societies to discontinue operations on the approach of winter. In 1929 Cossar had persuaded the New Brunswick authorities to allow his work to continue, but when he proposed to send out sixty boys between September 1930 and February 1931, the federal government warned the province that it would be financially answerable for any concessions it made, and stated vehemently:

> We killed the assisted farm labour movement by allowing unsuitable men to be included for assisted passage who were not farm labourers and never intended to be. This was on the pressure of transportation and other interests. The agricultural family movement was practically killed for the same reason. The trainee movement has come to an inglorious end because we allowed men to come who were not fit. Now pressure is concentrated on the juveniles and if we allow other interests than the interests of the boys themselves and the Province to which they are going, to govern the movement, we will put the juvenile movement where the others have gone.[79]

Increasing tension between Cossar and the Canadian immigration authorities was reflected in a long-running correspondence about the criteria on which boys were judged. James Malcolm, the Canadian agent in Glasgow – whom Cossar accused both of inconsistency in selection and a 'blasphemous and rough' attitude – complained that Cossar knowingly submitted delinquents and boys who were medically unfit, echoing Meiklejohn's earlier aspertions about the boys' dubious backgrounds. He cited two cases from Edinburgh – one of an epileptic who had been referred to Cossar by the Scottish Society for the Prevention of Cruelty to Children after earlier being rejected by the Canadian medical officers, the other of an illegitimate boy who, after being put on probation for theft, was one of forty 'problem cases' referred to Cossar by the Edinburgh Juvenile Organisations Committee between 1929 and 1931 with a view to emigration. According to the boy's mother, 'he had the choice of going to Canada or going to gaol, and he chose to go to Canada under Dr. Cossar's scheme'.[80] The Canadian immigration authorities, while sympathetic to Cossar's desire to befriend 'unfortunate waifs', were, not unnaturally, anxious 'that the material he helps from the gutter should be absorbed on the other side rather than sent to this country … if he is fishing in such muddy waters in Edinburgh, he is likely to be doing it elsewhere and the percentage of runts and failures that he sends out absolutely justifies us in applying all the tests that have been applied in the past and probably a few more.'[81]

The Canadians also alleged that Cossar was guilty of double standards in pressing for relaxed entry regulations while at the same time abusing the government-subsidized charity rate by returning boys whom he deemed unsuitable on some trifling and precipitate excuse. In 1931 twenty boys were sent back to Scotland, including eleven failures and four on health grounds. As one Canadian civil servant commented crossly, 'It is somewhat of an anomaly to find the Cossar people on the one hand asking us to help some more boys out this year and on the other hand having them send boys home whose only undesirability so far as I can see is requiring several placements.'[82] Cossar was unmoved by the advice of Frederick Blair, Secretary of the Canadian Immigration Department, to 'declare a holiday until conditions improve', and he remained determined to proceed despite the cessation of empire settlement funding in 1931.[83] In 1932, however, Craigielinn's increasing financial difficulties led to its free transfer to the Church of Scotland's Social Work Committee, and it was subsequently used as a training centre for youths on probation and potential delinquents until it was sold to Paisley Town Council in 1937.[84] At the same time the farm at Lower Gagetown – rebuilt after the original eighteenth-century building was destroyed by fire in December 1929 – functioned independently as a training centre for unemployed boys from eastern Canada under Cossar's renewed personal control and John Jackson's superintendence. In 1945 Jackson and two associates purchased the farm from Cossar's trustees, but in the changed post-war climate they were unsuccessful in their intention to re-establish assisted immigration from Scotland.[85]

Perhaps the most appropriate epitaph on Cossar was penned by the New Brunswick immigration agent D. J. Murphy, who, having observed his work in both Scotland and Canada, concluded in 1933 that 'he means well but does not know how to go about it'.[86] In particular, Cossar remained largely oblivious to the fact that his rescue work was not supplying the type of recruits demanded by either Canada or Australia. By 1926 he had fallen out with the Australian agents over their reluctance to accept Craigielinn trainees despite repeated efforts by the OSC to explain the reasons and work out a compromise, and he never achieved his intention of establishing a training and distribution farm in Australia.[87] Having operated the Canadian farm at his own expense from 1910 to 1928, he never really understood or accepted the principles of assisted migration under the ESA and was irked by the restrictions placed on his activities after Gagetown became a provincial training centre. For Cossar, state involvement in migration was a two-edged sword, offering financial assistance with one hand while taking away freedom of selection with the other, and in 1930 he complained to the Secretary of State for Scotland that Canada was dictating policy to the OSC, so that 'it is much harder for me to get boys away than it was before the Government gave assistance in the way of fares'.[88] G. Whiskard of the Oversea Settlement Department summed up the major problem of state-assisted emigration when he responded –

sympathetically but negatively – to Cossar's request that the Department should help him finance the passages of boys whom he regarded as suitable but who had been rejected by the Canadian authorities. The problem was one of divergent perspectives and priorities for, while Cossar strove to give individual boys a better chance in life, the OSD was 'concerned rather with the whole movement from the point of view of the economic advantage to the various parts of the Empire'.[89]

Yet, although Cossar's vision was frustrated, his achievements were not insignificant. For more than two decades his work, which saw around 900 boys sent to Canada and 200 to Australia – almost 800 of them from Craigielinn – was relatively untainted by complaints from employers or accusations of exploitation from recruits. He established the farm at Lower Gagetown both as a reception centre and also to set a fair wage level for the area, and some of his recruits preferred to stay there to 'have a good time' rather than seek independent employment elsewhere.[90] Not only were disadvantaged urban youths given opportunities that Scotland could not afford them thanks to training in the farming skills which the dominions required, but the good reputation earned by Cossar also enabled him to exercise exceptional influence over the wider juvenile immigration policy of the province of New Brunswick even as other philanthropists began to retreat from that type of enterprise. The great majority of his recruits were claimed to have become successful farmers in the Maritimes, while others attained prominent positions in a variety of professions.[91] Cossar himself died at Dunoon in 1942 as a result of exposure and heart strain suffered two years earlier when the ship on which he was escorting evacuee children to Canada was torpedoed in the Atlantic, and much of his estate was bequeathed to the juvenile rescue work he had so long supported.[92]

Just as Cossar's work provided a model for Cornton Vale, so Craigielinn and Gagetown were modelled on the longest-established and best-known juvenile migration agency operating in Scotland in the 1920s, that of the Orphan Homes of Scotland, established by William Quarrier in 1871 to rescue destitute children from the streets of Glasgow. After Quarrier's death in 1903, the work was maintained by his daughter and son-in-law, and between 1914 and 1939 836 children, predominantly boys, were sent overseas from the orphan village at Bridge of Weir, only a few miles away from Cossar's Craigielinn farm. Apart from the greatly reduced scale of the post-war exodus[93] and the occasional appearance of Australia and New Zealand as destinations, the practice and philosophy of emigration from Quarrier's Homes remained largely unaffected by the war and the ESA; orphans and other destitute children continued to be sent across the Atlantic in 'protected parties' and taken to the Fairknowe receiving home in the Scots-dominated town of Brockville, Ontario, before being sent out to households that had applied for a 'Home child' and had been vetted by the receiving home. Fairknowe staff attempted to monitor progress through regular inspections and promised that problems of incompatibility would be resolved by immediate relocation of the children. The emigrants were encouraged to keep in touch both with Fairknowe and with the Orphan Homes in Scotland, and their letters were reproduced in the annual report for the information of supporters in Scotland.

Throughout its existence the Quarrier organization has adhered to the Christian principles of its founder, although after the war its emigration policy was also influenced by the eugenic, imperialist climate of the age. In 1919 it was claimed, somewhat patronizingly, that thousands of emigrants had gone from Bridge of Weir 'to help solve the immense problems of our great Dominion across the seas',[94] and in 1922 patron Sir Joseph Maclay claimed that 'the day had gone by when it was necessary to contest the issue as to whether Canada was the place for these boys or not. Canada owed the Orphan Homes of Scotland much; some of the children from the Homes were its best citizens.'[95] Canadian scepticism about such claims seems to have been defused by Claude Winters, superintendent at Fairknowe, who worked hard to promote mutual understanding between the Canadian immigration authorities and the various voluntary societies while maintaining in his own institution a consistently high reputation for good placements and aftercare.

Winters was also realistic. He regularly admitted that his work was 'not all sunshine', for 'daily we are involved in the adjustment of wages, the settlement of accounts, the hearing and meeting of complaints concerning the human frailties of employed and employer, the reading and writing of letters, the jolting over concession roads, and the care of house and grounds'.[96] He acknowledged the problems of unemployment, low wages and dissatisfaction resulting from economic depression, and in 1929 referred explicitly to an unprecedented 'measure of unrest', which he attributed 'largely to the influence of boys other than our own who will not settle'. Although he named no individuals or organizations, it is possible that he may have been referring to a minority of Cossar boys who were trained at Craigielinn but then went to Canada in one of the Quarrier parties.[97] Not only in Winters' reports, but also in the positive correspondence selected by Quarrier's Orphan Homes for publication in the institution's annual report, the *Narrative of Facts*, there are sometimes traces of dark experiences in veiled references to loneliness and homesickness, 'undesirable' placements and runaway or footloose juveniles. Failure may have provoked the ultimate return to Scotland of some of the 284 Quarrier emigrants who came back between 1872 and 1939, but the most explicit admissions of failure are found in the unpublished files of individual emigrants.

These included the case of a 'foolish and wilful' girl from Edinburgh who was given a loan to return to her sister in Scotland in 1932 after her health and morale had been broken during six years of unsuccessful placements[98] and a Glasgow boy who petitioned without success to be sent back to a sister and brother-in-law in Coventry. According to the visiting inspector's report of 15 July 1932:

> William has changed very little. He has an exaggerated opinion of himself but is very critical of everyone and everything else. He has a grouchy disposition which after all is his worst fault and here as elsewhere he has become almost unbearable. He has a most unhappy manner. To me he has made no complaints about the home but his employer states that he is constantly grouching about the wages and on the whole he is being paid as well if not better than most of his capacity. It is doubtful if he will remain during the winter as Mr. Hutcheson is quite discouraged with trying to make anything of his disposition.[99]

Another Glasgow boy was deported in 1931 after being convicted of forging the signature of a fellow emigrant in order to steal money from his bank account, a crime for which he served a year's detention at the Ontario reformatory.[100] The same year saw the return of a third Glasgow boy, who was sent home after his father – described in the case file as 'much given to drink and always in debt' – threatened to take legal action on the grounds that his son had been removed to Canada without paternal consent. Despite several placements, the boy failed to settle and was, according to inspection reports, 'altogether disagreeable' and 'impertinent and self willed'. He 'swears like a trooper, will not attend Sunday School, and is reading trashy novels to such an extent that he is neglecting his duty'.[101] One of his fellow passengers on the SS *Scythia* in March 1931 was Norman R., another Quarrier emigrant from Glasgow, who in 1929 had assaulted his employer's wife and had then been imprisoned for ten days for vandalizing the railway track at Belleville. When he returned to Fairknowe after failing to settle in a subsequent situation, the Home, mindful of the prevailing political and economic climate, decided to return him to Scotland, since 'for our own reputation's sake we cannot turn him adrift, in view of the unemployment and general interest of the public in feeding and caring for the unfortunate'.[102]

Particular concern was expressed at the moral lapses of some of the female emigrants. One Glasgow girl was returned to Fairknowe two weeks after being placed at Gananoque on the grounds that 'she was not proving satisfactory especially in regard to her relationships to the children'. Two subsequent placements within a year both proved unsatisfactory, and in 1931, having become pregnant, she was sent home.

> The chap is of a worthless family, is a Roman Catholic and they are at least associated with the boot-legging fraternity referred to in a previous

report ... . Had Margaret's condition been caused by the right sort of people we could have sought redress but she herself was so foolish in her conduct and associations, and the man to blame of such an order that we could not take action and there was nothing to do but return her to Scotland in the way we did, as otherwise she would have been deported when she became a charge upon public charity.[103]

One of Margaret's fellow passengers on the SS *Letitia* was also being sent back to Kirkcaldy in disgrace after only a year in Canada, having aborted her illegitimate child and being suspected of following in her mother's footsteps by working as a prostitute. Her subsequent intention of returning to her Canadian employers in 1932 (at their expense) was vehemently opposed by Claude Winters, who suspected an illicit relationship between the girl and her employer and claimed that she was 'decidedly undesirable from the Canadian point of view and from the point of view of the reputation of our work'.[104]

Such examples can be misleading, for the case files are much more likely to discuss problem cases than the silent, uncontroversial majority who generated no correspondence. Indeed, on the whole, Quarrier's Homes' emigration work escaped scandal and official criticism, and relatively impartial sources (such as the Canadian Immigration Department) indicate that most of their recruits were well regarded, even in the antagonistic inter-war climate. In 1920 Claude Winters claimed that the vast majority of employers, whatever their original motives in petitioning for a Home child, in practice gave their charges a good education and 'homes in the strict sense of the term', and the following year he reported that 'in spite of the Canadian labour situation, which in many respects is critical, we have no trouble in placing our boys and girls'.[105] Although the glowing accounts of correspondents quoted in the promotional annual reports have to be treated with caution, some emigrants clearly benefited by going to Canada and petitioned the Homes to send out younger siblings.

> I am getting on fine out here in Canada and I feel very grateful for the opportunity which has been given to me through the Homes. I have often wondered where I would be to-day if there had been no Homes or if I had not been sent there when I was young ... . My sister is wanting very much to come to Canada as I have been keeping at her to come out here beside me as I am longing to see her. I will send the money to bring her out here if you will get in touch with her and let her come out with the lads this year.[106]

As far as it is possible to tell, many of the boys seem to have followed the advised career of farming, and several left Ontario to try their fortunes in the West. Of the others, some took a business training, while others became tradesmen, ministers or teachers. At least one became prominent in business and local government – according to the envious comment of a fellow Quarrier emigrant, who reported that he was 'extraordinarily well off', with a 'large auto, fine house, stores, and other property', and 'turns over more money in a day sometimes than I handle in a year'.[107] The girls were usually channelled, at least initially, into careers in domestic service, although those who had been given the opportunity to study sometimes became teachers or stenographers.

In 1930 Winters reported a keen demand for juveniles from Fairknowe, where 'our family is largely undisturbed by the unemployment situation'. His optimism was premature, for four years later the receiving home was sold to the local Children's Aid Society, as Winters discovered that neither long experience, independent commendation nor the acclaim of recruits could protect his endeavours from the chill wind of depression. It was not a unique experience. By then the Salvation Army, Cossar's Craigielinn and Gagetown farms, Cornton Vale and the YMCA, as well as the Ministry of Labour training centre at Carstairs, had all but ceased to send trainees overseas, and the demise of juvenile migration schemes belied A. G. Scholes' stubborn confidence in the enduring efficacy of the ESA. Its achievements, he claimed, 'were specially marked in the emigration of juveniles. The granting of free or reduced passages enabled increasing numbers to go overseas, while the greater security offered under schemes which earned the approval of government allayed the fears of parents, and attracted a type of boy who would not ordinarily have considered seeking a career overseas.'[108] Although such statements may have had some validity in the mid-1920s, by 1932 Scholes was clearly portraying the image rather than the reality of juvenile emigration, refusing to accept that one of the major pillars of the imperialists' inter-war programme had never aroused sufficient interest to match its funding and had within a decade come to a somewhat inglorious end.

Notes

1 *Aberdeen Journal*, 24 Aug. 1911; *All the World*, Oct. 1922, p. 427.
2 *P&J*, 30 Jan. 1924; *SG*, 23 Sept. 1927.
3 *Hansard*, vol. 153, 26 Apr. 1922, col. 582.
4 For further discussion of emigration under the auspices of the Salvation Army, see Anon., *Organised Empire Migration and Settlement. A Retrospect of Salvation Army Work for the Empire and its Citizens by a Privileged Observer* (London, The Salvation Army, Migration House, 1930); David Lamb, *Boys of Britain* (London, The Salvation Army, Emigration–Colonization and Shipping Office, 1923) and *General Booth's Scheme for Boys* (London, The Salvation Army, International Headquarters, 1925); and Marjory Harper, 'Emigration and the Salvation Army', *Bulletin of the Scottish Institute of Missionary Studies*, n.s., 3–4 (1985–7), pp. 22–9.
5 A. G. Scholes, *Education for Empire Settlement: A Study of Juvenile Migration* (London, Longmans, 1932), p. 138; Joy Parr, *Labouring Children. British Immigrant Apprentices*

to *Canada, 1869–1914* (London, Croom Helm, 1980), p. 151. Much of the general factual information for this chapter has been quarried from Scholes' book, which was sponsored by the Imperial Studies Committee of the Royal Empire Society.

6 Scholes, *Education for Empire Settlement*, p. 140. Since Scholes obtained most of his information from policy-makers who sought to justify their actions, he was, not surprisingly, optimistic.

7 *P&J*, 19 Dec. 1923.

8 *P&J*, 15 Apr. 1925.

9 Scholes, *Education for Empire Settlement*, p. 145.

10 *P&J*, 26 Aug. 1925; *HN*, 22 Aug. 1925.

11 *SG*, 21 Jan. 1926.

12 Scholes, *Education for Empire Settlement*, pp. 147–8.

13 *Ibid.*, p. 143.

14 *Ibid.*, p. 162.

15 *P&J*, 28 Jan. 1925.

16 *P&J*, 11 Nov. 1925.

17 Fifty public schoolboys a year were settled on the land in South Africa following training either at the Tarka Training Farm in Cape Colony or at Robian Estates in Radium, north Transvaal, and two years' practical experience (Scholes, *Education for Empire Settlement*, p. 163).

18 *Ibid.*, p. 94.

19 *P&J*, 10 July 1925; *SG*, 27 May 1926, 18 Mar. 1927.

20 *SG*, 16 Sept. 1927.

21 *The Scottish Red Triangle News* (*SRTN*), Oct. 1924, p. 11. This publication changed its name to *Scottish Manhood* (*SM*) in October 1926.

22 *SRTN*, May 1925, pp. 10–11.

23 G. F. Plant, *Oversea Settlement. Migration from the United Kingdom to the Dominions* (Oxford, Oxford University Press, 1951), p. 138.

24 *SRTN*, Sept. 1925, p. 23.

25 *P&J*, 2 Feb. 1926.

26 *SM*, Sept. 1927, p. 21.

27 *SRTN*, May 1926, pp. 14–15.

28 *SRTN*, June 1926, p. 21.

29 *SM*, July 1927, p. 19; Feb. 1930, p. 17.

30 *SM*, Sept. 1928, p. 16.

31 *SM*, Mar. 1929, p. 17.

32 *SM*, May 1929, p. 14.

33 *SM*, May 1929, p. 17.

34 *SM*, Oct. 1929, p. 16.

35 *SM*, Feb. 1930, p.7.

36 *Reports on the Schemes of the Church of Scotland – Committee on the Church Overseas*, 1925, p. 341.

37 *The Monthly Record*, Feb. 1927, p. 34.

38 NAC, RG76, C-10260, vol. 356, file 400652, 'Cornton Vale Trainees. Agreement with the Church of Scotland Committee on Social Work for Providing the Cost of Transportation etc.'.

39 *Reports on the Schemes of the Church of Scotland, with the Legislative Acts passed by the General Assembly, 1924 – Report of the Social Work Committee*, p. 887.

40 NAC, RG76, C-10236, vol. 323, file 310968, 'Fifteen parish trainees, Glasgow, allocated to Toronto'. Extract from the *Montreal Gazette*, 7 Sept. 1927.

41 *Ibid.*, J. G. Rattray, Superintendent, LSB, to W. R. Little, 11 Feb. 1928; A. O'Kelly, Assistant Director of Emigration, London, to the DIC, 8, 27 Mar. 1928. The seven recruits who sailed on the Anchor-Donaldson liner *Athenia* for Quebec on 26 August 1927 were James Campbell, Peter Chilton, Charles Robertson Lay, Edward McInnes, John Moore, Edward Murphy and William Porteous. Those who sailed on the *Cameronia* on 24 March 1928 were Robert Adams, Thomas Brown, Samuel Cameron, Matthew Clark, Thomas Connolly, Edward Cowan, George Davidson, George Discombe, John Docherty,

Charles Dolan, George Duggan, Walter Duggan, John Ferguson, Hugh Fitzpatrick, Robert Fullerton, James Gilchrist, Andrew Gillespie, Charles Green, Thomas Green, William Hay, James Henderson, William Henderson, Robert Kane, Patrick Keegan, David Kelly, James Kelly, Edward Kennedy, Alex Livingstone, Thomas McGlone, John McLaughlin, John McLean, Hugh Mallin, Robert Maloney, Thomas Miller, Arthur Muldoon, John Murdoch, Robert Murphy, James Platt, Hugh Ramage, Robert Sommerville, James Tweedie, Joseph Tweedie, David Wallace, John Williamson and James Wilson. A further thirteen recruits sailed on the *Letitia* on 18 May 1928: John Cockburn, William Davidson, James Entricon, Thomas Herbertson, John Leary, James McGibbon, Thomas McGibbon, William Munn, William O'Donnell, John Stein, William Thomson, George Watt and Henry Wilson. Another contingent on the same vessel, sailing on 13 July 1928, comprised Andrew Brown, James Dearie, John Dodds, Matthew Doris, Thomas Flannigan, James Lyons, Joseph McFinlay, Hugh McLaughlin, Donald McLeod, Thomas McMillan, Patrick Moffat, Thomas Murphy and Peter Rocks. Seven trainees sailed on the *Athenia* on 23 March 1929: William Corrigan, John Currie, Patrick Dillon, William Quinn, Robert Sproul, James Tracey and Robert Yuill; and five from Inverness under the same scheme by the same vessel on 12 July: Alexander Dowdles, William Grogans, John McCabe, Patrick Macdonald and Duncan McPhail.

42 NAC, RG76, C-10236, vol. 323, file 310968, E. M. Johnston to J. G. Rattray, 9 Apr. 1928.
43 *Ibid.*, J. B. Walker to W. J. Egan, 6 July 1928; Egan to Walker, 20 July 1928.
44 *Ibid.*, E. M. Johnston to J. B. Walker, 8 June 1928; LSB Commissioner at Winnipeg to CPR Steamship Passenger Agent, Montreal, 29 Dec. 1928; A. L. Jolliffe to Dr J. Page, 6 Sept. 1929; Jolliffe to Messrs the Robert Reford Company, Montreal, 19 Mar. 1930.
45 *Ibid.*, E. M. Johnston to J. B. Walker, 10 July 1928; unnamed Manitoba field supervisor to A. L. Jolliffe, 29 Oct. 1928.
46 *Ibid.*, J. B. Walker to W. J. Egan, two letters, both dated 24 Aug. 1928.
47 *Ibid.*, Andrew O'Kelly, Glasgow agent, to Anne MacDonald, 11 Feb. 1929; O'Kelly to Egan, 10 Dec. 1929; Egan to Little, 28 Dec. 1929. A total of 115 migrants had gone out under the scheme in 1928.
48 *Reports on the Schemes of the Church of Scotland, with the Legislative Acts passed by the General Assembly, Report of the Social Work Committee*, 1930, p. 422.
49 Church of Scotland, minutes of the Committee on Social Work, 17 Dec. 1930. Cornton Vale Farm functioned as a rehabilitation centre for destitute and delinquent youths and men throughout the 1930s. After the Second World War it was leased, and subsequently purchased, by the Scottish Home Department Prisons and Borstals Branch and later became a women's prison. For further details of its history, see Lewis L. L. Cameron, *The Challenge of Need. A History of Social Service by the Church of Scotland 1869–1969* (Edinburgh, St Andrew's Press, 1971), pp. 27–9, 68.
50 NAC, RG76, C-10467, vol. 568, file 811910, part 1, Cossar and William Hunter to the Minister of Agriculture, Ottawa, 31 Aug. 1909.
51 *Ibid.*, J. B. Walker to the DIC, 1 Sept. 1909.
52 Provincial Archives of New Brunswick (PANB), MC 2402, Vera Ayling records. The administration of Todhill Farm was subsequently handed over to the Scottish Labour Colony, and in 1922 the Trustees decided that it should be devoted to training boys for farming careers in Scotland (SRO, AF51/171, G. F. Plant to the Scottish Office, 18 Dec. 1924).
53 NAC, RG76, C-10647, vol. 568, file 811910, part 1, Cossar to W. J. White, Department of the Interior, Ottawa, 3 Nov. 1909.
54 *Ibid.*, report by G. B. Smart on Gagetown Farm, 15 Sept. 1913.
55 *GH, The Scotsman, Daily Record*, 3 Aug. 1922.
56 NAC, RG76, C-7821, vol. 282, file 234636, 'Agreement between the Secretary of State for the Colonies and Craigielinn Farm, 28 Aug. 1922'.
57 *P&J*, 15 Apr. 1924.
58 *Montreal Star*, 15 Aug. 1924. See also NAC, RG76, C-10647, vol. 568, file 811910, report by Charles Allan, Canadian government immigration agent, 14 July 1924.
59 *HN*, 31 Jan., 15 Aug. 1925; *P&J*, 29 June 1925.

60 *P&J*, 1 May 1925.
61 NAC, RG76, C-78221, file 234636, annual report of the Cossar Boys' Training Farms Inc., 1927–28, by Duncan Watson.
62 *Ibid.*
63 SRO, AF51/171, annual report of the Cossar Boys' Training Farms Inc., 21 Dec. 1923. Between 9 September 1922 and 31 October 1923 191 boys had been enrolled at Craigielinn, of whom sixty-five had gone to Australia and forty-two to Canada.
64 Undated letter from 'J.W.' in annual report of the Cossar Boys' Training Farms, Inc., 1927–8.
65 Annual report of the Cossar Boys' Training Farms, Inc.,1923.
66 NAC, RG76, C-10647, vol. 568, file 811910, part 1, Rev. William Smith, Gagetown, to Department of the Interior, 14 Oct. 1913; Cossar to W. D. Scott, 6 Dec. 1913.
67 *Ibid.*, C-7831, vol. 282, file 234646, deportation order of 26 Mar. 1929; C-10646-7, vol. 567, file 811910, part 2, Cossar to F. C. Blair, 8 Aug. 1931; C-10646-7, vol. 567, file 811910, part 1, John Jackson to Blair, 15 Aug. 1931; J. O. Smith to W. D. Scott, 22 Aug. 1917; Meiklejohn to G. B. Smart, 23 Oct. 1925.
68 *Ibid.*, C-10647, vol. 568, file 811910, part 1, Smart to Jackson, 17 Aug. 1928.
69 *Ibid.*, Waugh to Melvin, 14 Nov. 1924.
70 *Ibid.*, memorandum by Smart, 20 Jan. 1925; Cossar to W. J. Egan, 6 Mar. 1925.
71 *Ibid.*, vol. 567, file 811910, part 3, Scobie to Blair, 13 Jan. 1932.
72 *Ibid.*, vol. 568, file 811910, part 1, report by Smart on Cossar Farm, 21 Sept. 1929.
73 *Ibid.*, Jackson to Smart, 6 Apr. 1932.
74 *Ibid.*, D. J. Murphy to Smart, 4 July 1930.
75 *Ibid.*, Hugh Paterson to his mother, 'Sunday 6th' [Sept. 1924].
76 SRO, AF/41, 'Settlement of boys in Australia and elsewhere', 6 Feb. 1926, Cossar to Sir Joseph Cook, Australian High Commissioner, quoting a letter which he threatened to send to the press. See also *HN*, 15 Aug. 1925.
77 NAC, RG76, C-7821, vol. 282, file 234636, J. A. Murray, Minister of Immigration and Industry, New Brunswick, to W. R. Little, 7 Oct. 1927. See also *ibid.*, C-10260, vol. 356, file 397430, internal memorandum of the DIC, 3 Jan. 1934.
78 *Ibid.*, C-7821, vol. 282, file 234636, annual report of the Cossar Boys' Training Farms Inc., 26 Apr. 1929.
79 *Ibid.*, C-10647, vol. 567, file 811910, part 2, Blair to Egan, 8 Sept. 1930.
80 *Ibid.*, DIC memorandum, 10 Apr. 1930; Malcolm to Little, 21 May 1931; Cossar to Little, 30 May 1931.
81 *Ibid.*, Blair to Murray, 24 June 1931.
82 *Ibid.*, Blair to Little, 25 Aug. 1931.
83 *Ibid.*, Blair to Cossar, 31 Aug. 1931, Little to Blair, 7 Sept. 1931.
84 Church of Scotland, minutes of the Committee on Social Work, 11 Mar. 1931, 19 Oct. 1932; minutes of the Committee on Christian Life and Work, 7 Apr., 27 May 1937.
85 *Telegraph Journal* (St John, New Brunswick), 18 Dec. 1929; 13 Oct. 1948; PANB, MC 2402, Vera Ayling records.
86 NAC, RG76, C-10647, vol. 567, file 811910, part 1, Murphy to Blair, 14 June 1933.
87 SRO, AF511/174, G. F. Plant to Cossar, 16 Feb. 1926.
88 *Ibid.*, Cossar to Hon. William Adamson, 26 Mar. 1930.
89 NAC, RG76, C-10657, vol. 567, file 811910, part 1, Whiskard to Cossar, 24 Feb. 1930.
90 *Ibid.*, part 2, Blair to Little, 27 Mar. 1933.
91 PANB, MC 2402, Vera Ayling records. Success stories included a Beaverbrook scholar at the University of New Brunswick, a prominent fox rancher in Prince Edward Island, a high-ranking New York City police officer and a squadron leader in the Royal Canadian Air Force.
92 According to an article in the *Telegraph Journal*, 13 Oct. 1948, Cossar was also involved, just before the outbreak of the Second World War, in a 'cloak and dagger drama', rescuing more than 200 Jewish children from Nazi Germany. See also Cossar's will, registered in the Books of the Lords of Council and Session, Edinburgh, 26 Aug. 1942, copy in PANB.
93 Recruitment was suspended entirely from 1917 to 1919 and again from 1933 to 1937.

94 *Narrative of Facts*, 1919, p. 29.
95 *Ibid.*, 1922, p. 7, quoting from the *Glasgow Herald*, 29 Nov. 1922
96 *Narrative of Facts*, 1919, p. 32.
97 *Ibid.*, 1929, p. 44. Quarrier's emigration register for 1927 includes a list headed 'Cossar Boys'.
98 Jeanie Anderson, born 1910, entered 1919.
99 William Andrew, born 1913, entered 1927.
100 Herbert Clark, born 1911, entered 1915.
101 John MacPherson, born 1913, entered 1925. Visiting inspectors' reports of 23 Nov. 1929, 25 Jan. 1930.
102 Norman Roberts, born 1912, entered 1923. Fairknowe Report, 9 Dec. 1930.
103 Margaret Houston, born 1911, entered 1915.
104 Jessie Hunter, born 1911, entered 1923. Claude Winters to Agnes Burges, 17 Feb. 1932.
105 *Narrative of Facts*, 1920, p. 29; 1921, p. 28.
106 *Ibid.*, 1928, p. 21.
107 *Ibid.*, 1919, p. 3.
108 Scholes, *Education for Empire Settlement*, p. 75.

CHAPTER SIX

Evaluating emigration

The controversy that had always been a concomitant of emigration clearly did not cease with the passage of the Empire Settlement Act of 1922, which sharpened the debate from party political, ideological and practical perspectives. In a Scottish context, the youthful exodus from urban-industrial areas – which accounted for much of the country's inter-war emigration – also became one of the sharpest rocks on which formal schemes of empire settlement foundered, while simultaneously exposing the paradoxical attitudes of Scottish institutions, which, with one breath, bewailed the drain of population and, with the next, advocated coloniza-tion schemes. Domestic opposition from nationalists, communists and socialists was reinforced by colonial complaints of huge disparities between rural demand and urban supply but countered by the claims of agents and imperialists that overseas settlement was both beneficial to the adapt-able individual colonist and essential to the wellbeing and security of the empire.

The emigration of children and adolescents revealed particularly deep divisions – not just because of the recruits' predominantly urban origins, but because they seemed to symbolize all that was best and worst about assisted colonization. Most of the evangelical architects of juvenile emigra-tion had died by the First World War, but their achievements continued to be celebrated both in hagiographies and in the fund-raising publications of the agencies they had founded.[1] Significant government support for child emigration was first evident at a conference organized by the Royal Colonial Institute in 1910, as pressure to increase overseas recruitment under the English poor law was coupled with rising imperialist sentiments and a growing belief that juvenile emigration in particular could 'not merely palliate, but actually solve the problem of unemployment'.[2] But the emigrationists' determination to relocate town-dwellers in rural situations was not simply based on domestic ills and the economic argument that those removed from urban squalor and deprivation would – especially if they were young, malleable and well trained – be transformed into colonial producers of raw materials for British markets and consumers of British manufactured goods; both before and after the war it was also a reflection of their continuing confidence in the eugenic efficacy of rural colonial life as a means of regaining lost British values.

Such confidence was not universal. Once their work was underpinned by state subsidies, juvenile emigration societies were invested with much greater political sensitivity and, as a result, were praised and vilified all the more intensely by imperialists and socialists, respectively, in the press, in parliament and in official investigations. Opposition to the coalescence of support for emigration between emigrationists in the state and voluntary sectors came, as before the war, from colonial authorities and citizens – particularly in Canada – who complained about the calibre of the recruits and the difficulty of securing adult employment for emigrants who had outgrown their youthful placements. 'Van boys from Glasgow, butcher boys from Dundee and news boys from Bristol' were not welcomed in the Dominion,[3] where the Canadian Council on Child Welfare under its leader, Charlotte Whitton, collected sensational but sometimes question-able statistics from asylums, jails, VD clinics and reformatories and campaigned for a complete cessation of the movement. Perhaps the rescue societies had only themselves to blame for the increasingly vociferous hostility of the Canadian press and public since, in their fund-raising propaganda, they tended to highlight the contrast between the initial degeneracy of recruits and their subsequent rehabilitation. Labour repre-sentatives and middle-class spokesmen alike claimed that Home children 'failed the test of desirable immigrants on every score. As the dregs of British society, their fares underwritten by charity and government subsidy, their placement in rural Canada a payment for their poverty and depen-dence, and without a commitment to the land, these children and youths had no redeeming qualities.'[4]

At the same time, growing opposition in Britain was based partly on the practical argument that wartime mortality and a falling birth rate had solved the problem of overpopulation, while the Adoption Act of 1920 and, later, the payment of allowances to single mothers further reduced the number of candidates.[5] A more child-centred approach to young people's welfare also led to demands that problem children should not be separated irrevocably from their families and surroundings and sent to the empire as cheap labour but should be rehabilitated at home. Such arguments pre-dated the war, as did socialist opposition to child migration, but they were given added momentum with the election of a Labour government in 1924. Labour politicians, fiercely critical of a policy which they claimed was both ill-founded and deliberately designed to inhibit the extension of state welfare provision, regularly raised the issue in Parliament. J. C. Wedgwood and H. Snell were particularly adamant that the funding allocated to the 'deportation' of excess population to the empire should have been used to tackle domestic unemployment, and castigated their opponents for their unseemly determination – born, as they saw it, of expediency – to send other people's children to distant parts of the world. On one occasion Wedgwood tackled Sir C. Kinloch-Cooke on the grounds that 'the parents and relations of these children would prefer to have them settled on the land of this country rather than go where they are apparently not wanted, and where they will have as great a difficulty in getting land as they have here. What we have to do to solve the problem of finding work for these people is to open up the resources of this country, without bothering about sending them out to other parts of the world.'[6]

The suicides of three 'Home boys' in Canada in the winter of 1923 and five similar deaths in Australia led to the appointment of an investigative delegation, headed by Margaret Bondfield, Parliamentary Secretary to the Ministry of Labour in the MacDonald administration. During a six-week tour of Canada at the invitation of the Dominion government, it inspected receiving homes and situations in every province and talked to individual children, former children and officials, investigating allegations about lax inspections and exploitation. Despite expectations to the contrary, the Bondfield Report gave a balanced assessment of juvenile migration, commenting optimistically on the settlers' condition and prospects and highlighting the significance of secondary movement:

In many cases the children are regarded as members of the family and a real interest is taken in their future. Only in a very few instances did the delegation come across evidences of unhappiness, due possibly to the child proving unadaptable to its surroundings. Almost invariably the children stated that they were thoroughly happy in Canada and would, on no account, return to the Old Country. A number of the children interviewed anticipated their relatives joining them ... . We have no doubt that the prospects in Canada for the average boy or girl are better than they would be in the United Kingdom. The boy who is prepared to take farming seriously can with thrift and determination look forward to becoming an independent farmer in due course. We visited many farms which were owned by men who originally came to Canada as child migrants. In some cases the boys have been allowed to take over the farm of their original employer after gaining the necessary experience. In other cases they have saved enough from their wages to rent and stock a farm, and to purchase it by instalments over a period of years.

As a matter of fact, a large number of boys prefer to take up some other calling than farming after reaching the age of 18. We came across a considerable number of cases in which boys had secured good positions for themselves in the towns. The drift from the rural districts to the cities is as noticeable in Canada as it is in other countries, and the British immigrant boys and girls are not exempt from this tendency. At the same time we formed the impression that the years spent on the land were of great benefit to the boys in later life, both on account of the physical advantages gained and because those who have worked on the land are in a position to return at any time and secure employment as experienced farm workers.

As regards the girls, the majority of them marry and settle down satisfactorily either in the country as farmers' wives or in the towns.[7]

The delegation was generally satisfied with travel and reception arrangements, placements, inspection and supervision procedures. On the other hand, there was room for some improvement in selection to detect temperamental unsuitability, and the report claimed that training centres – on both sides of the Atlantic – were a waste of time and money, which should only receive official funding for the basic testing of applicants in Britain as a preliminary to selection. Distributing homes were urged to ensure that each child had a separate bedroom, or at least a separate bed, in a household of the same religion as itself, and societies should either work in separate spheres or co-operate to prevent unsuitable households receiving children from different organizations. The delegation was also struck by the variation in wage rates arranged by different societies for children of the same ages and qualifications working under similar conditions, a disparity which, they pointed out, caused discontent among the emigrants and could sour relations with their employers. Criticizing the societies' tendency to make cheap wage agreements on the basis of the farmer's wishes rather than their own estimate of the recruit's value, they recommended both that the societies confer with a view to standardizing wages and working conditions and that they adopt a firmer approach in the recovery of wage arrears from employers. The main reservation, however, was that children were rarely adopted legally into households but were recruited as wage labourers when they were too young to work, to the detriment of their education and general wellbeing.

> It seems to us that, recognising that the children are sent to Canada for working purposes, the general principle to be adopted is that the children should not leave this country until they have arrived at working age. At the same time there should be no undue interval between the date at which a child finishes school in the United Kingdom and the date of departure for Canada. The longer the interval in this case the more difficult will be the process of adaptation.[8]

In accordance with these recommendations, in April 1925 the Canadian immigration authorities fixed at fourteen years the age limit for the migration of unaccompanied subsidized children. The legislation was initially enacted for three years, but in 1928 it was made permanent as a consequence of the onset of worldwide depression coupled with Charlotte Whitton's continuing opposition.

In the Scottish context, Quarrier's Orphan Homes largely maintained in their inter-war emigration work the good reputation they had built up during the founder's lifetime, and although they welcomed the extra funding made available under the ESA, neither the integrity nor the continuation of their migration work depended on it. The same could not be said of many of the other agencies, which were lured into sponsoring juvenile and young adult migration from urban Scotland on the promise of shared funding, and which were subsequently faced not only with the practical problem of maintaining their momentum in the face of creeping depression but also with ethical dilemmas arising from their inconsistent attitudes to migration and their endorsement of popular eugenic, imperialist policies.

In the Scottish presbyterian churches especially, assisted colonization schemes sat uneasily alongside repeated outbursts of anti-emigration sentiment. Before the war the general assemblies of both the Free and United Free Churches had, in 1911, complained about the 'menace' of an 'exceedingly onerous' tide of emigration which was sweeping Scotland, claiming that since for a decade presbyterian emigration had largely surpassed the Roman Catholic Irish exodus from Scotland, both national stability and the future of Protestantism were under dire and imminent threat.[9] These xenophobic sentiments were reiterated much more stridently in the 1920s, when the Church and Nation Committee of the Church of Scotland regularly inveighed against the perceived threat to national presbyterian identity posed by Irish Catholic immigration into central Scotland set against a massive exodus of native Scots. Such was its concern that in 1923 the Committee was given a remit to investigate 'the menace to Scottish nationality and civilisation' caused by Irish immigration, and the following year this was extended to include a study of the effects of emigration on the relative position of native-born Scots and incomers in the Scottish population. In 1925 the Committee reported in some panic that

> The Scots are leaving their native land in tens of thousands every year, and the non-Scottish population come in every day, and neither they nor their descendants emigrate to any appreciable extent. It is noteworthy that though there has been a very great emigration of Scots from Glasgow, yet the number of unemployed has remained more or less stationary for the last two years. While immigration continues unregulated and unrestricted, emigration affords no remedy for unemployment.[10]

A year later, after consulting with the other presbyterian churches, the Church and Nation Committee reiterated its concern about unemployment, immigration and emigration. For many Scots, it claimed,

> the position is growing so hopeless that their only chance of a decent livelihood is to emigrate, with the result that the industrial areas are being largely recruited from a people whose whole social, mental, and moral outlook is on a lower plane than that of the stalwart sons and daughters of our native hills and glens ... . The Scot, who as a colonist is eagerly sought after by all the Dominions and by America, is being driven from his own shores, and his place taken by an immigrant who makes a very much less satisfactory citizen.[11]

Having witnessed no improvement in the situation by 1927, the Committee urged government, employers and trades unions to co-operate in regulating immigration and in creating conditions conducive to the retention of native labour at home. And the national church, it declared, should lead the way, having 'clearly an obligation to defend Scottish nationality such as no other institution or organisation has ... . If ever there was a call to the Church of Scotland to stand fast for what men rightly count dearest – their nationality and their traditions – that call is surely sounding now, when our race and our culture are faced with a peril which ... is the gravest with which the Scottish people have ever been confronted.'[12]

The national church's xenophobic hostility to emigration was echoed by the other presbyterian denominations. The Free Church in 1923 deplored the loss from the highlands in particular of 'young men and women in the freshness and vigour of early life' and complained in general that 'in many parts of the country there is a steady flow of undesirables who are taking the place of the emigrants'.[13] The United Free Church similarly argued that government attempts to relieve unemployment through assisted-emigration schemes were 'rendered futile by the fact that as fast as Scotsmen can be induced to emigrate Irishmen and others come over and fill their places ... and the peril is that our Protestant Church, in common with every other Scottish institution, will be swamped by an alien population having no sympathy with Scottish history, tradition, or custom.'[14]

But can the Scottish churches be accused of speaking with a forked tongue on these issues? If they were so implacably opposed to emigration on the grounds that it damaged Scotland's religious identity as well as its economy by substituting ignorant, indolent and subversive Irish for stalwart, honest, presbyterian Scots, why did they collaborate – with apparent enthusiasm – in so many schemes of assisted migration developed under the ESA? The answer seems to lie in the victory of expediency over ideology and a feeling that the two issues of immigration and emigration were only loosely related. In particular, the erosion of national identity at home made it all the more important to nurture that identity overseas, not least by fulfilling pastoral obligations to colonial brethren, particularly in group settlements.

> It is no part of the Church's duty to foster the departure of people from the Homeland, but the Empire Settlement Act of 1922 does encourage and seeks to regulate migration within the Empire, and very large numbers of people are leaving our shores. New groups of Scottish settlers are being formed in all parts of the world. Responsibility is laid upon us to provide them with the means of grace, for the Overseas Churches do not have ministers sufficient to meet the needs in old-established communities, far less to supply the immigrants with ordinances.[15]

The churches, however, went well beyond the passive delivery of religious ordinances. While deploring the economic ills which provoked much of the 1920s exodus, they admitted that not all emigration was a flight of unwilling refugees, and that even when unemployment was the trigger, emigration was both a palliative and a more desirable resort than the demoralizing 'dole'.[16] Furthermore, they acknowledged their Christian responsibility to protect and promote the temporal and spiritual interests of the adventurous and reluctant alike. Although this seemed to contradict their ideological opposition to emigration, they remained largely oblivious – at least in public – to the disparity between condemnatory rhetoric and positive pragmatism.

From such a perspective, ecclesiastical support for ventures such as the Cornton Vale and Craigielinn farms and the Church Nomination Scheme was a logical response to an existing demand, not an unsolicited and indiscriminate invitation to emigrate. If Scots were determined to leave, and were being encouraged by government incentives, then their duty, the churches argued, was to help channel that tide of emigration to the empire rather than to the United States, to recruit only surplus labour, and to ensure that would-be colonists were properly tested, trained and supervised in agricultural pursuits before, during and after their removal overseas. Despite inevitable mistakes, they were confident that the selection and training programmes which they set on foot, and their network of overseas contacts, had helped to turn many unlikely recruits from the less privileged ranks of Scottish society into nominees acceptable to the cautious dominion governments, and they blamed their early demise not on deficient policies but on economic circumstances beyond their control.

The divided mind of the Scottish churches over emigration was also evident in a clutch of familiar arguments in the secular press, which both reflected and moulded public attitudes. Since attitudes were generally based on domestic economic circumstances and self-interest rather than ideology or imperial visions, they tended to fluctuate according to whether the emigrating population was perceived as a threat or an asset to the local or national economy, and inter-war commentators – like their Victorian predecessors – frequently bemoaned the loss as one of enterprising citizens rather than surplus stock. The large readership of the *People's Journal* was exposed on 17 February 1923 to an editorial which opposed empire settlement as a remedy for unemployment on the grounds that all 'assisted and directed movements' down the ages had been 'streaked with failure' and that current arrangements provided overseas countries, including the United States, with the trained, educated élite of Britain's population. But not only was it 'a counsel of despair' to emigrate young people at the end of a costly educational process, the paper declared; experience had also shown that 'notoriously the emigrants of the assisted movements refuse to stick where they are placed', with up to 80 per cent gravitating to the towns instead of remaining on the land. A month later the *Press & Journal* gave partial endorsement to those sentiments. Catering for a rural constituency that deplored the depletion of the farm labour force but regarded the departure of skilled artisans as a means of relieving the dole queues, an editorial on 19 March 1923 acknowledged Sir Alfred Yarrow's lament that every young emigrant represented a national loss of £400 in terms of education but felt this was more than counterbalanced by transatlantic opportunities for engineers, miners and steelworkers, and welcomed the 'resumption of the westward flow of our surplus population' from central Scotland to Canada and the United States. Later that year, however, it bemoaned the tendency of too many emigrants to leave 'in a spirit of desperation rather than of hope ... with nothing more positive in mind than disgust at the lack of opportunities at home', an attitude which it claimed was simply 'a short cut to disaster'.[17] The massive Hebridean exodus of 1923 was regarded by the anti-crofter *Scotsman* as a positive effect of military service and the spread of education and 'a hopeful sign that a more enlightened view is now being taken by the islanders of their own interests'. It did, however, acknowledge the economic imperatives behind the often painful decision to leave islands that 'cannot support their population in the decency and comfort they have learned to seek' and deplored the impoverishment of Scotland through the loss of a 'sturdy, independent, and upright stock'.[18] The *Glasgow Herald* was also ambivalent about the Hebridean movement. On the one hand it deprecated the onset of a potentially serious leakage, which it blamed in part on especially extensive unemployment in those occupations which were not covered by the limited safety net of national insurance and in part on the collapse of Lord Leverhulme's schemes. On the other hand it remarked on the emigrants' cheerful demeanour and claimed that 'expatriation of the surplus population' was the only practicable solution to demographic pressure in islands afflicted by a 'chronic inadequacy of natural resources'.[19] Not surprisingly, given its constituency, it was more emphatic about the 'highly useful avocation in life' offered to demoralized city boys by George Cossar's colonial training scheme, although just a week later it also published the Scottish Land Settlement Association secretary's gloomy correspondence, which unreservedly deplored juvenile emigration as 'one of the most fatal mistakes that this nation ever made'.[20]

If expediency dictated that churches, newspaper editors and public were inconsistent in their attitudes to emigration, ideology dictated that in political circles Scottish Nationalists and the Communist Party were, for different reasons, unequivocal in their condemnation. From its establishment in November 1926 the Scottish National League's journal, the The Scots Independent, waged a relentless campaign against emigration, which it claimed arose from Scotland's failure to control its own affairs and the false assumption that the country was burdened with a surplus population. Comfort and prosperity in other lands, it asserted, were being won selfishly at the expense of continuing economic and political stagnation in Scotland as citizens with skill and ambition, believing that their homeland was 'done', abdicated their responsibilities of nationhood and, on settling overseas, degenerated into a sentimental nationalism and the constant, but futile, 'reiteration of undying affection for Scotland'.[21] Some, having unwittingly signed up for badly paid jobs in poor conditions, found that comfort and prosperity eluded them, while their departure did nothing to ease Scotland's economic ills. 'If emigration is the cure for unemployment, how comes it that Scotland is in such a plight?' The Scots Independent asked rhetorically in the context of an attack in 1927 on the Westminster government's tendency to encourage emigration rather than attempt to reconstruct Scottish industries, and a year later, after castigating the 'export' of Scottish domestic servants, it repeated its persistent refrain that 'Scotland is not over-populated: she is underworked'.[22] The Church of Scotland's Cornton Vale farm and the Ministry of Labour's training centre at Carstairs both came under nationalist attack for diverting the workless into unpromising overseas channels instead of encouraging them – somewhat questionably – to undertake land reclamation at home, and nationalists deplored the passivity of commentators who wrung their hands at the tragedy of emigration but did nothing to reverse the trend.[23]

One Dundee correspondent of The Scots Independent, appalled by the number of his friends who had emigrated in the previous three months, bemoaned the economic impoverishment of Scotland through the loss of skilled artisans to foreign competitors. His complaint was reinforced by an editorial five months later, which alleged that the emigrants' preference for such foreign competitors over the 'English Empire' was demonstrated by a waiting list of 60,000 Scots who wished to settle in the United States.[24] In February 1927 the Reverend Archibald Scott of Helmsdale, after making a robust attack on the government's failure to preserve the 'vitality and virility of the Scottish people' by obstructing the enlargement of holdings and preferring sportsmen and pastoralists to crofters and fishermen, offered a lengthy indictment of highland emigration, which included a criticism of the disingenuous proposal to send Hebridean fishermen to the Queen Charlotte Islands.

> The 'emigration' that is depriving the nation of its best types is not the way to Paradise – through fields of giant wheat, gigantic grape clusters, orchards and groves with 'sun-kissed' apples and oranges, as depicted in advertisements. The emigrated Highlander is a good correspondent, and the letters which he sends to the old home give pictures of another sort. Paradise is for the middlemen who exploit his labour, and for the agencies that order transport and implements, and for the banks into whose hands he falls sooner or later. There are regions where a full crop is not attained oftener than once in three years. Rigours of weather, drought, pests of various kinds exist on a scale that renders human effort, at times, utterly vain … . Many of the occupations into which agricultural and fishing emigrants have been inveigled are merely seasonable jobs. The work of the season over, a long spell of unemployment follows; and many men who have gone abroad with young families have bitter experiences to relate of hardships.
>
> Of course, the true corrective of emigration from the Highlands is to make it unnecessary, or to leave it to the young and venturesome spirits that have never been scarce among the Celts. In the present dependent state of our meat, butter, egg and cheese markets upon foreigners, to leave the Scottish Highlands unencouraged and undeveloped, and to incite the people to emigrate, is a token of national stupidity, and a sign of the utter bankruptcy of British statesmen in knowledge of how the homeland should be governed.[25]

In advocating the formation of overseas branches of the Scottish National League, columnist Joseph MacDonnell contrasted the positive outlook of Victorian emigrants with the pessimism of thousands of contemporary exiles, who were 'carrying away with them bitter memories of the land that bore them, memories of unemployment, of ill-requited war service and suffering, of accumulated grievances, especially of the post-war slaughter of wages'.[26] Although political collaboration and solid support for Scottish independence among Caledonian and St Andrew's societies and the Order of Scottish Clans proved hard to achieve, overseas subscriptions to *The Scots Independent* grew steadily, owing largely to the efforts of Arthur Donaldson of Detroit. Nationalists such as William Thomson and Scottish National League chairman Roland Muirhead periodically visited the United States and Canada to stimulate interest, Thomson undertaking regular promotional tours in the early 1930s, and expatriate Scots were urged to follow the example of their Irish counterparts in advancing the struggle for self-determination. Particular opprobrium was heaped on the

Westminster government in the wake of the unemployed miners' ill-starred prairie harvesting expedition of 1928 and the 'national crisis' demonstrated by the publication of the 1931 census, which showed particular depopulation in depressed towns such as Greenock, Motherwell and Coatbridge, from which there had been heavy emigration.[27] But, alleged the nationalists, it was not merely working-class Scots who were facilitating alien infiltration of their country by chasing overseas rainbows:

> Uncounted hundreds of able young men of the middle class are leaving the country every year for America, India, Australia, South Africa, London, as accountants, engineers, doctors, teachers, and so forth. It is admitted that there is not room for all of them at home. But the stream of departure has become a panic, it is a 'sauve qui peut.' It has taken on the colours of myth; there is a stupid legend abroad that it is impossible for a young Scotsman to 'make good' in his native land. A parrot-cry has arisen that El Dorados await young Scotland East and West, that crocks of gold lie at the rising and setting-places of the sun. Add to our educated youth the sum of the skilled mechanics who are leaving these shores in the illusion of receiving a better rate of wages where costs of living are three times greater and you swell enormously the host of the deluded fortune-hunters who, without probing the resources of their own country, unhesitatingly and thoughtlessly take wing for other climes on the strength of having seen a highly-coloured poster describing the Californian paradise, or a cleverly written brochure detailing the superiority of existence in Alberta or New South Wales.[28]

Some of the left-wing luminaries of the Scottish literary renaissance occasionally introduced anti-emigration sentiments into their writings, while the other end of the spectrum was represented by writers like Frederick Niven (1878–1944), Valparaiso-born and Glasgow-educated, who settled in British Columbia after the war and whose novels reflect both his pre-war experiences in western Canada's railway and lumber camps and his perception of the Scots as intrepid pioneers who successfully tamed the Canadian wilderness.[29] The nationalist Neil Gunn was relatively silent on the theme of exile, despite the emigration of three elder brothers to Canada before 1914 and his own denunciation of the highland clearances and nation-wide economic stagnation. His first novel, *The Grey Coast* (1926), makes passing reference (reproduced below) to Canada as a last desperate resort of failed fishermen, while part of *Morning Tide* (1931) portrays emigration to Australia in a similar light, as the unhappy and irreversible result of economic disintegration, which had dislocated family and community alike.

> No fishing, no croft. There remained the slums of Glasgow, or the remote world of Canada. And to Canada they all went. If you had a trade at your finger-ends you might do well; otherwise you took your chance, with a hand

ever ready to turn to anything. The young fisher fellows would be the worst off of all. For years they would go on living as they could, and working a terrible long day as hard as they could be driven. None of those who had gone out in the last six years had yet managed back to see the old folk. That was Canada.[30]

A more bitter disillusionment characterized the increasingly Marxist writings of Lewis Grassic Gibbon (James Leslie Mitchell). In *Sunset Song* farm servant Chae Strachan – later to be killed in the war – had by 1911 returned to Kinraddie after a period of unfocused and unfulfilled overseas wandering.

> For he'd been a fell wandering billy, Chae, in the days before he came back to Scotland and was fee'd his last fee at Netherhill. He'd been in Alaska, looking for gold there, but damn the bit of gold he'd seen, so he'd farmed in California till he was so scunnered of fruit he'd never look an orange or a pear in the face again, not even in a tin. And then he'd gone on to South Africa and had had great times there, growing real chieflike with the head one of a tribe of blacks, but an awful decent man for all that.[31]

Six years later the heroine's brother, Will Guthrie, after settling as a rancher in the Argentine but doing war service with the French Foreign Legion, declared his determination never to return to Scotland because 'it's dead or it's dying'; while by the 1920s a similar fate had befallen Canada and Australia as disillusioned emigrants returned 'from the starvation there to starve here.'[32]

Although *Workers' Weekly*, the mouthpiece of the Communist Party of Great Britain, approached emigration from a different ideological stand-point to the Scottish National League, it was just as unswerving in its hostility to a phenomenon which it regarded as a means of side-stepping domestic unemployment and aggravating labour problems overseas. The Australian free-passage scheme was condemned in February 1923 as simply a means of bringing out agricultural strike-breakers and soldiers, and later that year – in the light of a recruitment visit by Australian politi-cians – would-be emigrants were warned of serious unemployment in Australia, warnings which were reiterated in subsequent years.[33] Intending emigrants to New Zealand were similarly warned in 1925 and 1926 that 'things are not all milk and honey' for those without at least £1,000 capital – not only in terms of unemployment and an acute housing shortage but also because of a lack of free speech that had led to the prosecution of communists and the banning of *Workers' Weekly*.[34] Unemployment was also rife in South Africa, the United States and Canada. By 1924, as open-ings in the Detroit motor industry became more scarce, skilled mechanics either took up menial jobs or, if they could afford it, returned to Britain in their thousands. Meanwhile, on the other side of the border, the Canada Colonisation Association – alleged to be under the control of the CPR and CNR – was roundly condemned for trying to bring cheap labour into a country where one in ten was out of work.[35] Most of the 473 members of the National Union of Foundry Workers who emigrated in the first eight months of 1923 came from Scotland, and Scots were also heavily represented among the hundreds of harvesters who had been recruited by unscrupulous 'emigration-mongers' in the pay of the steamship companies and businessmen on both sides of the Atlantic. Men such as David Hendry of Dumbarton had left his wife and two children in response to an advertisement that promised work for inexperienced harvesters at four dollars per day, only to find that not only did his lack of experience prevent him securing farm work, but when he was offered alternative railway work at a minimal wage of forty cents per hour, with six dollars per week deducted for board, he believed he had fallen victim to 'a scheme to get men out here to build railways for nothing'.[36] The poor conditions and 'wage slavery' of railway construction work were confirmed in a letter from a Canadian navvy, while the Canadian National Association of Unemployed collaborated with its British counterpart in publicizing the complaints of disillusioned harvesters.[37] Emigrants were subsequently warned particularly against Alberta, scene of a miners' strike in 1924 and hunger marches by destitute farm labourers in 1925; and on two occasions correspondents complained about the treatment allegedly meted out by the Salvation Army to emigrants, including fifteen-year-old Kenneth Robertson from Glasgow, who claimed he had been evicted from a Salvation Army hostel at Brandon at 10.30 p.m. to walk three miles across the prairie to his new employment.[38]

From time to time during the 1920s *Workers' Weekly* publicized the anti-emigration propaganda of the Communist-dominated National Unemployed Workers' Committee Movement, created by Wal Hannington in 1921 to lobby on behalf of the workless by organizing hunger marches, preventing strike-breaking, and – particularly in winter 1923 – campaigning against emigration by sending members aboard Canada-bound ships in the Clyde to spread, among 4,000 emigrants, Hannington's message that the unemployed should not be 'shipped off to an uncertain future' simply because the system had failed them.[39] Although Hannington was disappointed at the limited impact of his anti-emigration campaign, it nevertheless contributed to the election of Britain's first Labour government in 1924. Four years later, when the subsequent Conservative administration mounted a lightning campaign to recruit 10,000 men – mostly unemployed miners – for the Canadian harvest, and threatened to deny benefit to those who refused to go, the NUWCM canvassed actively on board ship, as well as on both sides of the Atlantic, highlighting emigrants' grievances about squalid conditions and low wage rates and joining forces with Canadian trade unionists to expose exploitation. Their agitation not only resulted in many destitute men being repatriated at no charge in autumn 1928, but it also led the Canadian Labour Ministry to admit that exploitative wages had been offered to several recruits.

Despite these successes, Hannington's movement waned after the election of the 1929 Labour government, which for the first time clearly advocated a measure of emigration. From as early as 1923, however, *Workers' Weekly* had deplored the ambivalent stance which it claimed characterized the Labour Party, singling out for particular criticism Airdrie MP J. C. Welsh and J. H. Thomas at the Ministry of Labour for promoting emigration as a false remedy for unemployment.[40] Although such attitudes were uncharacteristic of Labour politicians, who throughout the 1920s generally tried to counteract the imperialist fervour of their Conservative and Liberal opponents and were particularly opposed to shipping out the unemployed, J. Wignall claimed in 1922 that his party's criticism of the Empire Settlement Bill was an attempt to safeguard and improve a scheme which they hoped would become 'a real power for good' and did not stem from a desire to destroy it.[41] But while J. R. Clynes expressed qualified support for the bill at its first reading – simply exhorting the government to avoid equating emigration with unemployment relief, to secure the co-operation of labour organizations in the dominions and to guard against unscrupulous private operators – much more explicit opposition was voiced by J. C. Wedgwood, who favoured domestic land reform, particularly in the Scottish highlands, over expensive overseas colonization schemes, which would create homes fit for heroes in the dominions at British expense.[42] In the opinion of Govan MP Neil Maclean, who had toured Canada in 1921, the bill was well-intentioned but misguided because town-bred recruits were likely to tire quickly of the hardships and loneliness of farm life and flock to Canada's overburdened cities, increasing their already grave unemployment problem. It was a theme to which he returned on subsequent occasions as Canada's unemployment crisis deepened in tandem with the increasing unsuitability of the predominantly urban-bred emigrants.[43]

Labour opposition became more vociferous with the implementation of the ESA. While some voiced concern about the effects of cheap fares and ill-thought-out settlement schemes on Canada and Australia, others drew attention to the deleterious eugenic implications of favouring a delusive short-term expedient over domestic social reform, and Sidney Webb warned that the spectre of economic coercion which had plagued nineteenth-century highland emigration continued to taint the post-war exodus.[44] Scottish MPs such as E. Shinwell (Linlithgow), W. Muir (Maryhill), G. Buchanan (the Gorbals), T. Johnston (Dundee), J. Maxton (Bridgeton), G. Hardie (Springburn) and D. Kirkwood (Clydebank) not only alleged that overseas colonization was an immoral and unworkable palliative for unemployment – particularly juvenile unemployment – and a drain on skilled and sturdy labour from Clydeside and the Hebrides, respectively; they also linked emigration with declining domestic land cultivation, drew attention to fraudulent Scottish press advertisements offering guaranteed employment in Canada and publicized the iniquities of the restrictive American quota.[45] Emmanuel Shinwell highlighted the impossibility of reconciling overseas demand with British supply in a way that was acceptable to both donor and destination countries, James Maxton pointed out the deficiencies and low take-up rate of the much-vaunted family settlement schemes, and David Kirkwood was particularly bitter about the loss of the flower of the Scottish population:

> Last year we had 60,000 people in Scotland who wanted to emigrate, who wanted to get away from their native land. Who are the type of people who go? Is it the ragtag and bobtail of city life that migrate from the cities of Scotland? No fear? [An Hon. Member: 'Landlords!'] If it were the landlords it would be all right. It is the best blood of our land, the young and the vigorous. You would really think that there was some malignant influence at work in this country of ours. When there is a war on it is the best blood of the country that is taken away – the young men, the strong, the vigorous and the intelligent. The old have-beens have been left behind or else they have been wiped out. It is the same with emigration. It is our young men, the best asset that any country ever had, the finest raw material in the world – the British working class. The raw material is being sent away across the seas instead of being retained at home and put upon our native land ... . Scotland is being denuded of its population. They [sic] only increase in the last census was in the number of gamekeepers; all because of the action of the present Government.[46]

Conservative support for the ESA was based partly on the recommendations of the Dominions Royal Commission and the Tennyson Committee and partly on the conviction that a state-assisted redistribution of population within the empire could at a stroke slash British unemployment figures and relief expenditure, consolidate imperial economic development, loyalty and security, and neutralize 'the bogey of the yellow peril'.[47] Its disappointingly low take-up rate was blamed by Sir C. Kinloch-Cooke on universal political apathy and tardiness in embracing a scheme that would reduce British overpopulation and counteract the influx of foreigners to the empire, by R. A. Eden on the deterrent effect of a minority of well-publicized failures as well as unnecessarily complex application procedures, and by W. J. I. Fraser on malevolent Labour condemnation.[48] But not all Conservative politicians endorsed exclusively rural recruitment campaigns. Echoing earlier press comments, C. M. Barclay-Harvey reflected the concern of his farming constituents in west Aberdeenshire and

Kincardineshire when he complained in February 1927 that aggressive agency activity was denuding the countryside of its best farm servants, and five months later Bradford MP E. J. Ramsden recommended that a delegation of Australian Scots which was due to make a recruitment trip to Britain the following year should be steered towards depressed industrial areas – particularly the Clyde – rather than the highlands, from which he admitted that it was 'highly undesirable that further depopulation should take place'.[49] Debilitating depopulation, alongside the expense of migration policies, was also a constant concern of politicians and bureaucrats in the Oversea Settlement Department, Conservatives included.[50]

Although Liberal politicians endorsed empire settlement, their support was generally cautious and qualified, particularly by the late 1920s. While Sir Donald Maclean, MP first for Peebles and then for Midlothian, predicted that the legislation would reduce sharp practice and bring shared economic benefits, he stressed the need to guard against any element of compulsion, protect women and children, and integrate co-operative government programmes with efficient voluntary aid, as well as avoid the temptation to make party political points about the abrogation of domestic responsibilities.[51] In his maiden speech on 25 July 1923, Western Isles MP Sir William Mitchell Cotts welcomed the assisted transfer of willing recruits from the overpopulated metropolitan centres to the underpopulated empire, but – referring to the recent extensive emigration of constituents disappointed by unfulfilled land settlement promises – warned that emigrants who left 'with bitterness in their hearts' were unlikely to be transformed into good advertisements for empire settlement however much they prospered.[52] Five years later his view was echoed by Swansea MP W. Runciman, who agreed that the reduction of passage rates would benefit the enterprising poor but warned against blanket application of artificially assisted colonization, a sentiment that was reinforced by the revelations of other Liberal MPs about the dissatisfaction of ill-trained and unsuitable recruits.[53]

Political and public criticism in the dominions, it has been observed, emphasized the economic and social dislocation created by an influx of settlers who were perceived as impoverished and incompetent recruits from Britain's dole queues.[54] One of the most contentious issues was the disparity between the demand for capable agriculturists and the supply of unadaptable, recalcitrant artisans and labourers. While many unsuccessful emigrants could not afford to retrace their steps, some returned – or were deported – to Scotland, where, according to a Glasgow agent in 1925, 'a few discontented misfits' were disrupting recruitment by employing 'all their time and misspent energy in spreading all the ills connected with our country'.[55] Rates of return increased significantly during the 1930s as depressed dominion economies contracted, and hopes of reviving emigration towards the end of the decade were thwarted not only by the outbreak of war but by a growing awareness that much of the demographic, economic and social rationale for empire settlement had been progressively and fundamentally eroded during the inter-war years. Throughout this period Canadian newspapers were particularly eager to deter unwanted settlers by detailed reporting of disappointments and misdemeanours, as in this 1929 storyline.

A ragged band of British immigrant youths, hungry and stranded in the land whose glowing promises had been held out to them a few months ago, were found sleeping in the old Union Station Tuesday night. Scantily clad and their faces revealing traces of months of privation, the majority of their number were openly envious of two companions who were sentenced in police court yesterday to deportation.

Unable to obtain employment of any sort, they had roamed the streets, hungry and cold, the youths declared. Drifting from place to place, they begged and stole their food, the search for which was their chief concern.

Nearly 50 of the youths migrated from Scotland last June, filled with enthusiasm at the prospect of life in a new land. They obtained farm work, which some found too strenuous. Others, more stalwart, worked for months, only to be dismissed when the harvest was in, and to be paid, they charge, only a fraction of the wages promised them.

The money was soon spent and they found themselves penniless and hungry and with no prospect of employment.

'Then things got bad,' the spokesman of the band told *The Star*. 'We used to go hungry day after day. At night we slept in empty box cars. We couldn't find food any place, and sometimes had to dig in the scrap pails at the back of restaurants.'

Then on a lucky chance, they found that the old Union Station was not locked at nights and that it was comparatively clean and warm. Here at night they would gather around the large radiators in the rotunda, that were kept going to warm the offices upstairs in the day time. They had no covering, but the warmth was something to be thankful for.

Then Tuesday night twenty of the forty that were clustered around the radiators were arrested. Wednesday they faced charges of trespassing and were turned over to the Salvation Army. But the army could not supply beds for all of them and many, rather than return to the shelter on Sherbourne St, to sleep on the floor, plan to return to the police cells.

Yesterday afternoon they gathered in the immigration office, hoping they might be deported back to their homeland.[56]

The question remains, however, of the extent to which gullible Scots put their faith in emigration as a result of heavily publicized overseas settlement schemes, only to be left disappointed – or even destitute – by the disparity between promise and performance. For how many Scots did the dream of new opportunity become the nightmare of exile, as they fell victim to the disputatious manoeuvrings of imperial and dominion politicians whose primary concern was rarely the welfare of the emigrants themselves? That some would-be participants regarded the prospect of assisted emigration as a convenient expedient, to be tried if other avenues of advancement had failed, is implicit in a letter sent to the Fishery Board for Scotland by W. J. Wiseman of Aultbea, Wester Ross, apparently on the spur of the moment.

> Here I apply to you again this Time regarding The Fishing business in Canada. Nova Scotia, as I have read about it in The Peoples Journal now as I am up to all the Fishing lines being at the fishing since I was eleven years old and now I am 25 years. Will you kindly do your best for me and get me fixed up in the Nova Scotia Fishing.
>
> I am ready to go any time that you could get me a birth [sic] or let me know where to write myself and if I could get assisted Passage. I have applied to you before for a loan for a dwelling house but the board of agriculture would not grant a loan the same as crofters get.[57]

Evidence suggests, however, that most Scots thought long and hard about the pros and cons of emigrating and did not let themselves be used as pawns on an imperial chessboard. While for some emigrants, particularly those going to Australia, official subsidy was the essential ingredient without which they could not have contemplated leaving home, for others it was simply a welcome aid to a decision that was rooted in other criteria. For many, however, it was a bureaucratic and debt-laden impediment to freedom of action, to be avoided if relocation could be privately facilitated and funded. Although the substantial exodus to the USA is the most obvious example of Scots' disregard for empire settlement strategies, even some of the agriculturists and domestics who were eligible for assistance to the dominions preferred to emigrate there independently, free of official obligations, and it is worth remembering that in the UK as a whole only 36 per cent of empire migrants made use of the ESA's facilities between 1922 and 1936. Perhaps the proverbially cautious Scots were particularly wary of its claims.

The ESA was undoubtedly a significant piece of legislation, representing an unprecedented long-term commitment on the part of the imperial and dominion governments to co-operate in stimulating and shaping emigration within a vulnerable empire. A measure of its importance is its success in circumventing the Geddes public expenditure cuts on the grounds that it was perceived as a viable tool for tackling social disquiet and unemployment in Britain, as well as enhancing imperial unity and continuity by sponsoring rural settlement programmes in unexploited areas of the empire. Not only did it occupy much parliamentary time and generate considerable parliamentary debate during most of its first fifteen years;

it was also serviced by a Whitehall bureaucracy that generated a continuous and wide-ranging paper trail throughout the 1920s, and its renewal
for a further fifteen years from 1937 marked the British government's
belief that improving economic conditions might reinvigorate schemes of
assisted passage.

It was not to be. Even in the halcyon days of the mid-1920s the high
profile of the ESA – at least in official circles – did not guarantee its success.
Assisted migration from Britain peaked in 1926 and 1927, but the exodus
of the 1920s was just a pale shadow of the massive outflow immediately
before the First World War, and it dwindled to a trickle in the face of international economic collapse in the 1930s, while expenditure always fell
short of the allotted budget. The disparity between rural demand and
urban supply which had inhibited the success of the legislation in its early
years was eclipsed by an increasing imperial preoccupation with unemployment and depression across all sectors of the economy, and renewal of
the act in 1937 was based on Westminster's misplaced faith in the future
rather than a confident assessment of past performance. Scottish emigrants, like their counterparts elsewhere in Britain, made use of the ESA
when it suited them, but they were just as likely – possibly more likely –
to ignore its facilities as irrelevant to their existing tradition of emigration.
For many, assisted relocation schemes were more of an optional extra than
an essential ingredient in planning their emigration, and they therefore
remained relatively unaffected by the fluctuating fortunes of empire
settlement legislation.

This study began by reviewing the tradition of emigration which, by 1914,
was firmly established within and beyond Scotland. The essential elements
of that tradition were not disturbed by war, reconstruction or the unprecedented injection of government funding and direction into the business of
overseas settlement. Just as in 1815 the high hopes that had marked the
end of a long and devastating war were dashed by economic downturn and
social dislocation, so in the 1920s the post-war vision of 'homes fit for
heroes' was soon replaced by images of unemployment, destitution and
unrest. In the 1920s, as 100 years earlier, emigration was perceived both
as a domestic safety valve and as a means of cementing the foundations
of the empire, although government funding in the latter period was
considerably more substantial, long-term and systematically administered
than in the 1820s. In each era, however, the interests of the emigrants
themselves were largely ignored by imperial and colonial authorities, who
continued to disagree about the economic, social and moral calibre of
recruits, for although the financial and strategic issues raised by the ESA
may have sharpened controversy, the controversy itself was not new.

But continuities were evident not only in official policy, which, as we
have seen, simply provided the framework for the development of a complex

and multifaceted phenomenon. Inter-war emigrants, like their nineteenth-century predecessors, were influenced primarily by personal persuasion, private assistance and increasingly sophisticated ethnic and regional networks, which both stimulated and sustained a long tradition of diaspora. Scots, who had been forging extra-European connections by such means with considerable success since at least the seventeenth century, did not change their approach in the 1920s, a decade which saw the already indelible imprint of emigration penetrate even more deeply into the fabric of modern Scottish history.

Notes

1 Hagiographical studies include J. H. Batt, *Dr Barnardo: The Foster Father of 'Nobody's Children'* (London, S. W. Partridge & Co., 1904), and J. Urquhart, *The Life Story of William Quarrier. A Romance of Faith* (Glasgow, S. W. Partridge & Co., 1900).
2 Speech by Professor W. L. Grant, 'Report of the Conference on Emigration convened by the Royal Colonial Institute, May 1910', p. 88, quoted in A. G. Scholes, *Education for Empire Settlement. A Study of Juvenile Emigration* (London, Longman, 1932), p. 67.
3 NAC, RG76, vol. 271, file 768363, part 1, DIC correspondence, Nov. 1929 and Feb. 1930, quoted in Patricia T. Rooke and R. L. Schnell, 'Imperial philanthropy and colonial response: British juvenile emigration to Canada, 1896–1930', *The Historian*, XLVI:1 (Nov. 1983), p. 71.
4 Rooke and Schnell, 'Imperial philanthropy', p. 77.
5 Joy Parr, *Labouring Children. British Immigrant Apprentices to Canada, 1869–1914* (London, Croom Helm, 1980), p. 151.
6 *Hansard*, vol. 154, 15 to 31 May 1922, cols 913–4, 927; vol. 174, 26 May to 30 June 1924, col. 552; vol. 187, 27 July to 7 Aug. 1925, col. 148.
7 PP 1924–5 Cmd 2285 XV 137, *British Oversea Settlement Delegation to Canada, 1924. Report to the Secretary of State for the Colonies, President of the Oversea Settlement Committee, from the Delegation appointed to obtain information regarding the system of child migration and settlement in Canada (Bondfield Delegation).*
8 *Ibid.*, p. 13.
9 *Aberdeen Journal*, 25, 27 May 1911.
10 *Reports on the Schemes of the Church of Scotland – Church and Nation Committee*, 1925, p. 724.
11 *Ibid.*, 1926, pp. 620–1.
12 *Ibid.*, 1927, pp. 1219–20.
13 *Monthly Record*, May 1923, p. 67.
14 *Reports to the General Assembly of the United Free Church of Scotland, Report of the Church Life and Social Problems Committee*, 1928, p. 16.
15 *Reports to the General Assembly of the United Free Church, 1923, Colonial Committee Report*, p. 4. See also *Reports on the Schemes of the Church of Scotland – Colonial Committee*, 1922, p. 218; *Monthly Record*, May 1924, p. 68; Sept. 1929, p. 230.
16 *Reports to the General Assembly of the United Free Church of Scotland*, 1926, pp. 619–20, 622; *Monthly Record*, May 1924, p. 96.
17 *P&J*, 25 Aug. 1923.
18 *The Scotsman*, 16, 24 Apr., 3 Nov. 1923.
19 *GH*, 14 Apr. 1923, p. 11; 16 Apr. 1923, p. 11; 17 Apr. 1923, p. 3; 23 Apr. 1923, p. 11.
20 *GH*, 6 Apr. 1923, p. 5; 14 Apr. 1923, p. 7.
21 *The Scots Independent*, I:9 (July 1927), p. 9; III:4 (Feb. 1929), p. 41.
22 *The Scots Independent*, II:2 (Dec. 1927), p. 20; III:1 (Nov. 1928), p. 1.
23 *The Scots Independent*, VI:2 (Dec. 1931), p. 18; VII:8 (June 1933), p. 120. The 507-acre

Ministry of Labour estate at Carstairs provided accommodation for 150 students, which, *The Scots Independent* pointed out, was far more than the total number of students enrolled at any of Scotland's three agricultural colleges. *The Scotsman's* comment of 24 April 1923 that 'Scottish sentiment has been touched by the emigration scenes in the Hebrides' was typical of what nationalists claimed was a prevalence of meaningless rhetoric in the public press and psyche.

24 *The Scots Independent*, I:2 (Dec. 1926), p. 4; I:7 (May 1927), p. 7.
25 *The Scots Independent*, I:4 (Feb. 1927), pp. 3–5. See also chapter 3, pp. 82–91.
26 *The Scots Independent*, II:1 (Nov. 1927), p. 7.
27 *The Scots Independent*, II:11 (Sept. 1928), p. 163; V:9 (July 1931), p. 129.
28 *The Scots Independent*, V:5 (Mar. 1931), p. 72.
29 Maurice Lindsay, *History of Scottish Literature* (London, Hale, 1977), p. 435; Marjory Harper, 'Adventure or exile? The Scottish emigrant in fiction', *Scottish Literary Journal*, 23:1 (May, 1996), pp. 21–32. John Buchan (1875–1940), appointed Governor-General of Canada in 1935, also clearly reflected the imperialist perspective.
30 Neil Gunn, *The Grey Coast* (Edinburgh, Porpoise Press, 1926), p. 237. See also *Morning Tide* (Edinburgh, Porpoise Press, 1931), pp. 117, 183–4, and Douglas Gifford, 'Neil Gunn and the mythic regeneration of Scotland: the two great epic cycles' in Dairmid Gunn and Isobel Murray (eds), *Neil Gunn's Country. Essays in Celebration of Neil Gunn* (Edinburgh, Chambers, 1991), pp. 82–3.
31 Lewis Grassic Gibbon, *A Scots Quair* (London, Penguin, 1986), vol. I, *Sunset Song*, p. 21.
32 *Ibid.*, p. 165; vol. II, *Cloud Howe*, p. 394. See also Lewis Grassic Gibbon and Hugh MacDiarmid, *Scottish Scene* (London, Jarrold, 1934), pp. 62, 124. Although MacDiarmid vehemently denounced the ills of twentieth-century Scotland from a nationalist and communist perspective, his writings rarely allude to emigration.
33 *Workers' Weekly*, 17 Feb., 21 July 1923; 24 July 1925.
34 *Workers' Weekly*, 15 May 1925, 17 Dec. 1926.
35 *Workers' Weekly*, 20 June 1924; 14 Apr., 11 Aug., 28 Sept. 1923.
36 *Workers' Weekly*, 8, 21 Sept. 1923.
37 *Workers' Weekly*, 19, 26 Oct. 1923.
38 *Workers' Weekly*, 13 June 1924, 17 Apr., 5 June 1925; 19 Sept. 1924, 31 July 1925.
39 Richard Croucher, *We Refuse to Starve in Silence. A History of the National Unemployed Workers' Movement, 1920–46* (London, Lawrence & Wishart, 1987), p. 66.
40 *Workers' Weekly*, 19, 26 Oct. 1923; 24 July 1925.
41 *Hansard*, vol. 153, 26 Apr. 1922, col. 655. For the constituencies and party affiliations of MPs, see F. W. S. Craig (compiler), *British Parliamentary Election Results 1918–1949* (London, Macmillan, 1977).
42 *Hansard*, vol. 153, 26 Apr. 1922, cols 592–5, 628–33; vol. 154, 22 May 1922, col. 925. See also above, pp. 196–7.
43 *Ibid.*, cols 929–30; vol. 216, 30 Apr. 1928, cols 1439–40. Maclean's recommendation in 1922 was that the Bill should make provision for disappointed recruits to be returned to Britain rather than released on to a saturated Canadian urban labour market.
44 *Ibid.*, vol. 174, 2 May 1924, cols 552–3; vol. 202, 17 Feb. 1927, col. 1209; vol. 182, 2 Apr. 1925, cols 1590–1.
45 *Ibid.*, vol. 160, 14 Feb. 1923, cols 184–5; vol. 163, 10 May 1923, col. 2615 (Muir); vol. 165, 26 June 1923, col. 2106; vol. 171, 1 Apr. 1924, col. 1957; vol. 182, 6 Apr. 1925, cols 1823–5 (Hardie); vol. 203, 16 Mar. 1927, col. 2917.
46 *Ibid.*, vol. 160, 14 Feb. 1923, cols 164–9; vol. 179, 19 Dec. 1924, col. 1482; vol. 213, 7 Feb. 1928, col. 59.
47 *Ibid.*, vol. 153, 26 Apr. 1922, cols 575–90, 598–616. The comment about eradicating oriental influence by promoting white settlement in Canada and Australia was made by R. Gee, Conservative Coalition MP for Woolwich.
48 *Ibid.*, vol. 187, 27 July 1925, cols 147–8; vol. 204, 23 Mar. 1927, col. 486; vol. 220, 24 July 1928, col. 1168; vol. 225, 11 Feb. 1929, cols 158–9.
49 *Ibid.*, vol. 202, 17 Feb. 1927, cols 1215–6; vol. 208, 4 July 1927, col. 860. See also chapter 2, pp. 44–5.

50 Michael Roe, *Australia, Britain and Migration, 1915–1940. A Study of Desperate Hopes* (Cambridge, Cambridge University Press, 1995), p. 14.
51 *Hansard*, vol. 153, 26 Apr 1922, col. 604.
52 *Ibid.*, vol. 167, 25 July 1923, cols 570–1.
53 *Ibid.*, vol. 222, 8 Nov. 1928, col. 276; vol. 188, 23 Nov., 1925, col. 959 (L. Hore-Belisha, Plymouth, Devonport); vol. 223, 20 Dec. 1928, col. 3300 (E. A. Harney, South Shields).
54 See chapter 1, pp. 19–21, and Roe, *Australia, Britain and Migration*.
55 NAC, RG76, C-4661, vol. 6, file 41, parts 2, 'Emigration from Britain, 1918–52': R. R. Rees, St Enoch's Station, Glasgow, to W. R. Little, 12 Mar. 1925.
56 *Toronto Daily Star*, 7 Nov. 1929.
57 SRO, AF62/1961/2, W. J. Wiseman to Fishery Board, 18 Mar. 1927. Wiseman, a native of Fraserburgh who had moved to the west coast after the war, did not emigrate.

BIBLIOGRAPHY

Unpublished manuscript sources

Aberdeenshire Archives
AC6/27/26–29	Fraserburgh Parish Council: record of applications, 1921–31.
AC6/61/8–9	Old Machar Parish Council: record of applications, 1911–26.
AC6/64/19	Peterhead Parish Council: record of applications, 1921–31.
AC6/67/9–11	Rathen Parish Council: record of applications, 1911–31.
GR6S/A47/3/1–4	Kittybrewster School, Aberdeen: register of 'lefts', no. 1, 1916–37.
GR6X/A71/3/1–4	Aberdeen Burgh School Board Lefts Register, Sunnybank Public School, 1912–30.

Archives in private hands
NRAS 1177	National Farmers' Union, Turriff and Deer group.
NRAS 1178	National Farmers' Union, Inverurie and Ellon districts.
NRAS 1202	National Farmers' Union, Strathbogie group.

Private letters and press cuttings from Port Dover, Ontario, in the possession of Dr Harry D. Watson, Edinburgh.

City of Vancouver Archives
Add MSS 453	The St Andrew's and Caledonian Society: minute books, vols 1 and 2, 1886–1933.
Add MSS 55	Queen Mary's Coronation Hostel, notes and correspondence, vols 1 and 2.
Add MSS 336	Vancouver Art, Historical and Scientific Association, vol. 28, file 330: The Scots Directory.

Alexander Begg Papers, 1887–1904.

Edinburgh City Archives
SL14/1/27–34	Edinburgh Parish Council minutes, 1920–28.

Glasgow University Archives and Business Records Centre
TSB14/1/1/3	Nairn Savings Bank minutes, 1913–41.
TSB29/1/1/3	Galashiels Savings Bank minutes, 1906–44.
TSB63/1/4/4	Glasgow Savings Bank annual reports, 1906–30.
TSB64/1/3/6	Greenock Savings Bank annual reports, 1916–30.
TSB71/1/2/4	Paisley Savings Bank annual reports, 1922–24.
UGD255/1/8/5–7	Anchor Line records: newspaper cuttings, 1920–27.
UGD255/1/26-2–5	Anchor Line records: saloon passenger lists of RMS *Caledonia* (May 1914), *Cameronia* (September 1914), *California* (January 1916), *Cameronia* (October 1922).

Glenbow Archives, Calgary, Alberta
Boxes 46 and 47, folders 520, 522, 527: Scottish Immigrant Aid Society; young
  Scottish immigrants.

Highland Council Archives, Inverness

CI7/15/5	Kingussie and Insh Parish Council: General Register of Poor, 1896–1927.
CI7/15/9–10	Kingussie and Insh Parish Council: record of applications, 1911–30.
CR6/1/6	Applecross Parish Council: record of applications, 1901–30.

National Archives of Canada, Ottawa

Record Group 25

A2, vol. 152, file C10/36	Proposed emigration to Canada of a group of Glasgow girls.

Record Group 76

C-4661, vols 5–6, file 41, parts 1–5	Emigration from Britain 1918–1952.
C-4709, vol. 46, file 1532	Orphan Homes of Scotland, Fairknowe, Brockville, 1914–24.
C-4713, vol. 49, file 1945, part 3	Lecturers in Britain, 1892–1923.
C-4734, vol. 65, file 3115, part 3	Inspection of British immigrant children, 1918–37.
C-4760, vol. 95, file 11365, part 2	Scotch fishermen, settlement in Canada, 1925–37.
C-4796, vols 132–3, file 30477, parts 1–2	State-assisted immigration by the government, 1920–23.
C-7303, vol. 147, file 34873	Glasgow. H. M. Murray, emigration agent, 1897–1909.
C-7327, vol. 170, file 54087, parts 1–2	G. Bogue Smart, Supervisor of juvenile immigration, annual reports on juvenile immigration, 1925–48.
C-7354, vol. 200, file 83981, parts 1–2	G. B. Smart and juvenile immigration, 1899–1933.
C-7355, vol. 200, file 85203, parts 1–2	Juvenile immigration (empire settlement), 1923–31.
C-7374, file 115272	Catholic Women's League Hostel, Toronto, 1932–35, 1939.
C-7380, vol. 230, file 127825, parts 1–2	Col. J. S. Dennis, CPR, selection of domestics under the Empire Settlement Act, 1924–37.
C-7385, file 135755, parts 13–18	British reduced rate settlers, 1928–30, applications for farm help.
C-7396–7, file 179046, part 1	3000 Families Scheme, 1924–25.
C-7401, vol. 252, file 182689	Re-union of Families settlement scheme.

Nominating dependents of persons already settled in Canada, 1924–29.

C-7401, vol. 252, file 186833 — Inverness agency, 1923–26.

C-7803, vol. 260, file 211873 — Clandonald colony, Vermilion, Alberta, 1925, 1929, 1954.

C-7808, vol. 260, file 211873 — J. S. Dennis, Chief Commissioner, CPR Department of Colonisation and Development, settlement scheme, Clan Donald [sic] and Extension at Vermilion (Scottish Immigrant Aid Society), 1925, 1929, 1954.

C-7831, vol. 282, file 234636 — Public schoolboys for New Brunswick, 1926–30.

C-10236, vol. 323, file 310968 — Fifteen parish trainees, Glasgow, allocated to Toronto.

C-10260, vol. 356, file 397430 — Provincial boys' scheme, 1929–33.

C-10260, vol. 356, file 400652 — Cornton Vale trainees, 1929–31.

C-10260, vol. 356, file 402561 — J. P. Ballantine, Cumnock, Scotland, bonus claims (lists), 1911–14, 1916, 1920–23, 1932.

C-10261, vol. 358, file 410827 — James Scott, Ayr, Scotland. Bonus claims (lists), 1905–14, 1920, 1923.

C-10261, vol. 358, file 411788 — Women's opportunities in Canada.

C-10264, vol. 362, file 453045 — MacKay Brothers, Edinburgh, booking agents. Lists, 1915–22.

C-10269, vol. 369, file 493191 — J. Wood, Lyron, Kirkwall, Orkney, Scotland. Bonus claims (lists), 1906–15, 1920–21.

C-10269, vol. 369, file 497599 — Walter Easton, Jedburgh, Scotland, Bonus claims (lists and pamphlets), 1906–14, 1919–21.

C-10275, vol. 378, file 524037 — A Warwick, Glasgow booking agent, 1923–27.

C-10294, vol. 404, file 589472 — British Passenger Agents' Association (pamphlets and reports), 1906–10, 1917–21.

C-10294–5, vol. 405, file 590687, parts 1–3 — John MacLennan, appointed immigration agent in Scotland, 1906–9, 1909–11, 1911–12, 1915, 1918, 1926.

C-10303, vol. 418, file 608438 — Overseas League, Scotland (brochures), 1936–37.

C-10309, vol. 426, file 629453 — D. Cumming, Glasgow, Scotland. Bonus claims (lists), 1907–15, 1918.

C-10311, vol. 429, file 635503 — J. & J. H. Rutherford, Kelso on Tweed, Scotland. Booking agent, 1908–9, 1912–15, 1921.

C-10311, vol. 430, file 636689 — Mary J. Farnon, Falkirk, Scotland. Booking agent, 1907–21.

C-10315, vol. 435, file 652801 — John Sinclair, Elgin, Scotland, booking agent, lists, 1907–14, 1923.

C-10315, vol. 435, file 652806, parts 1–3 — D. McFarlane, Glasgow, Scotland, booking agent, 1907–23.

C-10318, vol. 440, file 662655 — Hugh McKerracher, Paisley, Ontario, to take charge of an exhibition wagon in Scotland, 1907–17, 1920–21.

C-10324, vol. 450, file 682150, parts 1–2	Malcolm McIntyre, Canadian Government Agent, Glasgow, 1909–12, 1912–23.
C-10325, vol. 450, file 686431	Andrew Spalding, Blairgowrie, Scotland. Booking agent (lists), 1907, 1909–14, 1918–21, 1923.
C-10421, vol. 487, file 752538, part 4	Philanthropic societies which assist immigrants to Canada.
C-10446, vols 632–3, file 968592, parts 1–6	Scottish Immigrant Aid Society, immigration and settlement of Hebrideans.
C-10612, vol. 514, file 800180	James Moir, Bo'ness, Scotland. Booking agent, 1908, 1927.
C-10621, vol. 530, file 803485	W. G. Maitland, Longside, Aberdeenshire, Scotland. Booking agent, lists, 1908–17, 1919–21.
C-10644, vol. 564, file 808836	J. Obed Smith, Assistant Superintendent of Emigration, London, England. Provinces of the Dominion making special efforts in the British Isles to secure certain classes for their respective provinces.
C-10644, vol. 564, file 809010	Mackay Brothers, Aberdeen, Scotland. Booking agents, lists, 1910–19, 1921.
C-10646–7 vol. 568, file 811910, parts 1–2	G. C. Cossar, Glasgow, boy emigrants.
C-10680, vol. 679, file 41, parts 1–5	Emigration staff, Britain.

Provincial Archives of New Brunswick, Fredericton
MC2402	Vera Ayling records.

Public Record Office, London
BT27/1000–2	Selected Glasgow passenger lists, 1923.
BT27/1228	Selected Glasgow passenger lists, 1929.
BT27/1004	Selected Liverpool passenger lists, 1923.
BT27/1018	Selected London passenger lists, 1923.
BT27/1029	Selected Southampton passenger lists, 1923.
BT27/1151	Selected Leith passenger lists, 1927.
DO57/116 0057/2–15	Ministry of Labour trainees for Canada, 1929–30.
DO57/118 0164/1–2	Tour by K. M. Lindsay in the north of England and Scotland, 1929.
DO57/118 1069/A	Scottish Council for Women's Trades, training scheme.
DO57/119 0352/6–7	3000 Families Scheme: experiences of settlers.
DO57/121 1422/A	Glasgow Parish Council, boys' training.
DO57/132 0071/5–9	Scottish Council for Women's Trades.
DO57/134 0169/19–20	Scottish Council for Women's Trades training scheme.
DO57/139 0460/5–6	Church of Scotland, migrants' expenses agreement.

DO57/139 0491/6–7	Church of Scotland, Cornton Vale training farm.
DO57/139 0509/7–50	Clan Donald [sic] colony, land settlement scheme.
DO57/139 0547/9–42	Craigielinn Boys' training farm.
DO57/143 0987/6–33	Canada, Cossar Boys' training farms, aftercare.
LAB2/1237/9	Ministry of Labour, Employment and Insurance Department: oversea training, Canada.

St Francis Xavier University Special Collections, Antigonish, Nova Scotia

G5/9/6803–6815	Correspondence between Andrew MacDonell and Dr Hugh P. MacPherson, 1906–36.
RG12/5/230–237	The Scottish Immigrant Aid Society and the Catholic Society of Canada for British migration, 1933 Report.
RG30-2/1/2533–2549	Correspondence between Andrew MacDonell and Dr Moses Coady, 1929–52.

Scottish Catholic Archives, Edinburgh

DA9/26–27	Father R. A. MacDonell, Alberta immigration schemes.
DE132/1–7	Emigration to Canada: Catholic Emigration Society, Scottish Immigrant Aid Society, Catholic Society of Canada.

Scottish Record Office, Edinburgh

AF43/219	Emigration and migration from rural areas in Scotland (also in AF51/170).
AF51/167–87	Emigration files, particularly from crofting counties to Canada.
AF51/212	Emigration and empire settlement: memoranda on economic conditions in the Highlands and Islands.
AF62/1961/1–2	Fishery Board for Scotland: emigration of fishermen and fishworkers.
AF62/1962–1963	Fishery Board for Scotland: emigration of fishermen and fishworkers.
AF62/1964/1 & 4	Emigration of fishermen: proposed settlement of Scottish crofter fishermen in BC.
AF62/1964/2	Emigration of Scottish crofter fishermen to BC.
AF62/1964/3	Emigration of Scottish crofter fishermen to BC.
AF62/1965	Emigration of fishermen and fishworkers to Newfoundland.
AF62/1966	Emigration of fishermen: settlement of British fishing families in Australia.
AF70/123	Overseas settlement: training of boys on smallholdings.
CO4/32/7	Inch: General Register of Poor, 1845–1930.
DD10/190	Unemployment, emigration, assisted passages etc. General correspondence, 1925.
NRAS 1883	Skene, Edwards & Garson papers.

South Australia Archives, Adelaide

GRG7/8/793	Immigration Department, selected immigrants.

Western Isles Library, Stornoway
Lewis and Harris school log books, 1920s.
Stornoway Town Council minutes, 1920s.

Directories, newspapers and periodicals

Aberdeen Journal to 1922, thereafter published as *Press & Journal*.
Glasgow Herald
Highland News
John O'Groat Journal
Life and Work (monthly magazine of the Church of Scotland)
Monthly Record of the Free Church of Scotland
Oban Times
The Scotsman
Scottish Farmer, 1919–33
Scottish Farm Servant, vols 8–18 (1920–1931)
Scottish Red Triangle News, 1923–26, thereafter entitled *Scottish Manhood*
Stornoway Gazette
The Times

Contemporary printed books, articles and pamphlets

Anon., 'Some account of the Falkland Islands', *Colonial Magazine*, 7:28, April 1842, pp. 430–9.

Anon., *Organised Empire Migration and Settlement. A Retrospect of Salvation Army Work for the Empire and its Citizens by a Privileged Observer* (London, The Salvation Army, Migration House, 1930).

Belcher, E. A., and J. A. Williamson, *Migration within the Empire* (London, Collins, 1924).

Booth, William, *General Booth's Scheme for Boys* (London, The Salvation Army, International Headquarters, 1925).

Carrothers, W. A., *Emigration from the British Isles, with Special Reference to the Development of the Overseas Dominions* (London, Cass, 1929).

Church of Scotland, *Reports on the Schemes of the Church of Scotland, with the Legislative Acts passed by the General Assembly*, 1920–30.

Day, J. P., *Public Administration in the Highlands and Islands of Scotland* (London, University of London Press, 1918).

Department of Immigration and Colonisation, Canada, *Annual Reports of the Department*, 1919–36.

Department of Immigration and Colonisation, Canada, *Assisted settlement of approved British families on Canada government farms*, NAC pamphlets 2-5235 (Ottawa, DIC, 1924).

Department of Immigration and Colonisation, Canada, *Winning Through. Stories of Life on Canadian Farms, Told by New British Settlers* (Ottawa, DIC, 1929).

Gibbon, Lewis Grassic, *A Scots Quair* (London, Penguin, 1986).

Gregory, J. W., *Human Migration and the Future. A Study of the Causes, Effects and Control of Emigration* (London, Seeley, Service & Co., 1928).

Gunn, Neil M., *The Grey Coast* (Edinburgh, Porpoise Press, 1926).

Gunn, Neil M., *Morning Tide* (Edinburgh, Porpoise Press, 1931).

Lamb, D. *Boys of Britain* (London, The Salvation Army, Emigration–Colonization and Shipping Office, 1923).

Public Archives of Nova Scotia, *Annual Reports of the Agent General for Nova Scotia, 1909–30*, in *Journals and Proceedings of the House of Assembly* (Legislative Library).

Scholes, A. G., *Education for Empire Settlement. A Study of Juvenile Migration* (London, Longman, 1932).

Thomson, G. M., *Scotland: That Distressed Area* (Edinburgh, Porpoise Press, 1935).

United Free Church of Scotland, *Proceedings and Debates of the General Assembly*, 1919–30.

United Free Church of Scotland, *Reports to the General Assembly, Colonial and Continental Committee*, 1919–28.

British Parliamentary papers

PP 1917–18 X Cd 8462 *Final Report of the Royal Commission on the Natural Resources, Trade and Legislation of Certain Portions of His Majesty's Dominions (Dominions Royal Commission).*

PP 1917–18 X Cd 8672 *Empire Settlement Committee: Report to the Secretary of State for the Colonies of the Committee appointed to consider the measures to be taken for settling within the Empire ex-service men who may desire to emigrate after the war.*

PP 1920 XXII Cmd 745 *Report to the President of the Oversea Settlement Committee of the delegates appointed to enquire as to openings in Australia for women from the United Kingdom.*

PP 1920 XXII Cmd 933 *Report to the President of the Oversea Settlement Committee of the delegates appointed to enquire as to openings in New Zealand for women from the United Kingdom.*

PP 1924 XI Cmd 2132 *Report to the President of the Oversea Settlement Committee from the delegation appointed to enquire into conditions affecting British settlers in Australia.*

PP 1924 XI Cmd 2167 *Report to the President of the Oversea Settlement Committee from the delegation appointed to enquire into conditions affecting British settlers in New Zealand.*

PP 1924–25 XV Cmd 2285 *Report to the Secretary of State for the Colonies, President of the Oversea Settlement Committee, from the delegation appointed to obtain information regarding the system of child migration and settlement in Canada.*

PP 1926 X Cmd 2608 *Report to the Secretary of State for Dominion affairs of the inter-departmental committee appointed to consider the effect on migration of schemes of social insurance.*

PP 1926 XV Cmd 2760 *Report by the Rt Hon. the Earl of Clarendon, Chairman, and Mr T. C. Macnaghten, Vice-Chairman, of the Oversea Settlement Committee, on their visit to Canada in connection with British settlement.*

PP 1931–32 IX Cmd 4075 *Report of the Economic Advisory Council, Committee on Empire Migration.*

Fishery Board for Scotland, Annual Reports, 1917–33.
Ministry of Labour, Annual Reports, 1922–31.
Oversea Settlement Committee, Annual Reports, 1919–34.

Reports of societies and institutions

Craigielinn Boys' Farm Association, Annual Reports, 1925–26, 1927–28, 1928–29.
Quarrier's Orphan Homes of Scotland, *Narrative of Facts*, 1914–50, and case files
   of 152 individuals.

Oral history sources

Author's taped interviews with the late Gilbert Buchan and the late Annie Noble,
   Inverallochy, 16 September 1985.
Author's taped interviews with Mrs J. A. Coupland, Aberdeen, 24 July 1994 and
   16 October 1996.
Ellis Island Oral History Project, 'Scotland interviews':

Thomas Allan	NPS-149	Mary Kendrick	EI-492
Jack Carnegie	EI-729	Margaret Kirk	EI-440
Margaret Cook	EI-435	William McGuire	KM-77
Anne Cross	EI-357	Patrick Peak	AKRF-84
Joseph Daly	EI-558	Maisie Pedersen	EI-442
Joseph Delaney	AKRF-23	Anne Quinn	NPS-146
Mary Dunn	AKRF-127	Isabella Rohan	EI-823
Allan Gunn	EI-179	David Saltman	EI-97
Helen Hansen	DP-46	Agnes Schilling	EI-172
William Hopkins	EI-70	John Will	EI-547

Secondary books, articles and theses

Books

Baines, Dudley, *Emigration from Europe 1815–1930* (Basingstoke, Macmillan, 1991).
Baines, Dudley, *Migration in a Mature Economy. Emigration and Internal Migration
   in England and Wales, 1861–1900* (Cambridge, Cambridge University Press, 1985).
Cameron, Ewen A., *Land for the People? The British Government and the Scottish
   Highlands, c. 1880–1925* (Edinburgh, Donald, 1996).
Cameron, Lewis L. L., *The Challenge of Need. A History of Social Service by the
   Church of Scotland 1869–1969* (Edinburgh, St Andrew's Press, 1971).
Campbell, Mary E., *In Yesterday's Footsteps* (n.p., 1986).
Carrier, N. H., and J. R. Jeffery, *External Migration. A Study of the Available
   Statistics, 1815–1950* (London, HMSO, 1953).
Constantine, Stephen (ed.), *Emigrants and Empire. British Settlement in the
   Dominions Between the Wars* (Manchester, Manchester University Press, 1990).
Croucher, Richard, *We Refuse to Starve in Silence. A History of the National
   Unemployed Workers' Movement, 1920–46* (London, Lawrence & Wishart, 1987).

Devine, T. M. (ed.), *Scottish Emigration and Scottish Society* (Edinburgh, Donald, 1992).

Divine, R. A., *American Immigration Policy, 1924–1952* (New Haven, Yale Historical Publications Miscellany 66, 1957)

Dickson, Tony, and James H. Treble (eds), *People and Society in Scotland, vol. III, 1914–1990* (Edinburgh, Donald, 1992).

Elliott, Shirley B., *Nova Scotia in London. A History of its Agents General 1762–1988* (London, Office of the Agent General for Nova Scotia, 1988).

Erickson, Charlotte, *Invisible Immigrants. The Adaptation of English and Scottish Immigrants in 19th Century America* (Ithaca and London, Cornell University Press, 1972).

Erickson, Charlotte, *Leaving England. Essays on British Emigration in the Nineteenth Century* (Ithaca and London, Cornell University Press, 1994).

Fedorowich, Kent, *Unfit for Heroes: Reconstruction and Soldier Settlement in the Empire Between the Wars* (Manchester, Manchester University Press, 1995).

Ferenczi, Imre, and Walter F. Willcox, *International Migrations: vol. I: Statistics, vol. II: Interpretations* (New York, Gordon & Breach, 1969).

Ferguson, William, *Scotland, 1689 to the Present* (Edinburgh, Oliver & Boyd, 1968).

Glynn, Sean, and John Oxborrow, *Inter-war Britain: A Social and Economic History* (London, Allen & Unwin, 1976).

Flinn, M. W. (ed.), *Scottish Population History from the Seventeenth Century to the 1930s* (Cambridge, Cambridge University Press, 1977).

Gray, Malcolm, *The Fishing Industries of Scotland, 1790–1914. A Study in Regional Adaptation* (Oxford, Oxford University Press, 1978).

Gray, Nigel, *The Worst of Times. An Oral History of the Great Depression in Britain* (London, Wildwood House, 1985).

Harper, Marjory, *Emigration from North-East Scotland, vol. 1, Willing Exiles, vol. 2, Beyond the Broad Atlantic* (Aberdeen, Aberdeen University Press, 1988).

Hatton, Timothy J., and Jeffrey G. Williamson, 'What drove the mass migrations from Europe in the late nineteenth century?', Historical paper no. 43, working paper series on historical factors in long run growth (Cambridge, MA, National Bureau of Economic Research, Inc., 1992).

Jones, Maldwyn A., *American Immigration* (Chicago, University of Chicago Press, 1960).

Leneman, Leah, *Fit for Heroes? Land Settlement in Scotland after World War I* (Aberdeen, Aberdeen University Press, 1989).

Lynch, Michael, *Scotland: A New History* (London, Pimlico, 1992).

MacKenzie, Greta, *Why Patagonia?* (Stornoway, Stornoway Gazette, 1995).

MacKenzie, John M., *Propaganda and Empire. The Manipulation of British Public Opinion, 1880–1960* (Manchester, Manchester University Press, 1984).

Mainwaring, Michael J., *From the Falklands to Patagonia. The Story of a Pioneer Family* (London, Allison & Busby, 1983).

Malchow, Howard, *Population Pressures. Emigration and Government in Late Nineteenth-Century Britain* (Palo Alto, CA, Society for the Promotion of Science and Scholarship, 1979).

Marr, Andrew, *The Battle for Scotland* (London, Penguin, 1992).

Monk, Una, *New Horizons. A Hundred Years of Women's Migration* (London, n.p., 1963).

Moyles, R. G., and D. Owram, *Imperial Dreams and Colonial Realities. British Views of Canada, 1880–1914* (Toronto, University of Toronto Press, 1988).

Norton, Wayne, *Help Us to a Better Land. Crofter Colonies in the Prairie West* (Regina, Canadian Plains Research Center, 1994).

Parr, Joy, *Labouring Children. British Immigrant Apprentices to Canada, 1869–1914* (London, Croom Helm, 1980).

Perren, Richard, *Agriculture in Depression, 1870–1940* (Cambridge, Cambridge University Press, 1995).

Plant, G. F., *Oversea Settlement. Migration from the United Kingdom to the Dominions* (Oxford, Oxford University Press, 1951).

Pooley, C. G., and I. Whyte (eds), *Emigrants, Migrants and Immigrants. A Social History of Migration* (London, Routledge, 1991).

Pugh, R. B., *The Records of the Colonial and Dominions Offices* (London, HMSO, 1964).

Roe, Michael, *Australia, Britain and Migration, 1915–1940. A Study of Desperate Hopes* (Cambridge, Cambridge University Press, 1995).

Skilling, H. G., *Canadian Representation Abroad. From Agency to Embassy* (Toronto, Ryerson Press, 1945).

Smith, J. H., *Joe Duncan. The Scottish Farm Servants and British Agriculture* (printed by RCSS, University of Edinburgh, in conjunction with the Scottish Labour History Society, 1973).

Strange, Ian J., *The Falkland Islands*, 3rd edn (Newton Abbot, David & Charles, 1983).

Symon, J. A., *Scottish Farming, Past and Present* (Edinburgh, Oliver & Boyd, 1959).

Tinker, Hugh, *et. al.*, *The Diaspora of the British* (London, University of London, Institute of Commonwealth Studies, 1982).

Watson, Harry D. *Kilrenny and Cellardyke: 800 Years of History* (Edinburgh, Donald, 1986)

Wilkie, Jim, *Metagama. A Journey from Lewis to the New World* (Edinburgh, Mainstream, 1987).

Articles

Buchanan, Joni, 'Lewis families who made the long trek to Patagonia', *West Highland Free Press*, 22 Nov. 1996, p. 11.

Camm, J. C. R., 'The hunt for muscle and bone: emigration agents and their role in migration to Queensland during the 1880s', *Australian Historical Geography, Bulletin*, 2 (Feb. 1981), pp. 6–29.

Camm, J. C. R., 'The origins of assisted British migrants to Queensland, 1871–1892', *Australian Geographical Studies*, 23 (Apr. 1985), pp. 87–104.

Coull, James R., 'The Scottish herring fishery in the inter-war years, 1919–1939: ordeal and retrenchment', *International Journal of Maritime History*, II:1 (June 1990), pp. 55–81.

Harper, Marjory, 'Emigration and the Salvation Army', *Bulletin of the Scottish Institute of Missionary Studies*, n.s., 3–4 (1985–7), pp. 22–9.

Harper, Marjory, 'Crofter colonists in Canada: an experiment in empire settlement in the 1920s', *Northern Scotland*, 14 (1994), pp. 69–111.

Koroscil, Paul M., 'Soldiers, settlement and development in British Columbia, 1915–1930', *BC Studies*, 54 (summer 1982), pp. 63–87.

MacDonell, R. A., 'British immigration schemes in Alberta', *Alberta Historical Review* (spring 1968), pp. 5–13.

Macleod, Sheila, 'The day the *Metagama* sailed from Stornoway', *Eilean an Fhraoich Annual* (1973), pp. 25–30.

Milton, Norma J., 'The Scots in Alberta' in Howard and Tamara Palmer (eds), *Peoples of Alberta: Portraits of Cultural Diversity* (Saskatoon, Western Producer Prairie Books, 1985), pp. 109–22.

Reid, Richard G., 'From the old land to the new: a pioneer's impressions and recollections', *Alberta Historical Review*, 5, 1/2 (1957), pp. 3–9 and 15–21.

Rooke, Patricia T., and R. L. Schnell, 'Imperial philanthropy and colonial response: British juvenile emigration to Canada, 1896–1930', *The Historian*, XLVI:1 (Nov. 1983), pp. 56–77.

Schultz, John A., 'Finding homes fit for heroes: the Great War and empire settlement', *Canadian Journal of History*, 18 (1983), pp. 99–110.

Vance, Michael E., 'British Columbia's twentieth-century crofter emigration schemes: a note on new sources', *Scottish Tradition*, 18 (1993), pp. 1–27.

Wade, Jill, 'The "Gigantic Scheme": crofter immigration and deep-sea fisheries development for British Columbia (1887–1893)', *BC Studies*, 53 (spring 1982), pp. 28–44.

Theses

Kibblewhite, Elizabeth, 'The impact of unemployment on the development of trade unions in Scotland, 1918–1939: some aspects' (Ph.D. thesis, University of Aberdeen, 1979).

Sim, Diana, 'Clandonald: a rural Catholic colony' (unpublished undergraduate paper, University of Calgary, 1979).

INDEX

Note: Page numbers in bold refer to main entries. 'n.' after a page reference indicates the number of a note on that page.